Letterland

PROGRAMME TWO

TEACHER'S GUIDE

Published by Collins Educational
An imprint of HarperCollins*Publishers* Ltd
77-85 Fulham Palace Road
London W6 8JB

First published by Letterland Ltd 1987
This edition published 1999 by Collins Educational

ISBN 0 00 303306 6

British Library Cataloguing in Publication Data
A catalogue record for this book is available from the British Library.

Illustrations by David Eaton
Photographs by Martin Sookias
Design by Sally Boothroyd and Sylvia Kwan
Cover design by Sylvia Kwan
Printing and Bound by Printing Express Ltd. Hong Kong

Acknowledgements
The author and publishers would like to thank the following:
The staff and children at Peterborough Primary School, Fulham for their help with the photographs.
Stella Hopkins for providing the photograph on page 8.

Letterland™

PROGRAMME TWO

TEACHER'S GUIDE

by Lyn Wendon

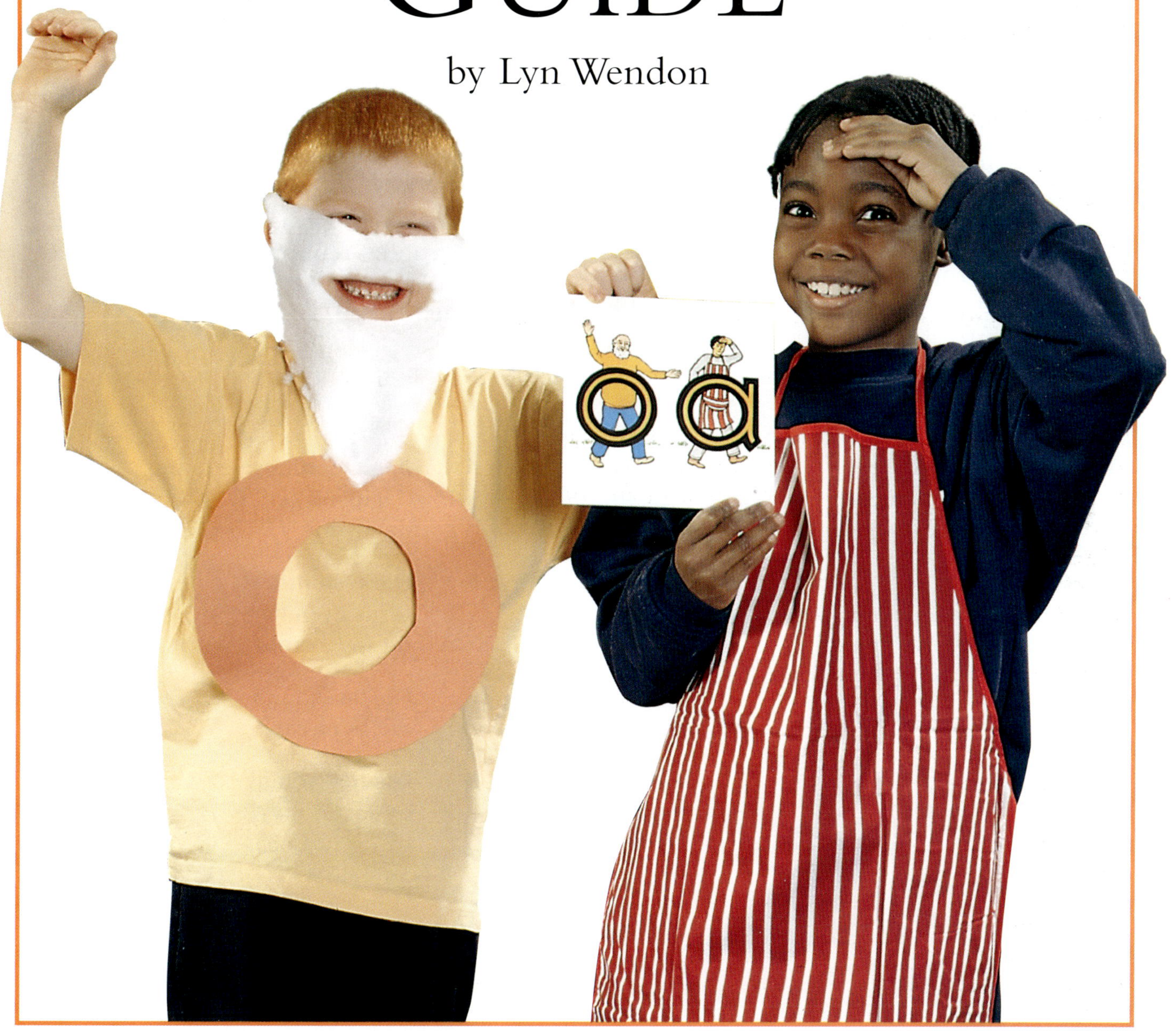

Collins Educational

An imprint of HarperCollins*Publishers*

Contents

Foreword

In the years prior to the introduction of the National Literacy Strategy, Letterland was one of the few published teaching programmes which upheld the central importance of phonics. It combined pictogram illustrations with alliterative stories, role play, rhythm and rhyme, music, art and crafts to engage the whole child, so that phonological awareness and early reading and spelling skills were the natural outcome.

Now that the National Literacy Strategy has endorsed the teaching of phonics by prescribing it, Letterland's distinction remains. One of Letterland's greatest strengths lies in the economy of learning it introduces by using a set of alphabet characters which serve twice over, first for single letter learning and second for the digraphs for 2-letter, 3-letter and even 4-letter units of sound.

In traditional phonic teaching, any visual cues for learning the **a–z** sounds become irrelevant as soon as any of the 26 letters combine to represent a new sound. First learning of **h** for house and **p** for parrot, for example, becomes a useless distraction when learning the **ph** combination. By contrast, for each new sound, Letterland teaching confirms and reutilises first learning. Taking **ph** again, here is an example of this economy.

In Programme One, children learn that **h** is the Hairy Hat Man who hates noise, so he never speaks above a whisper in words. He just say '**hhh**…'. They also learn that **p** is Poor Peter, a playful little puppy who is sad because instead of barking he can only make a little '**p**…' sound.

In Programme Two children learn that whenever Poor Peter and the Hairy Hat Man are next to each other in words, the Hat Man takes Peter's **ph**otogra**ph** to cheer him up. Then Poor Peter smiles and the Hat Man laughs happily, but quietly, with his mouth almost shut and his teeth on his lips. So he makes a 'fff…' sound, as in **ph**otogra**ph**.

The children can role-play the brief story, sing the **ph** song, draw the event where it happens in **ph** words (called picture coding, see page 19), paint it, or recreate it in clay, so that consolidation of this new learning is achieved without boredom and children with learning difficulties are not left behind.

Children learn the Letterland story reasons for new sounds quickly because they are using a logic which is within their own experience of real life. Letterland uses these phonic tales to teach not only many phonemes but also major structural principles so they can become clear and accessible to 5 and 6 year olds (e.g. the effect of a Silent Magic **e** on the previous vowel, or predicting the value of a vowel in an unknown word).

Letterland provides an opportunity for completing all the National Literacy Strategy requirements for Word Level work either in step with or ahead of the National Literacy Strategy timetable. Those who make full use of Programme Two will also find their children achieve earlier access to the rest of the school curriculum.

Lyn Wendon

Introduction to Letterland

From the perspective of a child, the alphabet is initially seen as a set of signs without significance. Although the letters are designed to signal and to signify meaning, they will not mean anything until the child has been initiated into the workings of the symbol system. Until then, the alphabet will be as inaccessible to children as ancient hieroglyphics are to us. From the perspective of adults, teachers and parents alike, the problem is how to explain the intricacies of our alphabetical system in a way which children can appreciate and will want to hear.

The introduction of an imaginary place called 'Letterland' has provided a solution to this communication problem. Letterland provides all that needs to be known about the alphabet, about correct letter formation, about the phonic system of spelling-sound translation, and about the rules of word structure. All this information is carried in the form of brief stories about letter characters who inhabit Letterland. For example, the different sounds of **a** in words like **pat** and **paw** are given reasons in story form, supported by pictograms fused into the letters, instead of abstract, unreasoned, rules.

Compare the difference between teaching an unfamiliar word by traditional phonic methods and by the Letterland route. In a word like **paw**, the respective sound values of **a** and **w** change for no apparent reason. Conventionally, children are taught a rule: '**a** beside **w** makes the 'aw' sound, as in **saw**'. But there is nothing in this phonic fact to capture children's interest. Nor is there anything to help them when they meet the **aw** pattern again in unfamiliar words. There is also nothing to prevent them confusing the **aw** sound with the two **ow** sounds or the **ew** sound, once these other **w**-controlled vowel digraphs have been introduced.

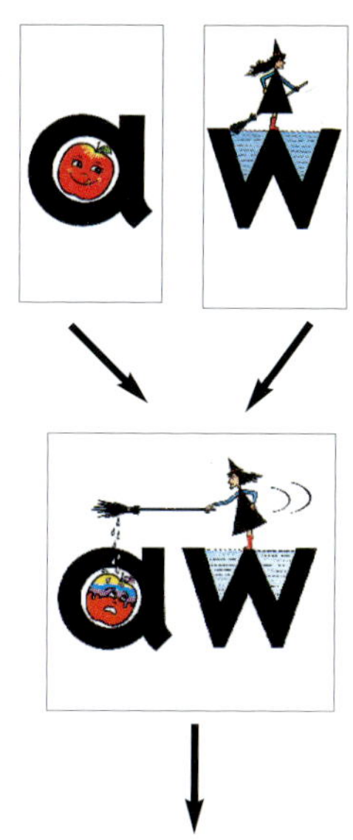

By contrast, Letterland uses Annie Apple and the Wicked Water Witch as picture clues for the basic sounds of **a** and **w,** and then builds on that prior knowledge to explain the new sound with an anecdotal story: in words like **paw** the **w**itch turns back and makes the **a**pple taste **aw**ful. The **aw** pictogram supports this information. The story reason and the illustration of this story fused into the letters make the new sound logical, dramatic, and therefore memorable, as well as uniquely associated with **aw** and no other **w**-controlled vowel digraph.

The Early Years Programme provided an introduction to the Letterland characters and their sounds. This introduction was developed in Programme One, with the addition of blends and first digraphs (**sh**, **wh**, **ng**) and, most importantly, with an emphasis on how letters function within words and on word building. Programme Two consolidates and extends this previous learning, introducing children to more phonemes, further blends, digraphs and double consonants, as well as suffixes, more complex spelling patterns and their exceptions.

Neither Programme One nor Programme Two attempts to cover all the skills that children need to acquire for full literacy. They concentrate instead on two important facets, namely:

* sound/symbol correspondences (the analysis and synthesis of letter strings)
* language development (both oral and written, listening and speaking skills, speculating, remembering, initiating and communicating ideas).

Letterland is entirely consistent with the National Curriculum in emphasising the importance of learning the sounds of letters, of developing a sight vocabulary and of learning specific spelling patterns through the medium of stories. It develops children's questioning and concentration skills, while providing a stimulus for different genres of writing. Letterland is a particularly valuable medium for implementing the National Literacy Strategy, in particular the word level strand. For more information, see page 10.

Letterland is widely used in Scotland and Northern Ireland and fully supports the Scottish 5-14 Guidelines and the Curriculum for Northern Ireland. It is particularly relevant as part of any Early Intervention programme because of its thorough and lively approach to teaching phonics.

SECTION 1

Letterland for everyone

Letterland and the National Literacy Strategy

The National Literacy Strategy sets out a framework of teaching objectives for each term and recommends that there should be systematic, regular and frequent teaching of phonics. Letterland provides the key to achieving those objectives on time, or even well ahead of time as thousands of schools currently using Letterland have shown.

A number of factors have contributed to this early achievement. The main factor is probably the ever expanding use of Letterland at the pre-school and nursery level. As a result, it is becoming more typical for children to arrive in Reception knowing all the **aA–zZ** shapes and sounds and correct letter formation. This allows the reception teacher to take full advantage of the Literacy Hour by teaching many of the Year 1 objectives ahead of time. This headstart can then be maintained as children progress on to Programme Two.

Other contributing factors are the economy of learning built into Letterland teaching (see Foreword, page 6), the informed support and back-up which parents are bringing through using Letterland at home, and the National Literacy Strategy's increased emphasis on whole class teaching, which has always been fundamental to Letterland teaching.

Cross-curricular links

Letterland can easily be incorporated into all areas of the curriculum, helping to strengthen and develop the understanding of specific phonemes or spelling patterns. The use of art, craft, role-play, music and songs developed in Programme One continues to contribute in Programme Two to ensure that lessons are enjoyed and remembered. In Section 2, you will find a variety of activities suggested to link with specific phonemes. These activities have been planned to combine a variety of different and important language skills with skills from other subject areas. They range from drawing maps and routes, to measuring shadows, growing plants and labelling diagrams. The activities relate to those suggested in the National Literacy Strategy and can be used in group work time during the Literacy Hour.

Regional and individual pronunciation

The picture-coded examples in this guide assume standard English pronunciation. However, where regional or individual pronunciation differs, the picture coding can easily be adapted. For example, in the case of the words **book** and **ask**, either of the picture codings on the right might be correct, depending on the pronunciation of the person adding the picture coding.

book
or
book

ask or ask

In a few cases, teachers may prefer to exclude certain pictograms as inapplicable in a particular area, e.g. the Vowel Stealer pictograms (see pages 94, 120, 132-137) in Scotland, where the pronunciation of **ar**, **or**, **er**, **ir**, and **ur** is scarcely different from the single letter sounds.

sport
or
sport

Where there is no correspondence between particular letters and their normal sounds, either because of idiosyncrasies in English spelling or because of regional or individual pronunciation, you can draw a wiggly line beneath the relevant letters. In these cases the wiggly line signals the disparity. (For more information, see **Picture coding** on page 19.)

thorough

Children with Special Needs

It was children with Special Needs who first inspired the idea of Letterland stories to explain the way letters behave in words. These children wanted explanations which they could understand and remember for the many variables in sound they needed to know.

The combination of story explanations and the fusing of a pictogram into each letter has also been shown to help the more severely disabled child, the visually impaired, the hearing impaired as well as the children who are physically disabled or have severe learning difficulties. The system reaches them not just through their eyes, ears or hands, but also by offering them a 'Letterland logic' to strengthen otherwise difficult rote-learning. Because the facts acquire reasons, they are easier to remember.

With older children who are behind in literacy skills, to start by going through the Letterland **a–z** in alphabetical order could make them feel awkward. First see which letters cause difficulties by analysing spelling errors. Do they confuse the vowels, **b** and **d**, **p** and **q**, or **s** and **c** or **ch**, and **sh.** If so, start with *The Vowels Poster* (illustrated on page 17) and those letters. They will soon want to know all the Letterland characters. Since Letterland reuses the single letter characters to explain digraph sounds they will be learning the complete alphabet as a natural progression on the way to more advanced phonic instruction.

English as an Additional Language

By suspending the use of traditional alphabet names in the early stages of teaching phonics, the Letterland approach saves EAL children from having to cope with the bewildering fact that no fewer than seven of the alphabet names are also high usage English words: **I**, **you**, **are**, **a**, **be**, **see** and **why**, not to mention **bee**, **sea**, **eye**, **oh**, **pea** and **tea**.

The catch-up time for EAL children can be achieved more swiftly than is normally possible because the clues for learning the alphabet are not a miscellany of 26 separate pictures which a child must link to 26 foreign shapes, but rather 26 pictograms with the sound/symbol link already designed into them.

EAL children can share immediately in the play-acting, art, craft and singing. Much of the story logic can be retold in their home language if necessary. Meanwhile, the Letterland characters mediate between the EAL children and the undeciphered letters, motivating them to master the new shapes, sounds and letter combinations.

For EAL children who are new to your class and are not already familiar with the Letterland characters, it may be useful for them to first discover the characters through the *Letterland ABC Book.*

Letterland and reading schemes

Years of experience by many teachers has shown that, no matter which reading scheme(s) a school prefers, the *parallel* introduction of Letterland makes for swifter progress.

Similarly, schools which prefer only non-scheme books report that Letterland provides a sense of structure and initial confidence which could otherwise be lacking where a school relies exclusively on non-scheme books.

Parental involvement

You can brief the children's parents about Letterland characters and any inter-connecting stories in gradual stages. Then each time their child comes home with something to tell them about Letterland (such as a new character or a new story), the parent is in an informed position to support the new learning. The key is for parents to be persuaded to let their child become the teacher!

The most effective approach to Programme Two involves, for example, the child coming home from school and telling his or her parent about Giant All and how the picture coding works in words like **all**, **tall**, **small**, **also** and **always**. The parent, by lending a willing ear and maintaining good eye contact, responds as a *learner*. He or she is impressed, shows it, and looks forward to the next story and the next picture coding. This parental listening role ensures that both school and home stay synchronised over the timing of the new sounds to be learnt, and allows the child to move into the novel and exciting position of teaching their parents for a change.

Throughout their early years, children are bound to experience most of their learning at the hands of those who know better than they do. They are always the passive receivers of adult input. Within the context of Letterland, the dynamics shift in favour of the child who becomes a more active contributor.

The role reversal of the 'child in the know' and the parent as 'the willing learner' can do wonders for a child's self-esteem. At the same time, the parent becomes a good role model by demonstrating daily an interested learning attitude. Another equally important benefit, is that the child's oral language skills are given scope to expand. Most important of all, however, is that as the children share their new knowledge at home *they consolidate their own learning*.

Parents and the National Literacy Strategy

Most schools have long welcomed the contribution that parents can make to children's progress by coming into school and listening to individual children read. That contribution is now likely to become more developed and focused as schools are encouraged, via the National Literacy Strategy, to invite parents to come in and help children with their group work. Many of the activities for **Group word work** contained in this book, are ideal for this purpose.

Letterland Programme Two

The materials

Essential

- *Letterland Programme Two Teacher's Guide*
- *Letterland Programme Two Picture Code Cards*
- *Letterland Programme One Picture Code Cards*
- *Letterland Programme Two Copymasters*
- *Letterland Programme Two Word Bank Copymasters*
- *Letterland Programme Two Songs Cassette*

Highly recommended

- *Letterland Vowel Scene Posters*
- *Letterland Programme Two Word Books*

What you will have achieved by the end of this Unit

Letterland materials needed for teaching this sound

Quick story summary

What you will need to prepare before the lesson

Sample picture coded sentence

UNIT 1.1

ee (as in feet)

Objectives

- To know that the letters **e** and **e** combine to represent long 'ē' (**ee** as in **feet**).
- To recognise and spell words containing **ee**.

What you need

- *Programme Two Picture Code Cards:* **ee**
- *Programme One Picture Code Cards*
- *Programme Two Copymaster:* 1
- *Programme Two Word Bank Copymaster:* 1
- *Programme Two Songs Cassette*
- *Vowel Scenes Poster:* Vowels Out Walking

Preparation

- **ee book**
  Have ready some sheets of paper for the children to prepare their **ee** book. Give the book a gr**ee**n cover.

Introducing the 'ee' sound

Introduce the concept of Vowels Out Walking by showing the children the *Vowels Out Walking Poster* and saying this rhyme together:

When two vowels go out walking
The FIRST man does the talking.
The first one says his name,
But his friend won't do the same.

This rhyme forms the basis for explaining all long vowel phonemes made by a vowel pair. It can be adapted to apply to the vowel pair you are teaching. In this case:

When two E's walk, the first E talks

When two E's go out walking.
The first Mr E does the talking.
He just says his name,
But his twin won't do the same.

The Vowels Out Walking song is on the *Programme Two Songs Cassette.* Verse 2 refers to the occasions when the vowel pair is affected by an **r** (and invalidates the Vowels Out Walking principle). It explains why the second vowel is silent: because the Vowel Man is busy looking out for **r**obbers (**r**'s). The children will need to look out for them too, because the letter **r** causes most of the exceptions to the Vowels Out Walking principle. The panel at the bottom of the *Vowels Out Walking Poster* shows some of the exceptions. (See also page 17.)

Whole class word work

- Listen to and sing the Vowels Out Walking song on the *Programme Two Songs Cassette*. The children raise their right arms and shout 'E!' after 'his name'.
- Write these sentences on the board and ask the children to help with picture coding **e** and **ee**.

Did we see ducks or geese between the trees?
That hole must be fifteen feet deep.

Did we see ducks or geese between the trees?

36

Notes about the materials

Programme Two Teacher's Guide

Section Two of this *Programme Two Teacher's Guide* provides strategies which enable all the National Literacy Strategy requirements for Year 1, Term 3 and Year 2 to be met on time or ahead of its scheduled time table. Units 1-17 follow the teaching order specified by the NLS, while Section 3 gives teachers detailed suggestions for teaching other important phonemes and principles of word structure used in the English language. It also includes some built-in revision of Programme One as appropriate. Section 4 comprises a range of photocopiable material, including a Teacher's Checklist, Pupil Record Sheet and useful templates for activities contained within the detailed teaching notes.

In Greenland it seems to get very cold indeed.
The queen agreed to give a speech at the meeting.

- Live spell: **free** → **flee** → **heel** → **steel** → **green** → **agree** → **degree**. Follow up by dictating these or other **ee** words.

Group word work

- Use *Programme Two Copymaster* 1 for further practice.
- Introduce *Word Bank Copymaster* 1. Ask the children to look for words containing **ee** in their books and to add them to their Word Banks.
- Make a class **ee** book using the colour gr**ee**n as a memory device. The children draw and label pictures of objects containing **ee** and colour them all green. Examples of these could be: gr**ee**n f**ee**t, thr**ee** gr**ee**n b**ee**s, a chimpanz**ee** with gr**ee**n ch**ee**ks and kn**ee**s, gr**ee**n b**ee**ch trees, sl**ee**py gr**ee**n sh**ee**p and gr**ee**n g**ee**se. These pictures could then be collated into a class spelling book for the children to read and use as a spelling resource.

Cross-curricular and other suggestions

- Ask the children to write sentences about the things that they will n**ee**d in order to go swimming, on a picnic, to the moon, to the zoo or to school. Make sure that they start each sentence of their list with "I will n**ee**d ... to go to the moon." They can decorate the borders of their writing with illustrations of the things that they n**ee**d.
- The children could also use collage materials to represent the **ee** objects used in their group work above.

Words containing ee

agree	knee
bee	kneel
been*	meet*
beetle	need*
between*	peel
breeze	peep
cheek	queen*
cheesecake	referee
cheetah	screen
chimpanzee	see*
coffee	seed
committee	seem*
creep	seen*
deed	sheep
deep*	sheet
degree	sleep*
eel	speech
feed*	speedy
feel*	squeeze
feelings*	steel
feet*	steep
flee	street*
free*	sweep
freeze	sweet*
geese	teenager
greedy	teeth*
Greek	three*
green*	toffee
heel	tree*
indeed	weed
keen	week
keep*	wheel

Challenge words

creek	settee
leech	sleek

* High usage words

References
Other vowel pairs: p38 **ēa**, p42 **ai**, p46 **ay**, p50 **ie**, p60 **oa**, p74 **ue**, p152 **ĕa**.

37

Example words containing the sound

Other relevant phonemes

Programme Two Picture Code Cards

The *Programme Two Picture Code Cards* consist of 85 cards featuring all the phonemes covered in Programme Two. Each card also includes a brief summary of the relevant story together with some example words containing the phoneme.

Programme Two Copymasters

These photocopiable sheets provide support activities for further practice and consolidation of the phonemes covered in each Programme Two lesson. They are ideal for group work, and help children to build their vocabulary, follow instructions and practise reading and spelling words containing the phoneme being studied.

Programme Two Word Bank Copymasters

The *Programme Two Word Bank Copymasters* provide examples of the spelling patterns taught in Programme Two. Children practise their skimming skills when collecting examples and create a useful reference list based on their own experience and investigations.

Programme Two Songs Cassette

The *Programme Two Songs Cassette* is a collection of songs featuring the most important phonemes covered in this guide. They support the story reasons for the new sounds and strengthen phonemic awareness through rhyme, rhythm and repetition. This helps to make lessons memorable, and particularly valuable for children with poor listening skills and poor auditory memories. They are also useful for assembly presentations and role-play/drama activities.

Programme Two Word Book

This advanced word book focuses on the letter patterns covered in Programme Two. It provides picture-coded examples on each page and spaces for children to build up their own personal resource of words they need to be able to spell.

Vowel Scenes Posters

These four A2 posters feature The Vowels (short and long), Vowels Out Walking, Silent Magic **e**, and The Vowel Stealers. Use each one as the central point in a wall display to provide a quick, on-going reference point for the children while they are learning these core spelling patterns.

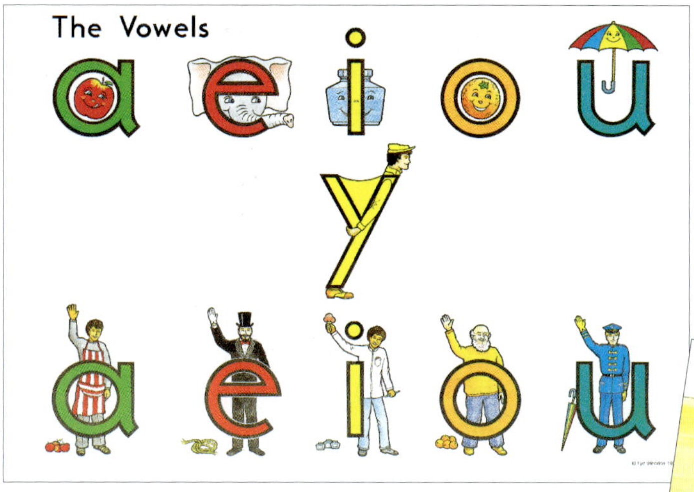

Teaching order

At first, you may prefer to follow the order of presentation given in this guide (see pages 4-5). This suggested teaching order correlates with the National Literacy Strategy's recommended time tabling. The difference lies in the fact that the term-by-term requirements of the Literacy Strategy are a list of contents *to be achieved by a given date*, not a required teaching order. It would be a wasted opportunity to hold back on telling the story explanation for **er** (as in dinn**er**) until Term 2 of Year 2 if you are doing a project on, say, My Family, in Term 3 of Year 1, where the children will need to spell a number of high usage words containing **er** (sist**er**, oth**er,** broth**er**, moth**er**). Likewise, if a Reception child called Rob**er**t wants to know why Eddy Elephant isn't saying '**ĕ...**' in his name, you may choose to praise him for noticing and reward him with a brief version of the **er** story.

Children are surrounded by words. If any one word arouses their curiosity (unless it is totally irregular) there is no need to postpone the relevant story which gives the *reason* for the new sound. Because the original mnemonics remain valid (**e** = elephant, **r** = robber), earlier facts are reinforced even as you tell the story for the new sound. So your teaching order can be highly flexible.

Be ready to introduce any part of Section 3 to individual children or to the whole class *at the time of need* to cure recurring spelling errors or to preclude other errors from occurring in the first place. For comments on the timing of the whole programme, see page 10.

Children new to Letterland

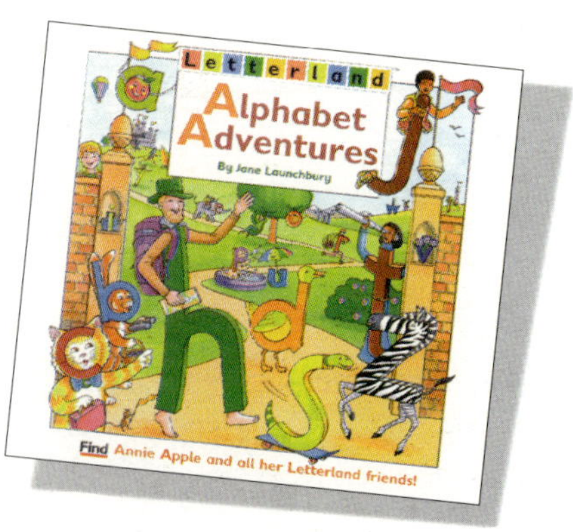

Any children in your class who have no prior knowledge of the Letterland Alphabet can be introduced to it swiftly using the *Letterland ABC Book* or *Alphabet Adventures.* All they need is a superficial acquaintance with the characters in order to appreciate the Programme Two stories, as most of the pictogram stories throughout Letterland revolve around the original **a–z** characters. As a result, children new to Letterland will find themselves rapidly learning 'who' the single letter characters are, and what sounds they make, on their way to learning their digraph sounds as well. Each new story provides a reason for the original Letterland characters to be making new sounds whenever they 'meet each other' in a word.

Teaching with Programme Two

Introducing each spelling pattern

Introduce each new spelling pattern with the help of the appropriate *Programme Two Picture Code Card.* In each section of this Guide, the text in colour provides you with a model for the story-like style which will make your teaching both interesting and memorable. To begin with you may like to read out the story, but you should also feel free to use your own wording and your own story-telling manner. Don't worry if you leave points out. A shortened version of each Letterland story is provided in the story title for each sound, making the titles into good summing-up sentences and useful reminders when revising sounds learnt so far. In a few cases, a shorter version of a longer story is provided in addition to the title.

Picture coding

Include some picture coding as a regular feature for each new sound you teach. It will enable you to progress more swiftly. Animating letters takes only a few easy pencil strokes. (See also page 21 of the *Programme One Teacher's Guide.*) As the children draw, they are illustrating with their own hands any key changes in letter behaviour.

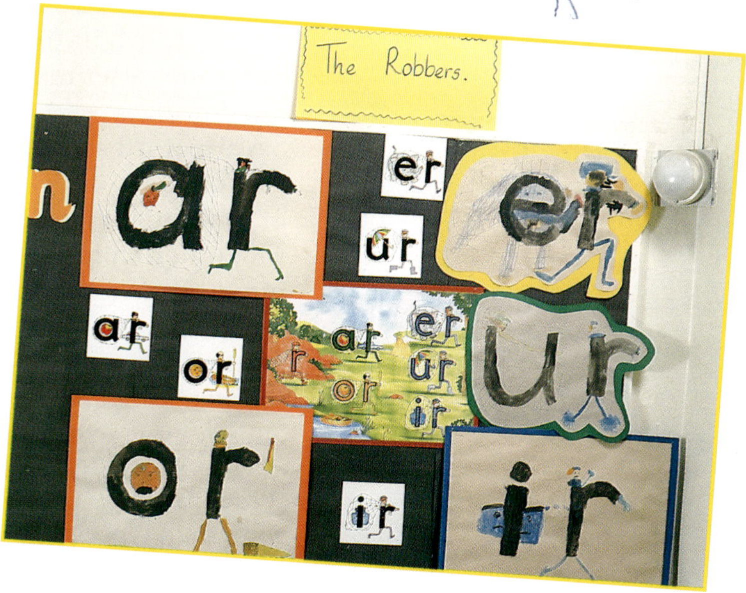

While the children may have the impression that all they have to do is to decorate some letters within a word or sentence, in fact they are doing much more. In order to add the picture code to any given letters, the child needs to:

* *read* the sentence (with help if necessary)
* *re-read* each word to be coded (providing repetition with a purpose)
* *listen* to their own pronunciation of the word, carefully enough to pick out the sounds made by the specific letters to be picture coded
* *relate* these sounds to the correct pictogram
* *confirm* the letter sounds in picture form.

Wiggly lines are a useful interim device for signalling any letter combination which does not conform to the information taught so far. Some sound changes will be explained by a pictogram story in due course, but for the time being your wiggly lines will save fruitless decoding attempts and alert the child to focus instead on whole word shapes and context and syntax clues.

Similarly, show the children how to use wiggly lines when they are picture coding irregular parts of words for themselves. They should not, for example, code **a** by drawing an apple if they cannot hear its '**ă**...' sound. Instead, they should use a wiggly line to show that they have discovered an irregular **a**.

Live spelling and dictation

Live spelling

In live spelling, each child holds a card which you have selected from your *Programme One* and *Programme Two Picture Code Cards*. The *Programme Two Cards* feature the phoneme being introduced in the lesson. The *Programme One Cards* enable the children to form whole words around the phoneme, using either pictogram or plain letter sides. Digraph cards may be held by one or two children.

Many of the suggested words for live spelling are set out in an order which enables just one child to completely change the meaning of the word, either by replacing another child or by joining the others as they stand. Here are two strategies for developing live spelling. The first one emphasises phonemic awareness; the second one decoding skills.

1. Emphasising phonemic awareness, spelling words

- Say the word, in this case **down**. Say it slowly and clearly.
- Put it into a sentence so that its meaning is clear, e.g. I saw him fall **down**.
- Say the word slowly again, exaggerating each phoneme.
- The children check their cards to see if they are holding one of the phonemes. If so, they come to the front.
- The other children can then guide them (turning word building into a cooperative effort).
- Direct each child to say their sound in sequence, adding miming gestures where appropriate. They repeat the whole word, then the watching children repeat it.
- Say the next word: **town**. The children must listen carefully to decide who must leave the word and who should come and take **d**'s place.
- Progressing on from **town** to **towel**, the **n**-child must realise it is time to go. *Two* other children join to create **towel**.

2. Emphasising decoding skills, reading words

- Give three or four children the cards needed to build a word, but without telling them what that word is. (Assume **down**.)
- Tell each child where to stand. Then help the card holders to discover, by blending their sounds, what word they have made.
- Ask the first child to sit down and the child holding **t** to take his or her place. What word has the new child helped to create? (**town**) Progress to **brown** in the same way.

Another option, in either sequence, is to appoint some watching children as record keepers. They copy the letter sequences as their friends make them, and then read all the words out at the end.

Benefits of live spelling

1 The *Picture Code Cards* make each phoneme division clear. For example, while **shower** is spelt with six letters, it is clearly made up of only three phonemes, each one a digraph. These can be held either by three children or six, who then mime the letter interaction that causes the new sound. (See illustrations in Sections 2 and 3.)
2 If a child makes a mistake, explaining the error will help all the children avoid it in the future.
3 Weaker spellers receive much needed help before they write anything down.
4 If the word is new vocabulary for any child, the live spelling routine provides a natural opportunity to explain its meaning.
5 Children with poor attention spans are likely to concentrate longer as they are looking at letters on their friends.

Dictation

Dictation is a valuable alternative to live spelling. The process is the same, but after you have said the word slowly, all the children write it. Write the correct spelling on the board *as soon as the children have written each word* so that they can immediately correct any mistake by crossing their word out and *rewriting the whole word correctly.* (With slightly more experienced children, you may prefer to write all the words out at the end for children to check for themselves.)

Dictation will take less time than live spelling but live spelling will continue to be important on and off throughout the year as a confidence builder because there are no mistakes on record. Meanwhile the children have exercised listening skills, practised linking sound to symbol and symbols to sounds, and improved their sequencing skills as they sort the phonemes into the right order.

Look, say, cover, write, check

The *look, say, cover, write, check* process is suggested as a way of helping children to learn spellings. Children are sometimes asked to learn spellings without any idea of *how* to go about this. Using the *look, say, cover, write, check* process, they copy the words in a list (or have them written), study and read each word carefully as many times as they need to, say it slowly out loud, then cover it and write the word again. They can then check for themselves whether they have written the word correctly.

Punctuation

Capital letters and full stops

Children become weary of endless reminders not to leave out capital letters and full stops. You may well become weary too, repeating yourself so often. Perhaps a change in your instruction language will help. For capital letters suggest that the children give their Letterland friends a chance to 'do their trick', to get bigger, or jump higher, and so on (as first described in Programme One). The Letterland characters then become the motivators. Encourage a 'full stop/then capital letter' habit.

Explain that ...

> *Authors of books use full stops together with 'big' capital letter shapes to signal to their readers to stop and take a deep breath before they read on. That is why the Letterland characters take a deep breath after a full stop too, and do their 'getting bigger trick'* [become capital letters] *to start the next sentence.*
>
> *The full stop usually means the end of the last thought. The capital letter signals an important new start, and the Letterlanders love feeling important, so don't forget to give them that pleasure.*

Ask everyone to scan old magazines to find, for example, just sentences that 'open with a Duck Door'. The children can then overwrite the preceding full stops and capital **D**'s in colour. They could then go on to look for sentences where, e.g. 'Poor Peter has popped up'. Also point out that to write *any* capital letter, they simply start at the top.

When correcting for omitted capitals, you could try talking along the following lines. If your sentence begins with the ['...'] sound, don't forget to ... (see the table on pages 23 and 24).

A Don't forget to…
put your apple on an Applestand.

B give Bouncy Ben a chance to do his balancing trick right there at the beginning!

C give Clever Cat a chance to do her 'getting bigger' trick.

D open it with a Duck Door!

E give Eddy Elephant a chance to do his 'elephant-on-end' trick.

F put Fireman Fred up front, with his letter all upright and straight,
the way he likes to look when he's doing an important job.

G give Golden Girl a go in her Go-Cart.

H show us how happy you can make the Hat Man
by letting him start it with a handstand!

I use an ink pen instead of an ink bottle!

J give Jumping Jim a chance to jump sky high.

K give Kicking King a chance to take a deep breath
and kick off this sentence with a nice big kick.

L give Lucy Lamp Lady a chance to rest her long, long legs on the line.

M let Munching Mike's Mum start it because Munching Mike is too little.

N give Naughty Nick a chance to bang in some nails without being
a nuisance, for a change.

let Oscar Orange take a deep breath and look big and important.

give Poor Peter a chance to pop up, even though his floppy ears will still droop.

let Quarrelsome Queen start the first word, sitting down in her Quiet Room.

let Robber Red show you how he looks when he has stuffed stolen goods under his jumper.

give Sammy Snake a chance to take a deep breath and look super-sized!

give Ticking Tess a chance to do her 'getting bigger' trick, making her so tall that her head disappears in a cloud.

give Uppy Umbrella a chance to do her 'getting bigger' trick.

decorate the beginning of the sentence with a very big Vase of Violets.

give Wicked Water Witch a chance to do her 'getting bigger' trick.

let Max and Maxine do their 'getting bigger' trick.

give Yo-yo Man a chance to step up on the line to begin it.

give Zig Zag Zebra a chance to do her 'getting bigger' trick. Maybe she won't feel quite so shy then.

Conversely, to cure bad habits (e.g. aBout or reaDy) your wording can be something along the lines of 'No tricks in the middle please!' Explain that the only time capitals occur inside words is when all the Letterland characters are helping to show how important that word is, e.g. DANGER, or in book titles.

Apostrophes – possession

To learn to use an apostrophe to signal possession requires a clear understanding of the purpose of this punctuation mark. Help the children to think of it like a coat peg where they hang their coats.

The 'belonging-peg' comma

When you see a comma hanging over a word, in Letterland it is called a 'belonging-peg' comma. This comma shows that something belongs to the word in which the comma appears.

The question in the uncertain speller's mind is, on which side to place the comma? Here are some guidelines:

Belonging to one

If you want the word to signal 'belonging to one', put the 'belonging-peg' comma behind Sammy Snake's back.

Belonging to many

To signal both 'several of something' and 'belonging to many', let Sammy say 'ssseveral' first. Then add your 'belonging-peg' comma in front of his nose.

Apostrophes – contractions

The incorrect placement of apostrophes is common among children and adults alike. Possibly **do'nt** for **don't** is the most frequent error, where the writer is not aware that the apostrophe should mark *the place of a missing letter and its missing sound*, not the space between two words compounded into one.

Exploding letters

The concept of 'exploding letters' will help prevent these errors. Plan a time gap between teaching about 'exploding letters' and the 'belonging-peg comma' (see page 25). Let necessity determine which type of apostrophe to teach first. While the other apostrophe signals belonging, this one acts as a place marker.

*Sometimes, when we speak quickly, the words tumble out of our mouths so fast that they bump into each other. When you see these words written down, the parts you can no longer hear will have disappeared. What has happened to them? They have exploded! For example, if you want to say 'do not!' quickly, you say '**don't**'. The words **do** and **not** bump together so hard that the **o** in **not** explodes, turning **do not** into **don't**. Although the explosion is very quiet, it is so great that most of the broken bits are never seen again!*

*Strangely enough, one of the exploded pieces (but only one) always comes floating down to hover over the spot where the explosion took place. This broken bit marking the spot looks like a piece of an **o**, but you never know. It might be a bit of some other letter, because **o** is not the only letter which explodes when it's bumped.*

*If you want to say '**I am...**' quickly, you say '**I'm...**'. Listen: **I'm**. Which letter explodes? The **a** explodes!*

I am → I'm

*If you want to say '**that is...**' quickly, you say '**that's...**'. Which letter explodes this time? The **i** explodes!*

that is → that's

*If you want to say '**Let us...**' quickly, you will say '**Let's...**'. Which letter explodes? The **u** explodes!*

Let us → Let's

*Sometimes more than one sound disappears, so more than one letter explodes. Even then, only one broken bit is ever seen again. Its job, it seems, is to mark the place where several explosions took place. Sometimes the first half of the word **have** explodes: **I've**.*

I have → I've

Sometimes the first half of the word ***will*** *explodes:* ***I'll.***

I will → I ’ll

The biggest explosions may include three or four letters or even a whole word. If you want to say ***'I would like it'*** *quickly, you say* ***'I'd like it'****. There is not much left of* ***would*** *after that explosion!*

I would → I ’d

When we say ***'o'clock'*** *we really mean* ***'of the clock'****. So not only* ***f****, but all the letters in the word* ***the*** *explode too!*

of the clock → o ’ clock

don't	hasn't	isn't	won't	can't	it's	he'd	she'll
doesn't	haven't	wasn't	wouldn't	couldn't	that's	you'd	we'll
didn't	hadn't	weren't	shouldn't	mustn't	what's	you've	they'll

Exception: Be careful in the following case: **it is** becomes **it's** as expected, but **its** means 'belonging to'. The only reason **its** has no 'belonging-peg' comma is because it would then look exactly like **it is** after the **i** has exploded.

it is → it ’s (as expected)	its = belonging to it (exception)

It's a pity that the dog cut its paw.

Special case: The words **you're** and **your** sound alike. The broken bit shows which one is really two words bumped together.

you are → you ’re   your = belonging to you

You're your own worst enemy.

Further ideas

Story-retelling

Few children enjoy repeating rules, but they do like retelling and acting out the Letterland story explanations, which take the place of rules. Recounting is an important part of language development. Retelling stories also provides a valuable form of revision and consolidation of information gained. Make narrating by the children a brief but regular feature of your Letterland sessions.

Visual memory training

To make plain letter(s) cue their own sounds use the following routine:

* Hold up the plain letter side of a *Picture Code Card.*
* Quickly flash the pictogram side and return to the plain side.
* Ask children to describe what they saw.
* Let them retell the relevant story in their own words.
* Follow up by letting them picture code some examples.

Linking words of a kind

Write out words of a kind on pieces of card, e.g. **phone**, **photograph**, **alphabet**, **dolphin**, **nephew**, **elephant**, **pheasant**, **paragraph**, **trophy** and hand them out to a group of children. Ask them to think up sentences using these words. This is more effective than simply memorising 'word families'. Younger children can draw or paint some of these objects around their own picture-coded **ph** digraph and then label the objects.

Spelling pictures

Choose words where children can both picture code all the letters in one word and illustrate its whole-word meaning (see also page 26 in the *Programme One Teacher's Guide*). A collection of these 'spelling pictures' bound into a book can become a special kind of classroom resource, a unique picture dictionary made, alphabetised and indexed by the children.

Help from older children

If you appoint older readers, say 7 or 8 year olds, to assist the younger ones, the opportunity arises to revise bits of Letterland logic with these older children first, to the ultimate benefit of both groups of children. For example, if the story a 6 year old will be reading includes the word **knight** in it, then the **kn** pictogram will be relevant. During reading, the older child should provide the whole word, **knight**, so as not to interrupt the flow of the story. *After* the story, however, he or she can help the younger child to construct the word **knight** using the *Picture Code Cards*, retell the **kn** story and show how to make a spelling picture which illustrates both the **kn** pictogram and the whole-word meaning of **knight**.

Creative writing

Because Letterland is an imaginary place, there is scope for all sorts of creative writing.

* Let the children choose from an early-level dictionary as many useful words as possible to include in a story about a favourite character, e.g. for Hairy Hat Man: **hunting**, **hut**, **helicopter**, **hippopotamus** and **hospital.** The chosen words can then help them to think of a plot.

* The children can write letters to the Letterland characters, making up addresses for them. They can then 'post' the letters to their classmates, who can reply in the style they imagine the characters might use.

* Let the children describe or invent any of the following:
- A special machine for getting to Letterland.
- Possible houses for favourite Letterland characters. (Here are some ideas from a group of 5 year olds for Jumping Jim: a **j**elly house, a **j**igsaw house, a **j**umping house, a **j**igsaw house on a **j**elly hill and a **j**ellybean house.)
- Favourite pastimes for various characters, such as Bouncy Ben: **b**lowing **b**ubbles or **b**uilding **b**ridges with **b**locks.

* The children can design Christmas cards with pictures of appropriate presents for Letterland inhabitants (for example, a 6 year old's idea for Hairy Hat Man was a **h**umming bird with only a very little **h**um, because he **h**ates noise).

* Suggest that the children describe a trip to Letterland: who they meet, what they say to the various characters, how the characters might reply and what adventures they might have together, and so on.

* Let the children flesh out any aspect of Letterland characters' lives they like. The result may be semi-autobiographical, for example:
Kicking King got hit in the tummy by a football and fell in the mud and his Mummy had to change his clothes!
It is, after all, very common for novelists to transpose personal experience on to fictitious characters!

Wipe-clean picture-coded words

To practise any difficult words or phrases, write them out clearly on one page, make as many photocopies as you need and then insert them into plastic pockets. Let the children add the correct picture coding (using non-permanent overhead projector pens) whenever they feel the need for picture support. They can then read the words, you can tick them and wipe off the coding. If they can re-read them without help you can turn your tick into a star! Finally, wipe off all the stars and check in a later lesson whether all the words remain readable. If so the child wins stars again.

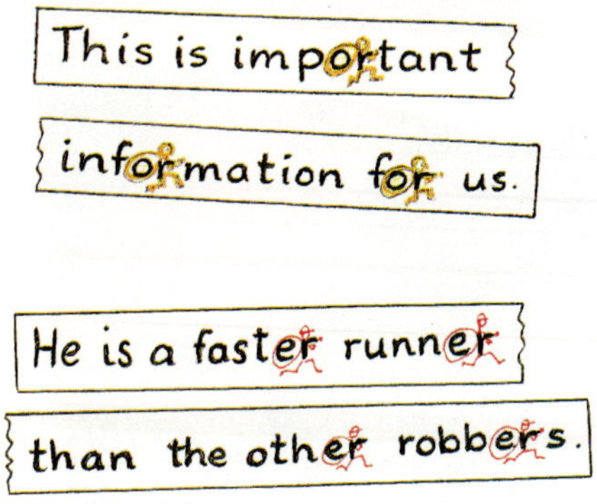

You may also like to write out some sentences for picture coding and cover them in clear plastic. These, too, can be picture-coded first, then wiped clean for re-reading without the picture coding support.

Making use of children's names

Names carry motivational strength and are frequently used in writing. They are, therefore, especially at the start, valuable for illustrating letter sounds. Some names are excellent examples of the Magic **e**, e.g. James, Jane and Kate. Others, like Charlotte, Martin and Edward, help in teaching the **ar** sound. (See also pages 188-9 of the *Programme One Teacher's Guide* for examples of picture-coded names.)

However, many names will contain irregularities or sounds you have not yet taught. Draw a wiggly line under any difficult groups of letters or sounds which you do not wish to teach yet. If the letter group appears on the **Contents** page or in the **Index**, you can promise a story later (see **Picture coding** on page 19). A few children, with names like Louisa or Sean, may be disappointed to be offered no story. Invite them, in due course, to think up their own 'one-off' little stories to explain the letter sequence where they would otherwise need to use a wiggly line.

'Wacky words' collection

Difficult words like **any**, **many** and **they** are good candidates for a 'Wacky words' collection. (Use an alternative name if you prefer.) Let the children write these words on cards, adding wiggly lines under the irregularities themselves.

From time to time, revise the collection to see which words can come out because now the children have learnt that there is some Letterland logic and picture coding to explain the irregular sound(s), e.g. Mr Mean-E sounding like an **a** in **they**.

Making tape recordings

Encourage language from reticent children by tape recording them, whispering like Hairy Hat Man, hissing like Sammy Snake, munching and saying 'mmm...' like Munching Mike, or pouting and making sad little 'p...' sounds like Poor Peter. Let them choose 'who' to be and what to say when they meet each other (on the tape) as Letterland characters. Some children will enjoy writing parts for themselves.

Stress liveliness of expression and encourage practice to reach fluency. It will make the final recording really good listening and provide the confidence boost which some children need.

Quick charades

Two or more children mime a Lettérland digraph or blend without props or letters, e.g. **mb**. (They should only add sound if the miming is not sufficient to identify the letter.) The other children must guess which spelling pattern or Letterland characters are being mimed, and then quickly think of as many words as possible with, in this case, **mb** in them. (With practice they will be able to list quite a few.)

Letterland plays

Some schools enjoy devising their own original plays based on Letterland. Their plots may incorporate songs from the Letterland audio cassettes or original songs, snatches of Letterland lore and their own ideas for adventures in Letterland. Christmas in Letterland, for example, can combine a seasonal theme with a light-hearted instructional element.

SECTION 2

UNIT 1

UNIT 1.1

ee (as in feet)

UNIT 1.2

ea (as in seat)

Long ē

UNIT 1

Resources for Unit 1

- *Programme Two Picture Code Cards:* **ee** (24), **ēa** (22)
- *Programme One Picture Code Cards*
- *Programme Two Copymasters:* 1-3
- *Programme Two Word Bank Copymasters:* 1
- *Programme Two Songs Cassette*
- *Vowel Scenes Posters:* The Vowels, Vowels Out Walking

The English language provides us with no less than seven different ways to spell the long 'ē' sound:

e (as in **we**, **de-**, **pre-**)
ee (as in **feet**)
ea (as in **seat**)
e–e (as in **these**)
ey (as in **key**)
-y (as in **body**)
ie (as in **field**).

This Unit concentrates on the **ee** and **ea** spelling patterns. These patterns occur in many high frequency words and they are the first examples of a generalisation which children can apply to other vowel pairs as well:

first vowel long ➜ second vowel silent.

To ensure that even very young readers can and *do* apply this generalisation (rather than just knowing but not using it), Letterland presents the rule as a rhyme which begins as follows:

When two vowels go out walking,
The FIRST one does the talking.

The Letterland *Vowels Out Walking Poster* brings this rhyme to life. It shows the children which vowel pairs usually follow the rule (several vowel pairs often do not) and ensures that the children see at a glance that the generalisation which it illustrates applies to other vowel pairs as well.

While the **ee** spelling almost always gives a regular sound, the **ea** spelling does not. The children should be prepared for the occasions when they come across the exceptions: **ea** saying 'ĕ' (as in **head**) or **ea** plus **r** (as in **bear** or **hear**). Keep separate lists for such words as children find them and be ready to explain that sometimes Mr E gives Eddy Elephant a turn with the talking (see page 152) and that at other times the two Vowel Men are captured by a **r**obber (see pages 116 and 148).

Before teaching this Unit, display *The Vowels Poster* as a conceptual organiser for the two basic vowel categories. Keep it on display as a reminder to children of the basic vowel sounds (*top row*), the vowel names (*bottom row*) and the fact that the Yo-yo Man often helps the Vowel Men in words.

UNIT 1.1

ee (as in feet)

Objectives

- To know that the letters **e** and **e** combine to represent long ē (**ee** as in **feet**).
- To recognise and spell words containing **ee**.

What you need

- *Programme Two Picture Code Cards:* **ee** (24)
- *Programme One Picture Code Cards*
- *Programme Two Copymaster:* 1
- *Programme Two Word Bank Copymaster:* 1
- *Programme Two Songs Cassette*
- *Vowel Scenes Posters:* Vowels Out Walking

Preparation

- **ee book**
  Have ready some sheets of paper for the children to prepare their **ee** book. Also prepare some gre**en** card for the cover.

Introducing the sound

Introduce the concept of Vowels Out Walking by showing the children the *Vowels Out Walking Poster* and saying this rhyme together:

When two vowels go out walking
The FIRST man does the talking.
The first one says his name,
But his friend won't do the same.

The rhyme forms the basis for explaining all long vowel phonemes made by a vowel pair. It can be adapted to apply to the vowel pair you are teaching.

When two E's walk, the first E talks

When two E's go out walking.
The first Mr E does the talking.
He just says his name,
But his twin won't do the same.

The Vowels Out Walking song is on the *Programme Two Songs Cassette.* Verse 2 refers to the occasions when the vowel pair is affected by an **r** (and invalidates the Vowels Out Walking principle). It explains why the second vowel is silent: because the Vowel Man is busy looking out for **r**obbers (**r**'s). The children will need to look out for them too, because the letter **r** causes most of the exceptions to the Vowels Out Walking principle. The panel at the bottom of the *Vowels Out Walking Poster* shows some of the exceptions. (See also page 17.)

Whole class word work

- Listen to and sing the Vowels Out Walking song on the *Programme Two Songs Cassette.* The children raise their right arms and shout 'E!' after 'his name'.
- Write these sentences on the board and ask the children to help with picture coding **e** and **ee**.

  Did we see ducks or geese between the trees?

  That hole must be fifteen feet deep.

Did we see ducks or geese between the trees?

In Greenland it seems to get very cold indeed.
The queen agreed to give a speech at the meeting.

☆ Live spell: **free** → **flee** → **heel** → **steel** → **green** → **agree** → **degree**. Follow up by dictating these or other **ee** words.

Group word work

☆ Use *Programme Two Copymaster* 1 for further practice.

☆ Introduce *Word Bank Copymaster* 1. Ask the children to look for words containing **ee** in their books and to add them to their Word Banks.

☆ Make a class or group **ee** book using the colour gr**ee**n as a memory device. The children draw and label pictures of objects containing **ee** and colour them gr**ee**n. Examples of these could be: gr**ee**n f**ee**t, thr**ee** gr**ee**n b**ee**s, a chimpanz**ee** with gr**ee**n ch**ee**ks and kn**ee**s, gr**ee**n b**ee**ch tr**ee**s, sl**ee**py gr**ee**n sh**ee**p and gr**ee**n g**ee**se. These pictures can be collated into a class spelling book for the children to read and use as a spelling resource.

Cross-curricular and other suggestions

☆ Ask the children to write sentences about the things that they will n**ee**d in order to go swimming, on a picnic, to the moon, to the zoo or to school. Make sure that they start each sentence of their list with 'I will n**ee**d ... to go to the moon.' They can decorate the borders of their writing with illustrations of the things that they n**ee**d.

☆ The children could also use collage materials to represent the **ee** objects used in their group work above.

References
For other vowel pairs, see p38 **ēa**, p42 **ai**, p46 **ay**, p50 **ie**, p60 **oa**, p74 **ue**, p152 **ĕa**.

Words containing ee

agree	knee
bee	kneel
been*	meet*
beetle	need*
between*	peel
breeze	peep
cheek	queen*
cheesecake	referee
cheetah	screen
chimpanzee	see*
coffee	seed
committee	seem*
creep	seen*
deep*	sheep
degree	sheet
eel	sleep*
feed*	speedy
feel*	squeeze
feelings*	steel
feet*	steep
flee	street*
free*	sweep
freeze	sweet*
geese	teenager
greedy	teeth*
Greek	three*
green*	toffee
heel	tree*
indeed	weed
keen	week*
keep*	wheel

Challenge words

creek	settee
leech	sleek

* High frequency words

UNIT 1.2
ea (as in seat)

Objectives

- To know that the letters **e** and **a** can represent long **ē** (**ea** as in **seat**).
- To recognise and spell words containing **ea** saying **ē**.

What you need

- *Programme Two Picture Code Cards:* **ea** (22)
- *Programme One Picture Code Cards*
- *Programme Two Copymaster:* 2
- *Programme Two Word Bank Copymaster:* 1
- *Programme Two Songs Cassette*
- *Vowel Scenes Posters:* Vowels Out Walking

Preparation

- Have ready an example word on a display stand and *Picture Code Cards* for making others (see page 39).

Introducing the sound

Point out to the children that **ea** is, like **ee**, a vowel pair. Study the *Vowels Out Walking Poster* together, looking especially at the Vowel Men's mouths to see who is talking. Then repeat the rhyme:

When two vowels go out walking,
The FIRST one does the talking.

In this instance, the verse changes as follows.

When Mr E and A walk, Mr E usually talks

When Mr E and A go out walking,
*Mr E **usually** does the talking.*
He just says his name,
But his friend won't do the same.

The word 'usually' is needed because of **ea**'s other sound (as in **head**) and the spelling patterns affected by **r** (as in **hear**). See pages 152 and 148 and the panel at the base of the *Vowels Out Walking Poster.*

Whole class word work

- Listen to and sing the Vowels Out Walking song on the *Programme Two Songs Cassette.* The children raise their right arms and shout 'E!' after 'his name'.
- Write these sentences on the board and ask the children to help with picture coding **e**, **a** and **ea**.

We dream of eating peaches and cream.
A beastly flea had eaten Ted's meat.
We made big heaps of leaves to leap into.
She gave them a hot meal of meat and beans.

We dream of eating peaches and cream.

- Live spell: **each** → **beach** → **reach** → **reason** → **season** → **stream**. Follow up by dictating these or other words where **ea** says 'ē'.

Group word work

- Use *Programme Two Copymaster* 2 for further practice.

- Introduce *Word Bank Copymaster* 1. Write a selection of words from the word box below on the board and add a few distractors. Each child chooses six words containing **ea** saying 'ē', to write in their Word Banks.

- Ask the children to write a menu for a r**ea**lly special m**ea**l or to describe a f**ea**st. It could include m**ea**t, p**ea**ches and cr**ea**m, p**ea**nut butter, b**ea**ns and p**ea**s. The children could decide how many of the items in the Meal words box they want and in what order. They could add extra ingredients and illustrate the borders with the ingredients of their meal.

Meal words

beans	peaches
cream cake	peanuts
lean meat	peas
lettuce-leaves	salad cream
meat	weak tea

Cross-curricular and other suggestions

- During a dance session, you could talk to the children about the four s**ea**sons in the year and their different weather conditions. Encourage the children to plan and perform their own dance, where their movements incorporate the elements of the four s**ea**sons. (Make sure they know the r**ea**son for the four s**ea**sons theme: the **ea** spelling in s**ea**sons!)

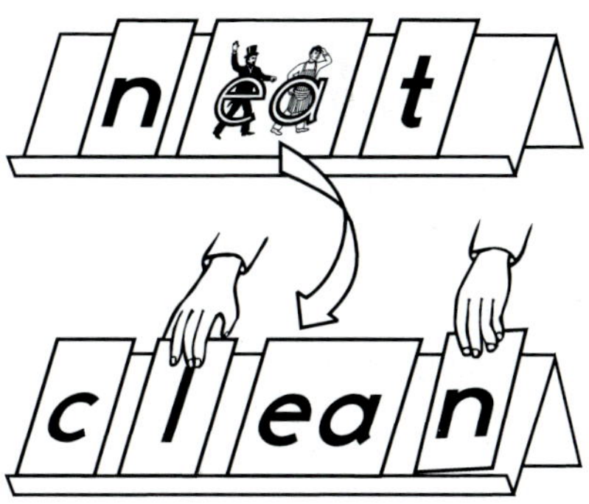

Words containing ea saying 'ē'

appeal	eager	lean	repeat
beach*	east*	least	reveal
bead	Easter*	leaves*	scream
beat*	eat*	meal	season
cheap	eaten	mean*	seat
cheat	flea	meat*	speak
clean*	grease	neat	squeak
cream	heap	peak	steal
deal	heat	plea	steam
dream	leaf*	reach	stream
each*	leak	reason	teach*

* High frequency words

References
For other vowel pairs, see p36 **ēe**, p42 **ai**, p46 **ay**, p50 **ie**, p60 **oa**, p74 **ue**, p152 **ĕa**.

UNIT 2

UNIT 2.1

ai (as in train)

UNIT 2.2

a–e (as in name)

UNIT 2.3

ay (as in play)

Long ā

UNIT 2

Resources for Unit 2

- *Programme Two Picture Code Cards:* **ai** (18), **ay** (45), **Mr A** (1), **Magic e** (9)
- *Programme One Picture Code Cards*
- *Programme Two Copymasters:* 4-7
- *Programme Two Word Bank Copymasters:* 2
- *Programme Two Songs Cassette*
- *Vowel Scenes Posters:* Vowels Out Walking, Silent Magic **e**

In the English language there are three particular spelling patterns that predictably contain a long **ā**: **ai**, **a–e** and **ay**. In all three cases, the second vowel is silent but it signals this important message: the vowel which precedes it will be saying its name. By becoming alert to these pronunciation signals, inexperienced readers can gain access to reading thousands of words long before they could ever hope to learn them as sight words.

The **ai** and **ay** patterns provide two opportunities to revise and extend the children's ability to use the Vowels Out Walking principle, first used in Unit 1 with **ee** and **ea**❖. It is worth establishing how well the children have grasped the generalisation that 'the first one talks and the second one is silent'. Ask the children to retell in their own words the Letterland reasons which help to make the rule memorable. Who talks? Who just walks? Why is the silent one's arm up? What is the danger? The answer to this last question paves the way for learning the major exception to the rule: when the next letter is an **r**.

The **a–e** spelling pattern provides an important opportunity to explain the Magic **e** principle: the effect of the final silent **e** on the previous vowel. Use the *Silent Magic **e** Poster* to emphasise its importance.

Children can be exposed to onsets and rimes containing the Magic **e** spelling patterns, e.g. **-ake**, **-ane**, **-ate**. Similarly, they can be taught the rule 'Silent Magic **e** makes the vowel before it say its name' and even repeat the rule accurately, yet still fail to relate the new word to those previously seen rhyming words by analogy. Letterland can help these children by presenting the **a–e** pattern in a story which breathes life into the rule and enables them to act it out. The time spent in role-playing the function of Magic **e** during Live Spelling will be worth every minute it takes.

❖ The letter **y** is regarded here as a vowel because whenever **y** is not making its usual sound (as in **yellow**), it takes on a vowel's role. In Letterland terms the Yo-yo Man is a part-time Vowel Man because he does jobs for them (see also pages 56 and 172-173).

UNIT 2.1

ai (as in train)

Objectives

- To know that the letters **a** and **i** can represent long **ā** (**ai** as in **train**).
- To recognise and spell words containing **ai**.

What you need

- *Programme Two Picture Code Cards:* **ai** (18)
- *Programme One Picture Code Cards:* **b**, **d**, **f**, **g**, **l**, **n**, **p**, **r**, **s** and **t**
- *Programme Two Copymaster:* 4
- *Programme Two Word Bank Copymaster:* 2
- *Programme Two Songs Cassette*
- *Vowel Scenes Posters:* Vowels Out Walking

Preparation

- **Rain poems**
  Find poems about the weather that you could read to the children, and some pictures of the rain or a rainy day to show them.

Introducing the sound

This is the third of the vowel pairs in which the first vowel 'says its name' while the second vowel remains silent. Point to the *Vowels Out Walking Poster* as everyone repeats the rhyme below.

When Mr A and I walk, Mr A talks

When Mr A and I go out walking,
Mr A does all the talking.
He just says his name,
But his friend won't do the same.

Whole class word work

- Listen to and sing the Vowels Out Walking song on the *Programme Two Songs Cassette.* The children shout 'A!' after 'his name'.
- Write these sentences on the board and ask the children to help with picture coding **ai.**

  "What a pain. It's raining again," said Mr A.

  I am afraid the paint has left a big stain.

  The old train still remains on the railway track.

- Live spell: **tail** → **snail** → **stain** → **brain** → **paint** → **faint**. Follow up by dictating these or other **ai** words.

"What a pain. It's raining again," said Mr A.

Group word work

- Use *Programme Two Copymaster* 4 for further practice.
- Introduce *Word Bank Copymaster* 2. Ask the children to look for words which contain **ai** in their books and to add them to their Word Banks.
- Help the children to explore onsets and rimes independently by giving them 10 consonants from the *Programme One Picture Code Cards:* **b**, **d**, **f**, **g**, **l**, **n**, **p**, **r**, **s**, **t** and the **ai** vowel pair from the *Programme Two Picture Code Cards*. The **ai**m is to build as many **ai** words as they can by combining the different consonants with the **ai** card. (There are over 30 possibilities.) Each child records the words on their own list. The children can then work together to compile a group list. In the plenary session, one or two children can be nominated to read out the final list.

Cross-curricular and other suggestions

- Ask the children to write a poem about the r**ai**n. You could discuss the noise that it makes, the clothes you have to wear, and the effect it has on plants. (See also *Letterland Ideas for Science and Technology*, page 54, on recording r**ai**nfall.)

Words containing ai

afraid*	explain	paint*	saint
again*	fail	plain	snail
aid	faint	praise	Spain
aim	faithful	raid	stain
brain	frail	rail	straight*
chain	gain	rain*	strain
claim	grain	rainbow	tail*
complaint	mail	raise*	trail
contain	maintain	raisin	train*
daily	nail	refrain	vain
daisy	paid*	remain	waist
drain	pail	retain	wait
entertain	pain	sailing	

* High frequency words

References
For other vowel pairs, see p36 ēe, p38 ēa, p46 ay, p50 ie, p60 oa, p74 ue, p152 ĕa.

UNIT 2.2

a–e (as in name)

Objectives

- To know that the letter **a** before a single consonant plus Magic **e**, is usually long (**a–e** as in **name**).
- To recognise and spell words containing **a–e**.

What you need

- *Programme Two Picture Code Cards:* **Mr A** (1), **Magic e** (9)
- *Programme One Picture Code Cards*
- *Programme Two Copymaster:* 5
- *Programme Two Word Bank Copymaster:* 2
- *Programme Two Songs Cassette*
- *Vowel Scenes Posters:* Silent Magic **e**

Preparation

- **Word game**
  Collect some magnetic letters and a board, or use *Picture Code Cards.*

Introducing the sound

The concept of Silent Magic **e** was introduced in Programme One. However, it is worth repeating the full story, serving as revision for some children and as new information for others in the class. As you tell the story, be ready to display the *Silent Magic* **e** *Poster* just before Mr E's rhyme.

Why Mr E invented a Silent Magic e

*The Vowel Men work so hard behind the scenes, putting **a**pples and **o**ranges, **e**lephants, **i**nk bottles and **u**mbrellas into words, that they seldom have the fun of appearing in words. Mr E decided that this would not do. He and his friends, the other Vowel Men, should have a chance to be in words more often. But how could he bring this about? He had to think up a new magic trick! Off he went to work on a very special kind of **e**. When it was ready, he called Mr A, Mr I, Mr O and Mr U together, and with a flourish, he announced his new invention:*

*'Introducing the **e** you cannot hear*
with power to make Vowel Men appear.'

*The brand new **e** was bright red and it had a top hat and wand, just like Mr E himself.*

tap tape

Write and picture code the word **tap** very large twice on the board. Ask a child to add a big Silent Magic **e** in red changing the second **tap** into **tape**. Add a top hat and wand to the child's red **e** and draw some magic sparks in yellow. Then rub out Annie Apple and put in Mr A by adding a yellow stick man right through the new **a**. Finally, all read and compare **tap** with the new word **tape.**

Whole class word work

- Listen to and sing the Magic **e** song on the *Programme Two Songs Cassette.*

Magic e makes the Vowel Man say his name.

- Write these sentences on the board and ask the children to help with picture coding **a–e.**

Magic **e** makes the Vowel Man say his name.
Jane had written her name on her maths book.
They ate a whole plate of biscuits!

- Live spell: **tap** ➜ **tape** ➜ **tap**, **plan** ➜ **plane**, **scrap** ➜ **scrape**. Play-act the exchange. The **a**pple-child backs away as Magic **e**'s sparks land on her and the Mr A child rushes in (from viewers' left) to take her place. When **e** leaves, so does Mr A and the **a**pple child returns.

Group word work

- Use *Programme Two Copymaster* 5 for further practice.
- Introduce *Word Bank Copymaster* 2. Ask the children to look for words containing **a–e** in their books and to add them to their Word Banks.
- Play a word g**a**m**e** with the children in which you choose a word from the **a–e** box below and, using magnetic letters or *Picture Code Cards*, muddle up its letters. (Alternatively, you could write them on the board.) Then ask the children to see if they can rem**a**k**e** the word.

Words containing a–e

age	crate	page
amaze	date*	pale
ape	escape	place*
awake	face*	plate
bake*	fame	race
base	flame	safe
behave	game*	sale
blame	gate	shake
brave	gave*	skate
cake*	grape	space
came*	lake	take*
case	late*	wake
cave	male	wave

Challenge words

demonstrate
educate
hurricane
operate

* High frequency words

References
For other Units on Magic **e**, see p52 **i–e**, p62 **o–e**, p70 **u–e**, p170 **e–e**.

Adding a Magic e to make a new word

at*	mat
ate*	mate*
can*	pan
cane	pane
cap*	plan*
cape	plane
fad	rat*
fade	rate
gap	Sam
gape	same*
hat*	scrap
hate	scrape
mad*	tap
made*	tape

Instruction words

Fire escape

illustrate	punctuate
make*	replace
name*	state
place*	trace

Note: For suggestions on how to deal with Magic **e** exceptions, e.g. **behave** but **have**, see page 171.

UNIT 2.3

ay (as in play)

Objectives

- To know that the letters **a** and **y** can represent long ā (**ay** as in **play**).
- To recognise and spell words containing **ay**.

What you need

- *Programme Two Picture Code Cards*: **ay** (45)
- *Programme One Picture Code Cards*
- *Programme Two Copymaster:* 6
- *Programme Two Word Bank Copymaster:* 2
- *Programme Two Songs Cassette*
- *Vowel Scenes Posters:* Vowels Out Walking

Preparation

- **My day**
  Take in a diary which has hour sections, to show the children. Prepare a diary page to photocopy, if needed.

Introducing the sound

The **ay** spelling is used at the ends of words instead of **ai**, but it sounds exactly like **ai**. The Letterland reason for **y** instead of **i** is as follows. (As you tell the story, be ready to display the *Vowels Out Walking Poster.*)

When Mr A and the Yo-yo Man go out walking, Mr A does all the talking

When Mr A and the Yo-yo Man go out walking, Mr A does all the talking. His usual walking partner is Mr I, but when Mr A goes out walking at the end of a word, it's no use taking Mr I with him because Mr I always feels dizzy at the end of words. So Mr I and the Yo-yo Man have agreed that the Yo-yo Man should always take over as Mr A's look-out man at the end of words.

Whole class word work

- Listen to and sing the Vowels Out Walking song on the *Programme Two Songs Cassette* to bring the rule to life. The children shout 'A!' after 'his name'.
- Write these sentences on the board and ask the children to help with picture coding **a** and **ay.**

  Mr I did say that he had to stay away.
  Did you say that we may play with clay today?
  Always keep away from the railway lines.
  Let's set up a display around that doorway.

- Live spell: **rain** → **ray** → **fray** → **stay** → **spray** → **stray**.
  Ask the **i**-child to mime feeling dizzy and almost falling as soon as the **n**-child leaves the word **rain**. Follow up by dictating these or other **ay** words.

Mr I did say that he had to stay away.

Group word work

- Use *Programme Two Copymaster* 6 for further practice.
- Introduce *Word Bank Copymaster* 2. Ask the children to look for words containing **ay** in their books and to add them to their Word Banks.
- Write a list on the board of some words which contain **ay** and some which do not. Ask the children to select, write and picture code those which contain **ay**.
- Write these phrases revising **ai** and **ay** on the board and ask a child to read each one. Select different children to explain why Mr A and Mr I go out walking in some words, but Mr A goes out walking with the Yo-yo Man in the others instead.

Main railway line.
Rainy day.
Entertaining May Day.
Afraid to stay.

Cross-curricular and other suggestions

- Explain to the children that the words **day** and **today** are important words. Show them one or two annotated pages from your hour-by-hour diary (see Preparation). Then work through an imaginary **day** together, on the board, to show them how you would fill it in. Now ask them to write their own diary of what they are going to be doing that **day**. Give out the photocopied diary formats for those who need them and ask the others to design their own.

Note: If children ask why **ay** is found *inside* some words, e.g. **payment** and **playing**, explain that the Yo-yo Man is still helping Mr A to finish the main, or root word.

Revision

Revise the sounds learned so far using the *Picture Code Cards* as cues and the story explanations as opportunities for the children to practise retelling and reflecting on the story content and purpose.

References
For other vowel pairs, see p36 **ēe**, p 38 **ēa**, p42 **ai**, p50 **ie**, p60 **oa**, p74 **ue**, p152 **ĕa**.

Words containing ay

archway	play*
away*	pray
betray	railway
birthday*	ray
clay	relay
day*	repay
display	runway
doorway	say*
gateway	saying*
hay	spray
highway	stray
jay	subway
lay	sway
May	today*
midway	tray
mislay	way*
pathway	yesterday*

Challenge words

decay
delay
dismay
fray
gangway

* High frequency words

Exceptions: they, **grey**, **obey**, **prey**, **osprey**, see page 176.

Main railway line.

UNIT 3

UNIT 3.1

ie (as in lie)

UNIT 3.2

i–e (as in bite)

UNIT 3.3

igh (as in high)

UNIT 3.4

y (as in fly)

Long ī

UNIT 3

Resources for Unit 3

- *Programme Two Picture Code Cards:* **ie** (29), **Mr I** (3), **Magic e** (9), **igh** (64), **y** (13)
- *Programme One Picture Code Cards*
- *Programme Two Copymasters:* 8-12
- *Programme Two Word Bank Copymasters:* 3-4
- *Programme Two Songs Cassette*
- *Vowel Scenes Posters:* Vowels Out Walking, Silent Magic **e**

When we hear an **i** saying its name in a word, it may simply need the letter **i** alone to spell it, e.g. **I**, **kind**, **bicycle**. However, in an unknown word, the clue to the long **ī** pronunciation is usually in a silent **e** (e.g. **lie** or **bite**) or a silent **gh** (e.g. **light**). Whether we realise the function of these silent letters as pronunciation signals or not, in spelling no-one can afford to leave them out.

The first long **ī** pattern, **ie**, occurs in relatively few words. It is another case of 'When two vowels go out walking, the first one does the talking'. The **e** is the Silent Look Out Man and the reader's signal that the **i** will be long. For exceptions (as in **field**, where the Vowel Men swap roles) see page 216.

The second long **ī** pattern, **i–e**, is the most important of the long **ī** spelling patterns, occurring in a large number of words including important instruction words, e.g. **write**, **divide**, **underline** and **describe**. It provides a good opportunity to go over the Magic **e** concept and for the children to act out the vowel shift from short to long using words like **pin/pine**. The *Silent Magic **e** Poster* will be useful to display at this time.

The third pattern, **igh**, occurs chiefly in the words **light**, **might**, **night**, **right** and **sight** and in compound words made with them, e.g. **midnight**. The Letterland story explanation rewards Golden Girl for being quiet and explains the resulting long **ī** sound.

The final spelling in this Unit is the letter **y**. This change of role for **y** is known in Letterland as 'the Yo-yo Man's business deal with Mr I'. Agreeing to do Mr I's job for him is in fact a small 'deal' compared with the amount of work the Yo-yo Man does for Mr E in thousands of words (see page 158 **-ly** and page 172 **y** as in **very**). Meanwhile, it is useful for the children to become familiar with the '**y** saying **ī**' spelling pattern.

UNIT 3.1

ie (as in lie)

Objectives

- To know that the letters **i** and **e** can represent long **ī** (**ie** as in **lie**).
- To recognise and spell words containing **ie**.

What you need

- *Programme Two Picture Code Cards*: **ie** (29)
- *Programme One Picture Code Cards*
- *Programme Two Copymaster:* 8
- *Programme Two Word Bank Copymaster:* 3
- *Programme Two Songs Cassette*
- *Vowel Scenes Posters:* Vowels Out Walking

Preparation

- **Look, say, cover, write, check**
  Make copies of the format on page 230.

Introducing the sound

Point out to the children that **ie** is, like **ai**, a vowel pair, and remind them of the rhyme:

When two vowels go out walking,
The FIRST one does the talking.

In this instance, the verse changes as follows.

When Mr I and E walk, Mr I usually talks

When Mr I and E go out walking,
*Mr I **usually** does the talking.*
He just says his name,
But his friend won't do the same.

The word 'usually' is needed because of **ie**'s other sound (as in **field**, see page 216). Show the *Vowels Out Walking Poster* to remind the children of the concept and explain that this vowel pair does not appear on the *Vowels Out Walking Poster,* because **ie** does not conform often enough to the rule 'the *first* one does the talking'.

Whole class word work

- Listen to and sing the Vowels Out Walking song on the *Programme Two Songs Cassette.* The children shout 'I!' after 'his name'.
- Write these sentences on the board and ask the children to help with picture coding **ie.**

  Mr I and Mr E love fried chicken and pie.
  Never tell a lie.
  I tied a knot in my tie.
  When this baby bird tries to fly, it flies badly.

- Live spell or dictate: **pie** → **lie** → **lies** → **flies** → **tries** → **tried** → **cried** → **relied**.

Mr I and Mr E love fried chicken and pie.

Group word work

- Use *Programme Two Copymaster* 8 for further practice.

- Introduce *Word Bank Copymaster* 3. Ask the children to look for words containing **ie** saying 'ī' in their books and to add them to their Word Banks. Keep any words they find that do not have a long **ī** (e.g. **studied**) on a separate list and be ready to explain that sometimes Mr E takes a turn doing the talking. Then Mr I becomes the silent look-out man. For more about Mr E's turn in **ie** words, see page 216.

- Give the children some **ie** words from the word box below and some words to revise from a previous Unit or Units. Ask them to complete the *look, say, cover, write, check* format (see Preparation).

Words containing ie saying 'ī'

allies	fried	simplified
amplified	justified	supplies
applies	lies	terrified
cried*	magnified	tied*
cries*	pie	tried
die*	replied	tries*
flies	satisfies	

* High frequency words

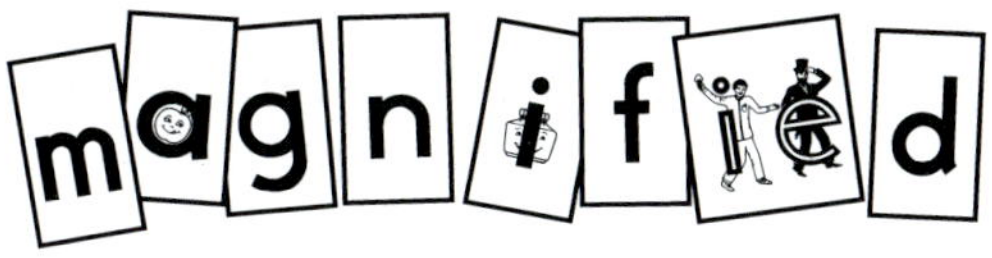

References
For other vowel pairs, see p36 **ēe**, p38 **ēa**, p42 **ai**, p46 **ay**, p60 **oa**, p74 **ue**, p152 **ĕa**.

UNIT 3.2

i–e (as in bite)

Objectives

- To know that the letter **i** before a single consonant plus Magic **e** is usually long (**i–e** as in **bite**).
- To recognise and spell words containing **i–e**.

What you need

- *Programme Two Picture Code Cards:* **Mr I** (3), **Magic e** (9)
- *Programme One Picture Code Cards*
- *Programme Two Copymaster:* 9
- *Programme Two Word Bank Copymaster:* 3
- *Programme Two Songs Cassette*
- *Vowel Scenes Posters:* Silent Magic **e**

Introducing the sound

The concept of final **e** as a Silent Magic **e** was introduced in Programme One and developed in Unit 2.2. Look together at the *Silent Magic e Poster* and remind the children of the following story which explains how Magic **e** works.

Magic e makes the Vowel Men appear

Mr E's special invention, his silent Magic ***e****, can make any Vowel Man appear in a word and say his name. The* ***e****'s magic sparks always jump back over one letter to land on a vowel.*

Use the same approach as on page 44 (showing how **tap** becomes **tape**) but working now with the words **pin**, **bit** or **slim**. This time it is Impy Ink who disappears in the shower of magic sparks and Mr I who appears in Impy's place, leading to the completely new words: **pine**, **bite** or **slime**. Give the children red and yellow chalk or board pens so they can help you to demonstrate the transformation:

pin   pin

Stress, too, how the Magic **e** has caused a transformation in meaning as well, from a tiny pin to a whole pine tree!

pin   pine

Whole class word work

- Listen to and sing the Magic **e** song on the *Programme Two Songs Cassette.*
- Write these sentences on the board and ask the children to help with picture coding **i–e.**

Mr I put his nice new bike beside the gate.

I like eating rice best.

It can be dangerous to slide on ice.

Mr I put his nice new bike beside the gate.

☆ Live spell: **pin** → **pine** → **pin** → **bit** → **bite** → **spin** → **spine** → **rip** → **trip** → **strip** → **stripe**. Role-play the changes with Impy Ink and Mr I swapping places. Follow up by dictating these or other **i–e** words from the word box below.

Group word work

☆ Use *Programme Two Copymaster* 9 for further practice.

☆ Introduce *Word Bank Copymaster* 3. Ask the children to look for words containing **i–e** in their books and to add them to their Word Banks. Check for any exceptions (e.g. **active,** see page 171).

☆ Ask the children to write a story about:

- Fire**man** Fred
- what it is **like** to be **five**
- m**ice**
- something special that they really **like**
- Munching **Mike**
- their b**ike**
- when they won a special pri**ze**
- or all the different food they can think of that is wh**ite**.

Words containing i–e

			Challenge words
alive	invite	side*	crocodile
arrive	kite	size	dynamite
beside	life*	slide*	televise
bike*	like*	smile	
bite	line*	stripe	
describe	mile*	time*	
fine*	mine*	underline	
fire*	nine*	while*	
five*	prize	white*	
glide	quite*	wide	
hide*	ride*	wise	
inside*	shine	write*	

* High frequency words

References
For other Units on Magic **e**, see p44 **a–e**, p62 **o–e**, p70 **u–e**, p170 **e–e**.

Adding a Magic e to make a new word

bit*	quit	shin	slim	trip*
bite	quite*	shine	slime	tripe
fin	rid	slid	strip	win
fine*	ride*	slide*	stripe	wine

UNIT 3.3
igh (as in high)

Objectives

- To know that the letters **i**, **g** and **h** can represent long **ī** (**igh** as in **high**).
- To recognise and spell words containing **igh**.

What you need

- *Programme Two Picture Code Cards:* **gh** (26), **igh** (64)
- *Programme One Picture Code Cards:* **b**, **f**, **h**, **l**, **m**, **n**, **r**, **s**, **t**
- *Programme Two Copymaster:* 10
- *Programme Two Word Bank Copymaster:* 4

Preparation

- **Look, say, cover, write, check**
  Make copies of the format on page 230.

Introducing the sounds

The first story explains why **g** and **h** are usually silent in words. The second one explains why Mr I often appears beside them with an **i**ce cream in the **igh** spelling pattern.

Golden Girl and the Hat Man are silent together

Golden Girl knows that the Hairy Hat Man hates noise. So every time he stands next to her in a word she keeps completely quiet. So does he. They just enjoy being silent together.

An ice cream for Golden Girl from the Hat Man

*Hairy Hat Man often asks Mr I to give Golden Girl an ice cream for being so nice and quiet beside him. In those words Mr I comes ri**gh**t up beside Golden Girl. Then you can hear him saying '**i**' for '**i**ce cream' as he holds out a delicious **i**ce cream for her. That pleases both Golden Girl and Hairy Hat Man very much, so they both smile – silently, of course!*

Whole class word work

- Write these sentences on the board and ask the children to help with picture coding **igh**.

She smiled brightly and looked delighted.

I like to have a night light on.

Her Highness, the queen, sighed a deep sigh.

She smiled brightly and looked delighted.

✪ Live spell or dictate these words: **high** ➔ **sigh** ➔ **sight** ➔ **night** ➔ **bright** ➔ **light**. During the live spelling, Mr I could mime handing Golden Girl an ice cream while she smiles br**igh**tly.

Group word work

✪ Use *Programme Two Copymaster* 10 for further practice.

✪ Introduce *Word Bank Copymaster* 4. Write a selection of words from the **igh** word list on the board. The children then choose the six words which they consider most useful to them and add them to their Word Banks.

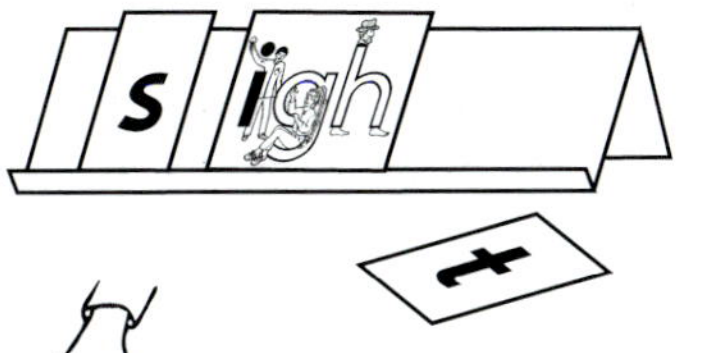

✪ Help the children to explore onsets and rimes independently by giving them **b**, **f**, **h**, **l**, **m**, **n**, **r**, **s** and **t** from *Programme One Picture Code Cards* and **igh** from *Programme Two Picture Code Cards*. The aim is to build 20 words with them by combining different single cards with the **igh** card. Each child records each word as it is made on his or her own list. If necessary, help them to discover that **s** can be used at either end (e.g. **right**, **rights**, **sight**, **sights**), so they can make eight more words.

✪ Give the children some **igh** words from the word box and some words to revise from a previous Unit or Units. Ask them to complete the *look, say, cover, write, check* format (see Preparation).

Words containing igh saying 'ī'

		Challenge words
bright*	midnight	Highness
delight	might*	hindsight
fight*	moonlight	plight
flight	night*	
fright	right*	
high*	sigh	
highest*	sight	
highway	slight	
knight	sunlight	
light*	thigh	
lightning	tight	

* High frequency words

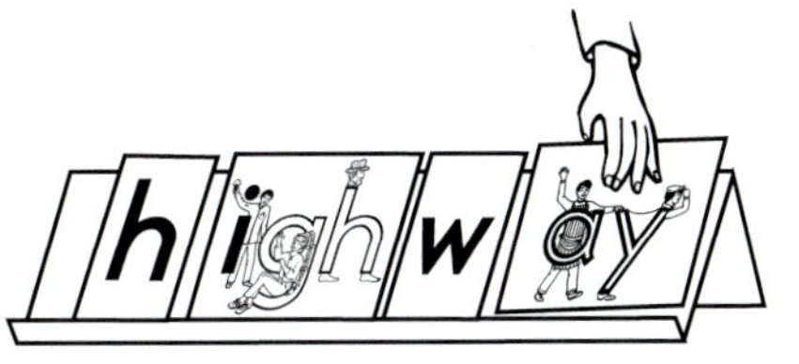

UNIT 3.4

y (as in fly)

Objectives

- To know that the letter **y** can represent long **ī** (**y** as in **fly**).
- To recognise and spell words containing **y** saying long **ī**.

What you need

- *Programme Two Picture Code Cards:* **y** (13)
- *Programme One Picture Code Cards*
- *Programme Two Copymaster:* 11
- *Programme Two Word Bank Copymaster:* 4

Preparation

- **Zig-zag books**
  Prepare some zig-zag books from thin card or stiff paper.

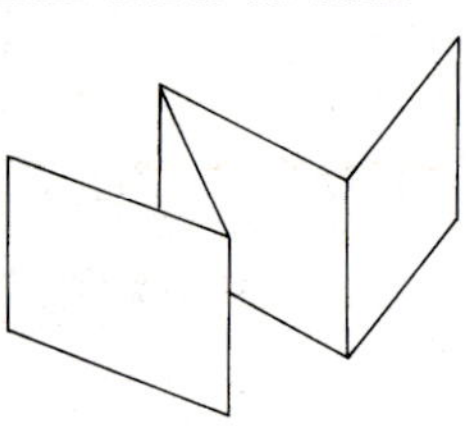

- **Classification activity**
  Fold some sheets of paper in half lengthways to create two columns.

Introducing the sound

Remind the children of the Yo-yo Man's normal job, selling yo-yos and making his usual 'yyy...' sound in words. Then go on to explain:

*Yellow Yo-yo Man has a problem. As it happens, there are not many words which need his 'yyy...' sound, so he has very few chances to appear in words and sell his **y**ellow **y**o-**y**os. He really needs to find more work to do! Let's look at some words to see if we can discover how he has solved this problem.*

Write these words on the board: **yes**, **try**, **yellow**, **my**, **yet** and **July**, and help the children to read them if necessary. Ask them if they notice anything about the **y** sound. Once they have discovered the long **ī** sound in **my**, **try** and **July**, the children are ready for the pictogram and story below.

Why the Yo-yo Man says "ī" for Mr I

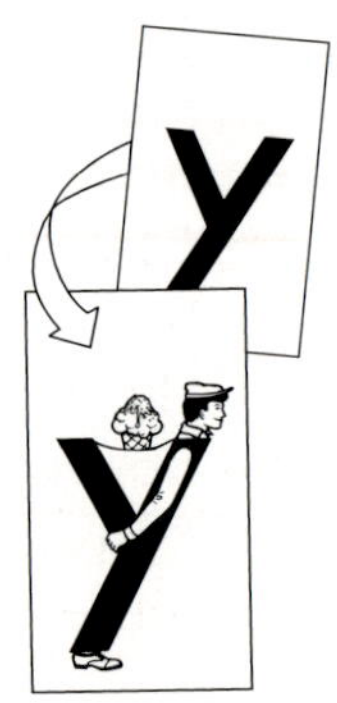

Luckily for Yellow Yo-yo Man, Mr I came rushing up to him one day, calling for help.

*"Oh, Yo-yo Man," cried Mr I. "Every time I stand at the **end** of a word to say my name I feel dizzy, as if I were about to fall off a cliff! Could you possibly stand at the end of a few words and say my name for me?"*

"Yyes, I'd be glad to have a go!" replied the Yo-yo Man. He put down his yo-yos carefully, took a deep breath and said, "ī". "That's fine," said Mr I, full of smiles.

*So from that day forward the Yo-yo Man was able to earn more money, working for Mr I at the end of words. He really enjoys the work because Mr I doesn't just give him money. He gives him a great big, free **i**ce cream every time the Yo-yo Man says "ī" for him.*

*Mr I even lets the Yo-yo Man say "**i**" for him inside quite a few words as well!*

Mr I said, "Why not try saying 'I' for me?"

Whole class word work

- Write these sentences on the board and ask the children to help with picture coding capital **I** and **y**.

Mr I said, "Why not try saying 'I' for me?"
She began to cry when she hurt her eye.
I'd love to fly in the sky all by myself.

- Live spell: **my** → **fly** → **fry** → **try** → **shy** → **why**.

Group word work

- Use *Programme Two Copymaster* 11 for further practice.

- Introduce *Word Bank Copymaster* 4. Ask the children to look in their books for words containing **y** working for Mr I and to add them to their Word Banks. They will find many more words where **y** sounds like long **ē** instead. Be ready to explain that it is Mr E, the Easy Magic Man, who often works for the Yo-yo Man in words as well! (See page 172, **y** as in **very**.)

- Write some of the words ending in **y** on a board, but omit the final **y**. Ask a child to come and write the **y** on the end of a word and then to read it out to their group. (Alternatively, you could ask a child to come and build the word using the *Picture Code Cards* or magnetic letters.)

- Give out the zig-zag books (see Preparation) and some of the high frequency words from the boxes on the right, so the children can write one sentence containing some of these **y** words on each page of their book. Ask them to picture code each **y** word. They could then read and compare each other's sentences.

Cross-curricular and other suggestions

- Talk to the children about the word **classify**. Give out the folded sheets of paper (see Preparation) and ask the children to make lists of various classifications. Some could, for example, classify which children in the class are boys and which are girls; who has brown hair and who has blonde hair; or which of the plants have flowers and which do not. Make sure that they label the columns of their classifications.

References
For more about **y**, see p172 **-y**, p174 **-y-**, p175-176 **ey**, p182 **y to i**, p195 **y** as a Magic Ending.

Words containing y

buy*
by*
cry*
fly*
my*
reply
shy
spy
try*
why*

Words containing medial y

buying*
bypass
crying*
cycle
drying
dye
dyed
dyeing
dynamite
eye*
flying*
frying
goodbye*
myself*
recycling
replying
rhyme
shyness
skyscraper
spying
style
type
typing
tyre

Challenge words

ally
amplify
apply
clarify
defy
hydrogen
hyphen
justify
lullaby
magnify
multiply
nylon
prying
sly

* High frequency words

UNIT 4

UNIT 4.1

oa (as in boat)

UNIT 4.2

o–e (as in pole)

UNIT 4.3

ow (as in show)

Long ō

UNIT 4

Resources for Unit 4

- *Programme Two Picture Code Cards:* **oa** (69), **Magic e** (9), **Mr O** (4), **ow** (78)
- *Programme One Picture Code Cards*
- *Programme Two Copymasters:* 13-16
- *Programme Two Word Bank Copymaster:* 5
- *Programme Two Songs Cassette*
- *Vowel Scenes Posters:* Vowels Out Walking, Silent Magic **e**

When we hear a long **ō** in a word, it may need the single letter **o** to spell it (as in **no, old** and **most**). More often than not, however, it will need **oa**, **o–e** or **ow**. In fact, to the reader, the silent **a** next to **o** (as in **boat**), a Magic **e** at the end (as in **pole**), or a silent **w** (as in **show**) are pronunciation cues, signalling the need to read the word as a long **ō** word.

The first long **ō** pattern, **oa**, occurs in relatively few common words apart from **boat, coat, goat, road, coast** and **toast**. Nevertheless, it is useful for the children to identify this vowel pair as another good example of two Vowels Out Walking. The sooner they grasp this concept (only the first one talks, and he just says his name) the more unfamiliar **oa** words will yield to phonic attack. The *Vowels Out Walking Poster* excludes those vowel pairs which only *sometimes* follow the rule (**ie**, **ue**, **ui**, **oe**), so the children can rely on the fact that if they see a vowel pair on the Poster, the concept *will* apply, unless a robber overpowers the pair (see the panel at the bottom of the *Vowels Out Walking Poster* and pages 110-117 **air**, **are**, **ere**, **ear** and pages 148-149 **ear**).

The second long **ō** spelling pattern, **o–e**, provides a further opportunity to strengthen the children's understanding of the Magic **e** concept introduced in Unit 2.2 with **a–e**. Now the children can act out the vowel shift from short to long, using new words like **hop/hope**. Return to the *Silent Magic* ***e*** *Poster* to remind the children how Mr E made his Magic **e**'s powerful enough to jump back over one letter to make any Vowel Man appear and say his name, in this case Mr O.

The third long **ō** spelling pattern is dealt with using a story about the Water Witch, who wants to get the orange out of the **o** so she can eat it. When old Mr O comes to the orange's rescue, we learn why the only sound we hear is 'ō'. A sequel story explains the 'ow' sound as in **cow** (see page 104).

For changes in the sound of **o** beside another vowel, see page 68 and page 90 **oo**, pages 98-101 **oy/oi**, page 106 **ou**, page 218 **ous**. For changes caused by **r** (**r**-controlled digraphs), see page 120 **or**, page 122 **oor** and page 124 **ore**.

UNIT 4.1

oa (as in boat)

Objectives

- To know that the letters **o** and **a** can represent long **ō** (**oa** as in **boat**).
- To recognise and spell words containing **oa**.

What you need

- *Programme Two Picture Code Cards:* **oa** (69)
- *Programme One Picture Code Cards*
- *Programme Two Copymaster:* 13
- *Programme Two Word Bank Copymaster:* 5
- *Programme Two Songs Cassette*
- *Vowel Scenes Posters:* Vowels Out Walking

Introducing the sound

Point out the **oa** vowel pair on the cover of this book and on the *Vowels Out Walking Poster* and remind children of the rhyme:

When two vowels go out walking,
The FIRST one does the talking.

In this instance, the verse changes as follows.

When Mr O and A walk, Mr O talks

When Mr O and A go out walking,
Mr O does the talking.
He just says his name,
But his friend won't do the same.

Whole class word work

- Listen to and sing the Vowels Out Walking song on the *Programme Two Songs Cassette.* The children shout 'O!' after 'his name'.
- Write these sentences on the board and ask the children to help with picture coding **oa**.

  Watch out for goats and toads crossing the road!

  They moaned when they had to wash with soap.

  Mr O and Mr A saw six boats floating by.

- Live spell: **boat** ➜ **coat** ➜ **coast** ➜ **toast** ➜ **throat**. Dictate these or any other words from the box on the opposite page.

Watch out for goats and toads crossing the road!

Group word work

- Use *Programme Two Copymaster* 13 for further practice.
- Introduce *Word Bank Copymaster* 5. Ask the children to look for words containing **oa** in their books and to add them to their Word Banks. Prepare them to expect a few exceptions and to avoid adding these to their word list (e.g. **roar**, **soar**, **board**).
- Write this selection of **oa** words on the board and ask the children to try writing a story which uses as many of them as possible. They could also illustrate their story and label the things in the story that contain **oa**.

boat	coach	coast	coat	float	goal	goat
loaf	road	soak	soaked	soaking	soap	throat

Cross-curricular and other suggestions

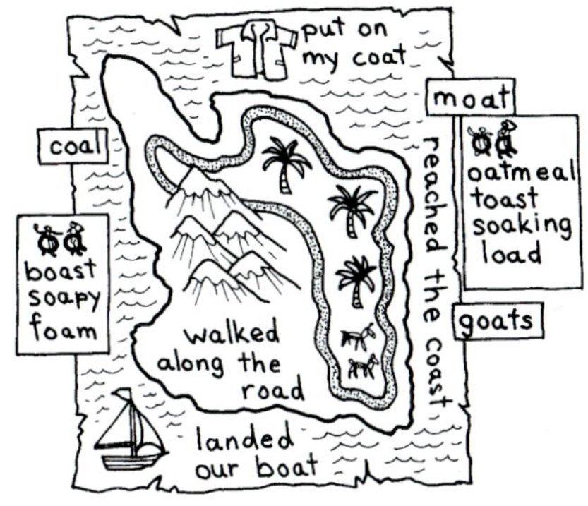

- Ask the children to draw and label a map of their **oa** story. It could be either a route map or a treasure island map.

Words containing oa

			Challenge words
approach	foam	oatmeal	bloated
boast	goal*	poach	hoax
boat*	groan	poached	loathsome
coach	load	road*	
coal*	loaf	roam	
coast	loan	roast	
coat*	loathe	soap*	
coated	loaves	stoat	
cockroach	moan	throat	
float	moat	toad	
foal	oath	toast	

* High frequency words

References
For other vowel pairs, see p36 **ēe**, p38 **ēa**, p42 **ai**, p46 **ay**, p50 **ie**, p74 **ue**, p152 **ĕa**.

UNIT 4.2

o–e (as in pole)

Objectives

- To know that when the letter **o** comes before a single consonant plus final **e**, the **o** is usually long (**o–e** as in **pole**).
- To recognise and spell words containing **o–e**.

What you need

- *Programme Two Picture Code Cards:* **Mr O** (4), **Magic e** (9)
- *Programme One Picture Code Cards*
- *Programme Two Copymaster:* 14
- *Programme Two Word Bank Copymaster:* 5
- *Programme Two Songs Cassette*
- *Vowel Scenes Posters:* Silent Magic **e**

Introducing the sound

Remind the children of the *Silent Magic* ***e*** *Poster* scene and the following story which explains how Magic **e** works.

Magic e makes the Vowel Men appear

Mr E's special invention, his silent Magic ***e****, can make any Vowel Man appear in a word and say his name. The* ***e****'s magic sparks always jump back over one letter to land on a vowel.*

Use the same approach as for **tap/tape** (page 44) and **pin/pine** (page 52), but working now with **hop/hope**, **not/note** or **rod/rode**. This time it is Oscar Orange who disappears and old Mr O who takes his place.

Whole class word work

- Listen to and sing the Magic **e** song on the *Programme Two Songs Cassette.*
- Write these sentences on the board and ask the children to help with picture coding each **o** and **o–e**.

Old Mr O likes to close his eyes and doze!

I spoke to my Granny on the phone.

He woke up, wrote a note and then left home.

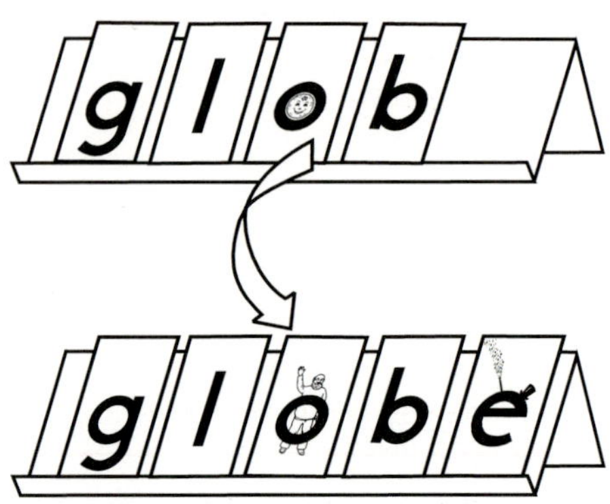

Old Mr O likes to close his eyes and doze!

✩ Live spell: **hop** ➜ **hope** ➜ **not** ➜ **note** ➜ **glob** ➜ **globe** ➜ **mop** ➜ **mope**.

✩ Dictate: bone, stone, joke, broke, stroke, nose, hose.

Group word work

✩ Use *Programme Two Copymaster* 14 for further practice.

✩ Introduce *Word Bank Copymaster* 5. Write a selection of words from the **o–e** word list on the board. The children then choose the six words which they consider most useful to them and enter them in their Word Banks.

✩ Write this list of **o–e** words on the board and ask the children to write them in their own books in rhyming pairs.

alone choke cone doze froze hole hope

mole nose phone slope rose throne woke

As an extension to this activity, the children could use their rhyming pairs to make up a nonsense poem.

Words containing o–e

alone*	drove	nose*	stole
awoke	expose	note*	stone*
bone	froze	phone	stroke
broke*	globe	poke	suppose*
choke	grope	pole	those*
close*	hole*	quote	throne
code	home*	robe	tone
coke	hope*	rope*	whole*
cone	hose	rose	woke*
cope	joke	slope	zone
dose	mole	smoke*	
doze	mope	spoke	

Exceptions: one, see p166, **done**, **gone,** see p171.

* High frequency words

References
For other Units on Magic **e**, see p44 **a–e**, p52 **i–e**, p74 **u–e**, p170 **e–e**.

UNIT 4.3

ow (as in show)

Objectives

- To know that the letters **o** and **w** can represent long ō (**ow** as in **show**.)
- To recognise and spell words containing **ōw**.

What you need

- *Programme Two Picture Code Cards:* **ow** (78)
- *Programme One Picture Code Cards*
- *Programme Two Copymaster:* 15
- *Programme Two Word Bank Copymaster:* 5

Preparation

- **Ow windows**
  Prepare a yell**ow** wind**ow** display space. Leave space beside it for the Brown Owl display (see Unit 10.1)
- **Growing seeds**
  Sort out some soil, plant pots, old spoons and seeds.
- **DANGER, SLOW signs**
  Collect some card.
- **Shadows**
  Collect some different coloured chalks.

Introducing the sound

When Mr O surprises the Witch, they both cry "O"

Mr O knows that the Wicked Water Witch is after his oranges. "Oh no you don't!" he cries, whenever he sees her next to one of them.

Now, although Mr O is very old, he manages to stop the Witch by calling out his name "O" to show that this orange belongs to him. At the very same moment, she cries out "Oh" in surprise.

Whole class word work

- Write these sentences on the board and ask the children to help with picture coding **o** and **ow**.

Old Mr O shows her who owns the oranges.
The snow is blowing in the window.
Look, my seeds are slowly growing.
I could see the sparrows in the garden below.

- Live spell: **lot** ➜ **low**, **rod** ➜ **row**, **shop** ➜ **show** ➜ **shadow** ➜ **own**.
- Dictate: grow, blow, below, flow, flown, own.

Old Mr O shows her who owns the oranges.

Group word work

- Use *Programme Two Copymaster* 15 for further practice.
- Introduce *Word Bank Copymaster* 5. Ask the children to look for words containing **ow** in their books. Before they add them to their Word Banks, help them to sort out any words with the second sound of **ow** (as in **cow**), see page 104.
- Make a yell**ow** wind**ow** display where the children can stick on their own picture-coded words to help make this **ow** sound distinct from other words spelt with **oa** or **o–e** or long **ō**.

Cross-curricular and other suggestions

- Gr**ow** some seeds and ask the children to draw and label the plant as it gr**ow**s.
- Ask the children to make their own **DANGER, SLOW** signs, either in 3D or out of paper.
- The children work in pairs, outside. Ask one of the children to draw around the shad**ow** of the other one and to mark where he or she was standing. Come back an hour later and repeat this, asking the children to note if their shad**ow** has moved, gr**ow**n or stayed the same. (See also *Letterland Ideas for Science and Technology*, page 63.)

Words containing ow

arrow*	flown	shown
below	follow	slow*
blow	grow*	snow*
borrow	know*	sparrow
bow	low*	throw*
bowling	owner	thrown
bungalow	pillow	window*
crow	shadow	yellow*
elbow	shallow	
flow	show*	

* High frequency words

References
For **ow** as in **cow**, see p104.

UNIT 5

UNIT 5.1

oo (as in boot)

UNIT 5.2

u–e (as in tune)

UNIT 5.3

ew (as in flew)

UNIT 5.4

ue (as in blue)

Long ū

UNIT 5

Resources for Unit 5

- *Programme Two Picture Code Cards:* **oo** (70), **Mr U** (5), **Magic e** (9), **ew** (59), **ue** (36)
- *Programme One Picture Code Cards*
- *Programme Two Copymasters:* 17-21
- *Programme Two Word Bank Copymasters:* 6-7
- *Programme Two Songs Cassette*
- *Vowel Scenes Posters:* Silent Magic **e**

The focus in this section is on the four most common spelling patterns for the phoneme 'o͞o' (as in **boot**, **tune**, **flew** and **blue**). However, regional pronunciations may differ, ranging between 'o͞o' and long 'ū'.

Since 'o͞o' (as in **boot**) is only one of two different sounds which **oo** can represent, (the other being 'o͝o' as in **foot**), the children are bound to find examples of either sound pattern in their reading and spelling. The names Boot and Foot Twins contain both sounds, so while this section features Boot Twin words, you can praise any child who finds a word with 'o͝o' in it for discovering a 'Foot Twin word'. The 'o͝o' sound is covered in Unit 7.2 on page 90. The Boot and Foot Twin song on the *Programme Two Songs Cassette* will help both 'o͞o' and 'o͝o' sounds to linger in the children's auditory memories.

The **u–e** spelling pattern in this Unit provides a good opportunity to review the signalling power of a Silent Magic **e** when it sends its sparks flying back over one letter. When children see the Magic **e**, they can expect the previous vowel to be saying a Vowel Man's name, in this case 'U'! (or Mr U's name shortened to 'o͞o').

The **e** in the **ew** digraph is a **w**-controlled vowel. Therefore, as the children will have found already with **ōw** (Unit 4.3), it is the Water Witch who is to blame, now causing them to have to learn yet another way to spell both the 'oo' and 'you' sounds. They will find her behaving in an equally interfering way with vowel sounds again in Units 10.1 (**ow** as in **cow**) and 12.4 (**aw** as in **awful**).

The **ue** spelling pattern also represents either the 'oo' or 'you' sound (compare **blue** and **argue**). When Mr U and E go out walking, Mr U says his name, either very clearly 'U' or else he shortens it to 'o͞o'. But it seems that Mr U is not all that keen on going out walking. All the most useful **ue** words can be learnt together in one sentence: Is it tr**ue** that the bl**ue** gl**ue** was d**ue** to arrive on T**ue**sday?

UNIT 5.1

oo (as in boot)

Objectives

- To know that the letters **o** and **o** can combine to make the long 'ōō' sound (**oo** as in **boot**).
- To recognise and spell words containing **oo** (as in **boot**).

What you need

- *Programme Two Picture Code Cards:* **oo** (70)
- *Programme One Picture Code Cards*
- *Programme Two Copymaster:* 17
- *Programme Two Word Bank Copymaster:* 6
- *Programme Two Songs Cassette*

Preparation

- **oo collections**
  Have ready enough sheets of paper for each child to make pictures of the Twins and add illustrated words around them.
- **Word cubes**
  Have ready four blank cubes that letters can be written on.

Introducing the sound

Programme One introduced short ŏ (Oscar Orange), long ō (Mr O, the Old Man) and **o** as in **brother** (Oscar's Bothersome Little Brother). When two **o**'s appear together in a word, the more usual sound they make is the long vowel phoneme 'ōō'. The second 'ŏŏ' sound (**oo** as in **foot)** is covered in Unit 7.2.

Two new pictogram characters represent the two **oo** sounds. They are the Boot and Foot Twins, two mischievous boys whose personalities are best expressed by their song on the *Programme Two Songs Cassette.* The chorus is excellent for reinforcing the two sounds of **oo**. The sounds may be taught separately or together, depending on the children in your class.

Note: Regional pronunication can vary the **oo** sound, leading to some overlap between the two sounds.

The Boot and Foot Twins always fight over their boots

*The Boot and Foot Twins are the grandsons of Mr O, the Old Man. In Letterland, everyone calls them the Boot and Foot Twins because they spend so much time arguing over their b**oo**ts. In many words you will hear the B**oo**t Twin teasing his brother by saying, "**OO**! I have your b**oo**ts!"*

Whole class word work

- Listen to the Boot and Foot Twins song on the *Programme Two Songs Cassette.*
- Write these sentences on the board and ask the children to help with picture coding **ōō**.

OO! I have your boots!
That afternoon they went to the zoo.
They saw a racoon and a baboon.

OO! I have your boots!

☆ Live spell or dictate these words: **boot** ➔ **too** ➔ **tool** ➔ **cool** ➔ **stool** ➔ **spoon** ➔ **moon**.

Group word work

☆ Use *Programme Two Copymaster* 17 for further practice.

☆ Introduce *Word Bank Copymaster* 6. Write a selection of **oo** words on the board. Ask the children to choose the ones which they consider the most useful to enter into their Word Banks.

☆ Hand out paper for the children to make a Boot Twin Words collection. Ask them to ch**oo**se ones which can be illustrated from the words already on the board. (You may want to add more choices.) The children can illustrate these around their own central picture of the Boot and Foot Twins.

☆ Write this list of **oo** words on the board:

bloom	cool	moo	root	spoon	tooth
boot	hoop	moon	shoot	too	zoo
broom	loot	room	soon	tool	

Write the letters **oo** on all sides of one blank cube (see Preparation), then the letters **r**, **b**, **c**, **h**, **m** and **s** on the second cube, and **m**, **t**, **l**, **n**, **th** and **p** on the third cube. On a fourth cube write the letters **l**, **n**, **r**, **s**, **t** and **z**. The children throw the cubes to see what words they can make from the **oo** word box. They could also try reading any non-words they make or real words which are not listed on the board. Ask two children to record each throw. When they re-read the list the group can decide which are the real words and cross out the non-words.

References
For **o͝o** as in **foot**, see p90. For **o** as in **who**, see page 167.

Words containing oo as in boot

afternoon*	cool*	moon	shampoo
baboon	droop	moose	shoot*
balloon	fool	mushroom	soon*
bamboo	goose	noodles	spook
bedroom*	hoop	proof	spoons*
bloom	igloo	racoon	stool
boot	kangaroo	room*	swoop
booth	loot	roost	too*
broom	macaroon	rooster	tool
choose*	maroon	root	tooth*
cocoon	moo	school*	zoo*

* High frequency words

UNIT 5.2

u–e (as in tune)

Objectives

- To know that the letter **u** before a single consonant plus Magic **e** is usually long (**u–e** as in **tune**).
- To recognise and spell words containing **u–e**.

What you need

- *Programme Two Picture Code Cards:* **Mr U** (5), **Magic e** (9)
- *Programme One Picture Code Cards*
- *Programme Two Copymaster:* 18
- *Programme Two Word Bank Copymaster:* 6
- *Programme Two Songs Cassette*
- *Vowel Scenes Posters:* Silent Magic **e**

Preparation

- **Look, say, cover, write, check**
  Make copies of the format on page 230.

Introducing the sound

Use the *Silent Magic* ***e*** *Poster* to remind children of the principle which underpins the Magic **e** story.

Magic e makes the Vowel Man appear

Mr E's special invention, his Silent Magic ***e****, can make any Vowel Man appear in a word and say his name. The* ***e****'s magic sparks always jump back over one letter to land on a vowel. So when you see the letter* ***u*** *in a Magic* ***e*** *word, you can be sure it will be Mr U himself saying his name. Listen carefully, though, because sometimes he seems to shorten his name, so it sounds less like 'you' and more like 'oo'.*

Regional accents may determine how some **u–e** words are pronounced, e.g. **tube** as **t**'you'**b** or **t**'oo'**b**. When picture coding Mr U in the sentences below, you may like to add a little speech bubble with **oo** in it coming from Mr U's mouth in words like **June** and **include**.

Whole class word work

- Listen to or chant the Magic **e** song on the *Programme Two Songs Cassette.*
- Write these sentences on the board and ask the children to help with picture coding **u** and **u–e**.

  Mr U played a beautiful tune on his flute.
  She decided to buy a huge tube of toothpaste.
  June will include us on the space capsule visit.

- Live spell: **us → use**, **cub → cube**, **tub → tube**, **cut → cute**. Role-play Uppy Umbrella disappearing and Mr U taking her place as soon as Magic **e** joins the word (see page 71).
- Dictate: use, fuse, confuse, refuse, amuse, June, tune.

Mr U played a beautiful tune on his flute.

Group word work

- Use *Programme Two Copymaster* 18 for further practice.
- Introduce *Word Bank Copymaster* 6. Write some **-use**, **-ume**, **-ule**, **-une**, **-ute** words on the board for the children to sort into onsets and rimes. Ask the children to look for words containing **u–e** in their books and to add these to their Word Banks.
- Give the children some **u–e** words from the word box below and some words to revise from a previous Unit or Units. Ask them to complete the *look, say, cover, write, check* format.

Words containing u–e

accuse
acute
amuse
assume
capsule
confuse
dispute
excuse*
fuse

huge
minute
module
mule
perfume
reduce
refuse
tune
volume

Words sounding more like **oo**

brute
exclude
flute
include
June*
Luke
prune
rude

Challenge words

attitude
attribute
consume
distribute
gratitude
immune
institute

latitude
longitude
magnitude
multitude
schedule
tribute

* High frequency words

References
For other Units on Magic **e**, see p44 **a–e**, p52 **i–e**, p62 **o–e**, p170 **e–e**.

UNIT 5.3

ew (as in flew)

Objectives

- To know that the letters **e** and **w** combine to represent long **ū** (**ew** as in **few** or **flew**).
- To recognise and spell words containing **ew**.

What you need

- *Programme Two Picture Code Cards:* **ew** (59)
- *Programme One Picture Code Cards*
- *Programme Two Copymaster:* 19
- *Programme Two Word Bank Copymaster:* 7
- *Programme Two Songs Cassette*

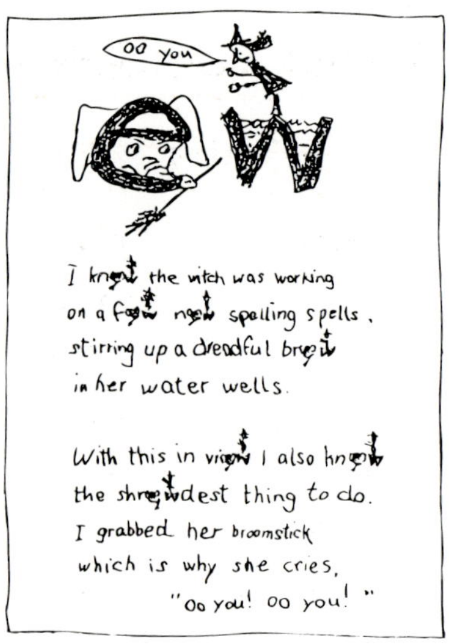

Introducing the sound

The letter **w** can cause a change in the sound of any vowel to its left, creating the **w**-controlled vowels in words like **few**, **flew**, **saw**, **dawn**, **owl** and **vowel**. In Letterland terms, the Wicked Water Witch is behaving in character: being a trouble maker. She loves confusing everyone!

This Unit focuses on the two sounds made by the letters **ew**: 'oo' and 'you'. Regional pronunciation of words in this group vary, so you may wish to adjust the words in the boxes on page 73 accordingly.

When Eddy grabs her broomstick, the Witch cries, "Oo! You!"

When you see Eddy Elephant before Wicked Water Witch, don't expect him to be saying "ĕ..." as usual. He'll be far too busy trying to outwit the Witch. You see, she would love to turn him into a wicked elephant if she could! To make sure that she can't, Eddy grabs away her broomstick whenever he sees her coming into a word beside him. That makes the Witch furious because she needs her broomstick for her spells.

*"**Oo!**" or "**You!**", she cries, and that is why when we see Eddy and the Witch together we will always hear "**Oo!**" or "**You!**".*

Whole class word work

- Listen to and sing the Eddy Elephant and the Witch song on the *Programme Two Songs Cassette* to increase phonemic awareness of the 'ōō' and 'you' sounds.
- Write the following sentences on the board and ask the children to help with picture coding **ew**.

The elephant knew a few shrewd tricks.
Andrew drew a picture of the birds as they flew by.

The elephant knew a few shrewd tricks.

He threw the jewels on the floor.

We had a good view of the crew as the ship drew in.

- Live spell: **few** ➔ **flew** ➔ **blew** ➔ **grew** ➔ **chew**. Follow up by dictating these or other **ew** words.

Group word work

- Use *Programme Two Copymaster* 19 for further practice.
- Introduce *Word Bank Copymaster* 7. Write a selection of words from the **ew** word lists on the board. The children can then choose the six words which they consider most useful to them and enter them into their Word Banks.
- Ask the children in the group to make their own **ew** picture code cards. Say aloud some of the **ew** words from the box, interspersed with other words. Ask the children to lift up their code card and say 'oo' or 'you', as appropriate, when you say an **ew** word.
- Play a type of hangman game with the children. First, write several of the **ew** words on the board, then choose one of these to be 'your' word. Write the letters **ew** in their appropriate spaces and put dashes in for the other letters. Ask the children to look at the **ew** words on the board, then in turn to offer suggestions for the letters in your word. Make sure that the children attempt letters in order from left to right. You could also use a timer and the children could see how quickly they can guess the word. Then you could ask one of the children to take on your role.
- Ask the children to try and think of headlines for n**ew**s items which use **ew** words, e.g. An elephant fl**ew** by!, or An Interv**iew** with Prince Andr**ew**.

Cross-curricular and other suggestions

- Make a class n**ew**spaper and give it a name, e.g. N**ew**s and V**iew**s. Then ask the children to report on the event of Eddy Elephant stopping the Witch's spell by grabbing her broomstick, or to write a brief report of an event that you are covering in History this term as though it were today's n**ew**s.

References
For other **w**-controlled vowels, see p126 **aw**, p64 **ow** as in **cow** and p104 **ōw** as in **show**.

Words containing ew saying 'oo'

blew, brew, chew, flew, grew, jewel, threw

Challenge words

Hebrew, shrewd

Words containing ew saying 'you'

dew, few*, interview, knew*, new*, newspaper, pew, phew, review, stew, view

Challenge words

ewe, honeydew, renewed

* High frequency words

UNIT 5.4
ue (as in blue)

Objectives

- To know that the letters **u** and **e** represent long **ū** (**ue** as in **blue**).
- To recognise and spell words containing **ue**.

What you need

- *Programme Two Picture Code Cards:* **ue** (36)
- *Programme One Picture Code Cards*
- *Programme Two Copymaster:* 20
- *Programme Two Word Bank Copymaster:* 7
- *Programme Two Songs Cassette*

Preparation

- **Zig-zag books**
  Prepare some zig-zag folded books from thin card or stiff paper.

Introducing the sound

As we have seen in the other sounds in this Unit, Mr U sometimes shortens his name, so instead of hearing a clear **ū**, the sound we hear is more like 'oo'. So for this vowel pair the usual 'out walking' rhyme is as follows:

When Mr U and E walk, Mr U talks

When Mr U and E go out walking,
Mr U does all the talking.
He just says his name, "U",
Or else he just says "oo!".

The *Vowels Out Walking Poster* does not include **ue** in the scene, as this vowel pair appears in relatively few words. Most of them are listed in the word boxes opposite. The most important ones to read and spell are **blue** and **true**.

As a reading strategy, it is useful to know that for any vowel pairs which are *not* shown on the *Vowels Out Walking Poster*, the 'first one does the talking' rule nearly always applies, e.g. **tōe**, **hōe**, **sūit**, **nūisance**, **pēople**. However, there are a few words in which the second vowel is not silent, e.g. **dūĕt**, **pōĕm**, **nēŏn**, **vidēŏ**, **sūĭcide**.

Whole class word work

- Listen to and sing the Vowels Out Walking song on the *Programme Two Songs Cassette*
- Write these sentences on the board and ask the children to help with picture coding **ue**. Add a speech bubble with **oo** in it when the sound is **ōō** rather than Mr U saying his name.
  Mr U and Mr E made the statue on the avenue.
  Is it true that Sue spilt glue on the blue carpet?
  I haven't a clue so don't argue.
- Live spell or dictate: **true** ➔ **glue** ➔ **blue** ➔ **clue** ➔ **rescue**.

Mr U and Mr E made the statue on the avenue.

Group word work

- Use *Programme Two Copymaster* 20 for further practice.
- Introduce *Word Bank Copymaster* 7. Write a selection of examples from the **ue** word list on the board and add a few distractors. Each child chooses six words to write in their Word Banks.
- Ask the children to write sentences containing some of the words from the board. They could write them out again in a zig-zag book, picture code the words containing **ue** and illustrate their sentences.

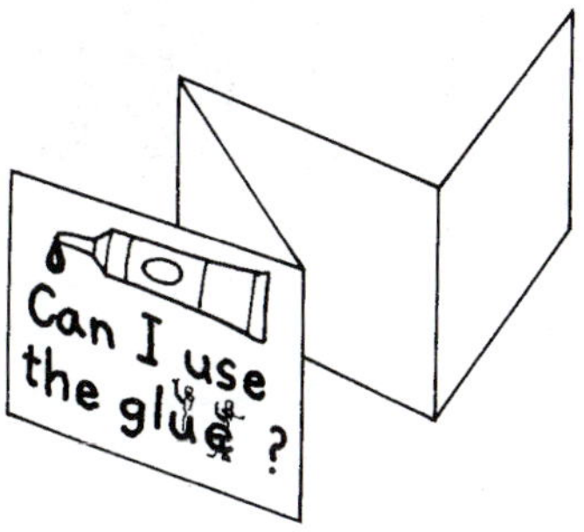

Words containing ue saying 'oo'

blue*	glue
clue	rueful
flue	true

* The only high frequency word

Words containing ue saying 'you'

argue	pursue
avenue	rescue
cue	rueful
due	statue
issue	tissue
queue	

References

For other vowel pairs, see p36 **ēe**, p38 **ēa**, p42 **ai**, p46 **ay**, p50 **ie**, p60 **oa**, p152 **ĕa**.

UNIT 6

UNIT 6.1

Magic –ed

(as ĕd, d or t)

UNIT 6.2

Magic –ing

Magic Endings

UNIT 6

Resources for Unit 6

- *Programme Two Picture Code Cards:* **ed** (50), **ed** (51), **ed** (52), **ing** (65)
- *Programme One Picture Code Cards*
- *Programme Two Copymasters:* 24-26
- *Programme Two Word Bank Copymasters:* 8, 9
- *Programme Two Songs Cassette*

The concept of Magic Endings is a strategy for alerting children to the on-going signalling power of a Magic **e**:

- when **e** is no longer the final (easy-to-notice) letter
- when **e** is no longer silent, and
- when **e** is dropped in favour of **-ing**.

flat but inflate
inflated
inflating

rip but ripe
ripen
ripest
riper

The suffixes **-ed**, **-en**, **-est** and **-er** usually contain Magic **e**'s, and **-ing** invariably replaces a Magic **e** (avoiding awkward spellings like 'inflateing'), so in Letterland these suffixes are called Magic Endings.

This Unit focuses on the two most used Magic Endings in the English language: **-ed** and **-ing**. For more about Magic **en**, Magic **est**, Magic **er**, and also final **y** when it is functioning like an **e**, see pages 190, 193 and 195 respectively.

This Unit also looks at the three sounds of **ed**: 'ĕd', 'd' and 't' (as in **expected**, **disappeared** and **vanished**) particularly to help those children who spell by ear and make typical errors such as 'huntid', 'livd' and 'hopt'.

On introducing **-ing**, attention is first given to the **ng** digraph in **-ang**, **-eng**, **-ing**, **-ong**, **-ung** words. This will be revision for most children and perhaps new phonic information for some. The introduction of **-ing** as a Magic Ending follows. As usual it comes in the form of a story. Knowing that **-ing** is just as 'magic' as a Magic **e** also helps children to understand why they need to drop **e** before **-ing**.

UNIT 6.1
Magic -ed
(as ĕd, d or t)

Objectives

- To know that the letters **e** and **d** combine to make one of three different sounds: 'ed', 'd' or 't' (as in **expected**, **disappeared** or **vanished**) and that **-ed** is a Magic Ending.
- To recognise and spell words ending **-ed**.

What you need

- *Programme Two Picture Code Cards:* **-ed** (50), **-ed** (51), **-ed** (52)
- *Programme One Picture Code Cards*
- *Programme Two Copymasters:* 24, 25
- *Programme Two Word Bank Copymaster:* 8

Preparation

- **TV reporters**
  Make a 'TV' by cutting a hole in an old cereal box. Remove the back. Paint the box. Attach some bottle tops or buttons for controls.

Introducing -ed as a Magic Ending

The **-ed** suffix often replaces Silent Magic **e**, as this story explains.

How ed became a Magic Ending

*When Mr E first invented his special Silent Magic **e**'s, Eddy Elephant was full of **e**nvy. "Can't I learn that trick, too?" he asked. "I want to shoot magic sparks as well. "What a good idea!" said Mr E. "Wear my hat and take my wand. But you'll need a partner for this trick."*

Just then, Dippy Duck came along. "Ah, Dippy Duck, would you like to come and help?" called Mr E. "I'm putting Eddy Elephant in charge of some Magic Endings from now on, but he'll need the help of at least one other letter to end the words with him. Would you help?"

*"Yes, I'd love to!" replied Dippy Duck, waggling her tail with delight. "Good!" said Mr E. "First Eddy will go to the end of the word. Then the moment you arrive to finish the word, Eddy Elephant will let the magic sparks fly. Hey presto! An **a**pple (or an **o**range or **i**nk or **u**mbrella) will disappear and a Vowel Man will appear to say his name instead - exactly as with my Silent Magic **e**!"*

Magic -ed works just like Magic e

code	flute	invite	side
coded	fluted	invited	sided
crate	hate	mute	skate
crated	hated	muted	skated
divide	include	quote	vote
divided	included	quoted	voted

Whole class word work

- Write these sentences on the board and ask the children to help with picture coding **-ed** and the previous vowel.

Mr E decided that Ed could help.

They invited the people included on the list.

Mr E decided that Ed could help.

☆ Live spell or dictate: **cod** ➜ **code** ➜ **coded**, **side** ➜ **sided**, **divide** ➜ **divided**, **skate** ➜ **skated** ➜ **fad** ➜ **fade** ➜ **faded**.

Introducing the three sounds of -ed

Once the children are familiar with the concept of **-ed** as a Magic Ending, introduce them to its three different sounds.

Coding the three different sounds of **-ed** is a good exercise in auditory discrimination. Don't be surprised if some children need quite a lot of help at first. Each word ending in **-ed** should be pronounced out loud, with a little exaggeration on the final syllable. The children should avoid whispering because a whispered **-ed** will always sound like 't'!

Learning the three sounds of **-ed** helps children to work back from understandable errors such as 'usd', 'trid', 'raind', 'stopt', 'snapt', 'helpt', 'crasht'. Tell them that *for a few words* **t** will be correct (e.g. **slept**, **wept**) but **-ed** is more likely whatever sound **ed** is making. (It sometimes sounds like **-id** as well.)

The following story explains why sometimes Eddy Elephant and Dippy Duck say 'ed' as usual, but at other times we hear 'd' or 't'.

Eddy Elephant and Dippy Duck can say 'ed', 'd' or 't'

*Eddy Elephant and Dippy Duck have found another way to make it exciting to be together in this Magic Ending. Quite often they play a disappearing game! You may find them each making their own sound, as expecte**d**.*

*On the other hand you may find Eddy Elephant has disappeare**d**, leaving not a trace of sound behind him!*

*Even more amazing, sometimes both Eddy Elephant and Dippy Duck have vanish**ed**. The only person who ever sees them vanish is Ticking Tess. She is so astonish**ed** that all she can say is 't…' as usual.*

*So the three sounds of this Elephant Ending are **ed, d** and **t**. But have you noticed? Even though the **e**lephant and the **d**uck disappear, the Magic never disappears.*❖

❖ This means that a single vowel may need protection from Eddy's sparks! See Blocking Magic, page 187.

Words containing Magic -ed making Vowel Men appear

faded

'ed'	commuted	graded
	completed	hated
	decided	skated
	faded	voted

blamed

'd'	blamed	supposed
	lined	surprised
	phoned	tamed
	saved	used

based

't'	based	produced
	choked	scraped
	coped	stroked
	priced	used (to)

Whole class word work

- Write the following sentences on the board and ask the children to help with picture coding the three sounds of **-ed**. Display all three *Picture Code Cards* to help the children in deciding which coding to apply.

  I supposed he wished to be collected at two.
  We hopped, skipped and jumped in the park.
  I'm not used to the rules she used in the game.
  Mum gripped my hand and patted me on the back.

- Live spell these words: **lifted** ➜ **limped** ➜ **filmed** ➜ **mixed** ➜ **mashed** ➜ **handed**. Remind the children that magic sparks can only reach back over one consonant to land on one vowel. If there are two consonants before Magic **-ed** the short vowel is protected from being replaced by a Vowel Man. This is useful information in preparation for understanding why many short vowel words need double consonants before Magic **-ed** to protect them from Eddy's sparks, too. See page 187.

Two consonants before -ed

Eddy's magic sparks cannot reach the vowel

ended		banged		bumped	
ended	lifted	banged	killed	bumped	jumped
handed	melted	farmed	longed	clicked	milked
hunted	rented	filled	smelled	cracked	thanked
landed	shifted	filmed	warmed	crashed	wished
				helped	
attracted	expected	alarmed	performed	addressed	immersed
converted	invented	belonged	pretended	attacked	remarked
discarded	reported	hardened	uncurled	embarrassed	reversed

I supposed he wished to be collected at two.

Group word work

- Use *Programme Two Copymasters* 24-25 for further practice.

- Introduce *Word Bank Copymaster* 8. Select words from the first row in each section on page 80 and write them in random order on the board. Ask the children to plan, on a piece of paper, which words should go under each of the three headings: **ed**, **d** and **t**. Check their lists before they enter the examples beside the correct *Word Bank* pictograms. Remind them that to hear the difference between the 'd...' and 't...' sound, they must *speak*, not whisper the word because all **d**'s sound exactly like **t**'s when whispered.

- Read out one of the sentences below. Ask a child to come to the front. He or she can stand behind the 'TV' (see Preparation) and be a TV reporter, reporting the sentence to the other children using past tense **-ed** words. For example, the sentence 'Cow jumps over the moon!' could be: 'News Flash, cow jumped over the moon!'.

  We all work very hard and finish late.

  The rocket turns and lands on the moon.

  Our school will raise lots of money for charity.

  Sally skates and Rob races for Britain.

- Play a game with the children where you give them a letter and ask them to think of **-ed** words (verbs) that begin with that letter. The children could point to the **-ed** *Picture Code Card* that matches the sound of the past tense words.

References
For Best friends to the rescue, see p185.
For Magic **en** and **est**, see p190.

UNIT 6.2

Magic -ing

Objectives

- To revise the 'ng' sound and to know that the **-ing** ending (as in **exciting**) can function like a Magic **e**.
- To recognise and spell words ending in **-ing**.

What you need

- *Programme Two Picture Code Cards:* **-ing** (65)
- *Programme One Picture Code Cards:* **ng** (61)
- *Programme Two Copymaster:* 26
- *Programme Two Word Bank Copymaster:* 9
- *Programme Two Songs Cassette*

Revising the 'ng' sound

The 'ng' sound was introduced in the *Programme One Teacher's Guide*, where it explains how Naughty Nick and Golden Girl together make a new, almost s**inging** sound whenever they meet in a word. The following activities can be used for quick revision before going on to look at **-ing** as a Magic Ending.

- Write some words from the word box below on the board. Read them aloud together so that the children identify the recurring 'ng' sounds. As a class, play with these words by making up sentences which everyone repeats, e.g.

  Nick and Golden Girl saw an orang-utan ...

  ... banging a gong and singing a song.

  ... flinging a boomerang.

  Picture code some of the words on the board.
- Play an **ng** game. The children each say something end**ing** with **-ing** which they like do**ing**. Each child has to repeat what the previous child said and then add their own suggestion. For example, I like ... dancing, skipping, eating, sewing, running, reading, swimming, knitting, cooking, singing, painting, drawing, watching TV, riding my bike, gardening, making things.
- Following this game, the children could draw a picture of themselves do**ing** some of the **-ing** th**ing**s.

* High frequency words

Words containing -ang, -eng, -ing, -ong, -ung

along*	cling	dong	hang	rang	spring*
bang*	clung	fling	hung	ring*	string*
clang	ding	flung	long*	rung	strong*
angry	clanging	length	longing	singing	tingling
belonging	fungus	lightning	oblong	slinging	triangle
boomerang	hanging	lungs	ping-pong	stinging	wingling
bungalow	jingle			strength	wringing

Introducing -ing as a Magic Ending

The power of **-ing** as a predictive signal is exactly the same as with Magic **e**, in that it causes the previous vowel to say its name. In fact there are fewer exceptions than in Magic **e** words, i.e. fewer power failures! So Magic **-ing** is a very reliable signal. As long as a previous *single* short vowel is only *one* letter away, the sparks will shoot over and make a Vowel Man appear.

How -ing became a Magic Ending

*The most exciting thing about the **-ing** ending has still to be told: **-ing** is a Magic Ending, just as magic as Magic **e**! So why doesn't Magic **-ing** begin with **e**?*

*It happened by chance. One day, not long after Mr E had invented his Magic **e's**, he took off his hat and absent-mindedly put it down on an **-ing** ending. His head must still have been very full of magic because suddenly the **-ing** ending started zzz**inging** with magic! Mr E was amazed, but then he decided it might be quite excit**ing** to keep **-ing** as a Magic Ending. So he left a spare wand and top hat right there. Ever since then **-ing** has been a Magic Ending! Naughty Nick and Golden Girl find that very excit**ing**.*

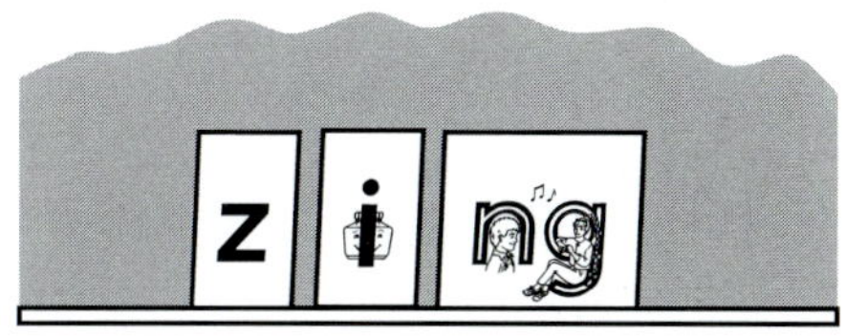

Whole class word work

- Sing or chant the Magic **e** song on the *Programme Two Songs Cassette*. Its words apply to Magic **e**, Magic **-ing** and every other Magic Ending. Stress that the magic sparks can only transform *single* vowels.

- Show the children how Magic **-ing** words are really Magic **e** words that have changed to Magic **-ing**. Use the word **escape** as the first example. Write it on the board three times, as in the table below. Ask how the second syllable would have to be pronounced if there were no Magic **e** or Magic **-ing**. Do the same with **collide**, **explode**, **presume** and **complete** or **delete**.

Magic -ing behaves just like Magic e

take tak.. taking	like lik.. liking	hope hop.. hoping	compete compet.. competing	use us.. using
name nam.. naming	drive driv.. driving	joke jok.. joking	delete delet.. deleting	include includ.. including
escape escap.. escaping	collide collid.. colliding	explode explod.. exploding	complete complet.. completing	presume presum.. presuming

Magic e words drop e before Magic -ing

Use some of the same example words on page 83 to help children to understand that, since Magic **e** and Magic **-ing** both do the same job, it would be a waste of magic to keep Magic **e** *and* then add on a Magic **-ing**. Magic is precious stuff in Letterland and shouldn't be wasted!

The phrase 'Naming Game' (the Vowel Men's way of describing the fun they have appearing whenever a Magic **e** is placed at the end of a word) applies equally to Magic **-ing**, as the coding of these two words demonstrates.

Naming Game

Whole class word work

Write these sentences on the board and ask the children to help with picture coding Magic **-ing** and the previous vowel.

Using magic is quite exciting.

They were smiling and joking while skating.

The film was amazing and really amusing too.

Live spell or dictate: **name** → **naming** → **make** → **making** → **ride** → **riding** → **hope** → **hoping** → **use** → **using**.

Using magic is quite exciting.

Group word work

- Use *Programme Two Copymaster* 26 for further practice.
- Introduce *Word Bank Copymaster* 9. Ask the children to look for words ending in Magic **-ing** in their books and to add them to their Word Banks. They may need help in choosing only words where the preceding vowel is long. Words with e.g. **nt**, **ck** already causing **-ing** to be out of reach do not count, neither do words with two vowels side by side (e.g. **speeding**, **raining**, **reaching**).
- Explore the structure of some longer words that inexperienced readers might trip up on because the middle syllable is a recognisable word in itself, e.g.

frust**rat**ing	fabri**cat**ing	en**twin**ing
cor**rod**ing	distri**but**ing	com**pet**ing
ro**tat**ing	dis**put**ing	des**crib**ing
de**fin**ing		

Unless the children apply their new Magic **-ing** knowledge, these three and four syllable words can be discouraging. By adding **-ing**'s magic sparks and drawing in the Vowel Man, they demonstrate to themselves **-ing**'s power as a Magic Ending.

rat	frustrat...	frustrating
but	distribut...	distributing
pet	compet...	competing

The children will soon discover that they can read long, difficult words before they even know their meaning: a good demonstration of the value of **-ing** as a predictive signal. This strategy is also an important precursor to predicting when to double the consonant (see page 185).

UNIT 7

UNIT 7.1

u (as in pull)

UNIT 7.2

oo (as in foot)

The ŭ sound

UNIT 7

Resources for Unit 7

- *Programme Two Picture Code Cards:* **u** (12), **u** (Uppy Umbrella – back of 5), **oo** (71)
- *Programme One Picture Code Cards*
- *Programme Two Copymaster:* 27
- *Programme Two Word Bank Copymaster:* 10
- *Programme Two Songs Cassette*

In the high-frequency words **put**, **push**, **pull**, **full** and in many words ending with **-ful**, the letter **u** makes a different sound. Why this irregular **u**? In Letterland terms the question becomes: 'Why isn't Uppy Umbrella making her usual 'u' sound (as in **up**)?'

The answer in this Unit leads the children to a new Letterland character, Giant Full, a towering fellow who is sometimes, but not always, helpf**u**l in words. In Letterland lore he takes the blame for the irregular 'u' sound. (For more about Giant Full and about words ending in **-ful,** and when to drop one **l**, see page 156.)

This irregular 'u' sound is actually spelt far more often by using **oo** ('oo' as in **good**). Given the greater number of high frequency words in this group, a good case can be made for teaching Unit 7.2 before Unit 7.1. In Letterland this **o͝o** spelling pattern provides an opportunity to revisit the Boot and Foot Twins (see page 68). The focus is now on the Foot Twin. Whereas before the Boot Twin was talking, this time we hear from the Foot Twin, loudly complaining about his foot in the key phrase, 'O͝O, just lo͝ok at my fo͝ot!'

Once again, take advantage of the Boot and Foot Twins' song on the *Programme Two Songs Cassette* to strengthen phonemic awareness of both sounds made by the letters **o͝o**, but especially this time, of the final sound in the refrain which ends so emphatically with **o͝o**!

UNIT 7.1

u (as in pull)

Objectives

- To know that the letter **u** can make the short 'ŏŏ' sound (**u** as in **pull**).
- To recognise and spell words containing **u**.

What you need

- *Programme Two Picture Code Cards:* **u** (12), **u** (**Uppy Umbrella** – back of 5)
- *Programme One Picture Code Cards:* **p**, **b** or **l**, **l**
- *Programme Two Copymaster:* 27
- *Programme Two Word Bank Copymaster:* 10

Introducing the sound

If an umbrella is pushed into its letter too roughly, it will say "ŏŏ"!

In Letterland there are two towering giants. One is Giant All and the other is called Giant Full. Unlike his friend Giant All who doesn't help matters at all, Giant Full can be a very helpful fellow. He loves helping Mr U by filling his u's full of umbrellas for him. In fact, Mr U calls him "Giant Fill-U-Full", because he fills so many u's full of umbrellas! The trouble is that he sometimes pushes and pulls the umbrellas about so roughly as he throws them in, that you might hear an umbrella puffing 'ŏŏ!' Then you will know who probably put it there too roughly – Giant Full!

Use *Picture Code Card* 5 for the regular short vowel sound made by Uppy Umbrella when she is the right way up, and *Picture Code Card* 12 with the upside-down picture of her to show how her sound changes in just a few words to the 'ŏŏ' sound (as in **put**).

c u t but p u t

There are not many words with this irregular **u**. The ones the children will come across most are given in the word box opposite.

Whole class word work

- Write these sentences on the board and ask the children to help with picture coding **u** sounding like 'ŏŏ'.

Giant Full thinks he fulfils his job well.
You can try pulling that bull, but don't push it.
Please put this notice up on the bulletin board.

Giant Full thinks he fulfils his job well.

☆ Demonstrate this sound with the *Picture Code Cards* at this point, saving the live spelling for Unit 17.1 (**full** and **ful**). You can either use the single irregular **u** (Card 12), plus two plain single **l**'s from *Programme One Picture Code Cards*, or Giant Full (Card 60) with **p** or **b** (*Programme One Picture Code Cards*) placed before the **f**, and an upside down Uppy Umbrella (Card 12) placed over **fu** beside the Giant's legs. (On the Giant Full card, the **u** is shown **fu**ll of umbrellas, signalling the same 'o͝o' sound as one upside down umbrella p**u**shed in too roughly.)

☆ Dictate: but, bull, pull, pulling, putting, cutting, push, bush, bushes, fun, full, comparing the sounds of the **u** in the different words.

Group word work

☆ Use *Programme Two Copymaster* 27 for further practice.

☆ Introduce *Word Bank Copymaster* 10. Write a selection of words from the word box below on the board. The children then choose the six words they consider to be the most useful to them and enter them into their Word Banks.

Words containing u saying 'o͝o'

bull	cushion	pulling
bullet	fulfil	push
bulletin	full*	pushed
bush	pull*	put*
bushes	pulley	putting

Most of the other words containing this irregular **u** end in the suffix **-ful**.

* High frequency words

References
For more about Giant Full and the suffix **-ful**, see page 156.
For more about Giant All, see p163.

UNIT 7.2

oo (as in foot)

Objectives

- To know that two **o**'s can combine to make the short 'ŏo' sound (**oo** as in **foot**).
- To recognise and spell words containing **oo**.

What you need

- *Programme Two Picture Code Cards:* **ōo** (70), **ŏo** (71)
- *Programme One Picture Code Cards*
- *Programme Two Copymaster:* 27
- *Programme Two Word Bank Copymaster:* 10
- *Programme Two Songs Cassette*

Preparation

- Prepare an area for a Boot and Foot Twins display. Have ready some card for the children to make one large picture of each of the Boot and Foot Twins.

Introducing the sound

The long 'ōo' sound as in **boot** was covered in Unit 5.1. If you were able at that point to play the Boot and Foot Twins' song on the *Programme Two Songs Cassette* and to encourage children to sing along with it, they will already have some familiarity with this short 'ŏo' sound, as represented by the Foot Twin.

The Foot Twin steps in a puddle and says "ŎO!"

*Remember that the Boot and Foot Twins are the grandsons of Mr O, the Old Man. They spend a lot of time arguing over their **boo**ts.*

*In most words you will hear the **Boo**t Twin teasing his brother by saying "**ŌO**! I have your b**ōo**ts!"*

*Sometimes, however, you will hear the second twin instead, complaining, "**ŎO**! Just l**ŏo**k at my f**ŏo**t!" as he steps in a puddle. He is the **Foo**t Twin.*

Whole class word work

- Listen to the Boot and Foot Twins song on the *Programme Two Songs Cassette* and sing along on a second playing.
- Write these sentences on the board and ask the children to help with picture coding **ŏo**.

  OO! Just look at my foot!

  We gave our grandmother a good cook book.

  You could also display both the **ōo** and **ŏo** *Picture Code Cards* and try picture coding these sentences which combine the two sounds.

  He is in too bad a mood to eat good food.

  I feel like a fool in this woolly hat.

- Live spell or dictate these words: **foot** ➜ **good** ➜ **wood** ➜ **wool** ➜ **book** ➜ **brook** ➜ **crooked**.

OO! Just look at my foot!

Group word work

- Use *Programme Two Copymaster* 27 for further practice.

- Introduce *Word Bank Copymaster* 10. Write a selection of words from the **oo** word box below on the board. The children then choose the six words they consider to be the most useful to them and enter them into their Word Banks.

- Help children to discriminate between the long and the short sound of **oo** by creating a display for collecting Boot and Foot Twin words. The children picture code and then mount their Boot and Foot Twin words under two large **o͞o** and **o͝o** pictures which you can ask two children to make with picture coding as shown on *Picture Code Cards* 70 and 71.

Words containing oo as in foot

book*
brook
childhood
cook*
crook
crooked
foot*
football*
good*
goodbye*
goodness
hood
hook
likelihood

look*
looks*
looked*
looking*
nook
overtook
rook
soot
stood*
took*
wood*
wool*
woollen

Challenge words

likelihood
withstood
undertook

* High frequency words

Revision

Use the *Picture Code Cards* from the Units covered so far to revise the sounds. Hold up each card, asking for that letter's sound. Turn to the pictogram side only to help or to confirm correct responses. Go through the cards more than once, aiming for speed of responses. The ultimate goal is automatic responses so that when reading, the child's mind is able to process with ease not only the letters and words, but the message as well.

References
For **o͞o** as in **boot**, see page 68.
For **o** as in **who**, see 167.

UNIT 8

UNIT 8.1

ar (as in car)

The 'ar' sound

UNIT 8

Resources for Unit 8

- *Programme Two Picture Code Cards:* **ar** (40)
- *Programme One Picture Code Cards*
- *Programme Two Copymasters:* 28
- *Programme Two Word Bank Copymasters:* 11
- *Programme Two Songs Cassette*
- *Vowel Scenes Posters:* The Vowel Stealers

This Unit focuses on **ar**, known in Letterland as Arthur Ar, the Apple Stealer. Meeting him paves the way for introducing the other Vowel Stealers (already in view on the *Vowel Stealers Poster*) by alerting the children to the concept of **r**-controlled vowels.

The 'ar' phoneme provides a good first occasion to introduce a remarkable fact about the English language. Almost every time a single vowel is to the left of an **r**, that **r** will alter the vowel's sound. Consider **tap** but **tar**, **hen** but **her**, **fist** but **first**, **pot** but **port**, **fun** but **fur**. The vowels all become **r**-controlled vowels the moment they are placed behind the robber's back, creating the new phonemes: **ar**, **er**, **ir**, **or** and **ur**.

Letterland explains this phonic fact at a child's level by depicting all **r**'s as running **r**obbers. Robber Red, introduced in Programme One, represents the regular growling sound, 'rrr...', found at the start of many words and in all the consonant blends with **r**, e.g. **br**, **cr**, **dr**, **fr**. But Robber Red also has a gang of five Vowel Stealers who steal away the five vowel sounds. They represent three new sounds: 'ar' (as in **farm**), 'or' (as in **corn**) and 'er' (spelt three ways, as in **fern**, **third** and **turn**).

The challenge to the children is to become sharp-eyed detectives and catch these five lawless robbers in the act of stealing, so they cannot stop the children from reading the words they appear in! The children identify the three new sounds by learning the Vowel Stealers' surnames, Arthur Ar, Orvil Or and the three Er/Ur/Ir Brothers: Ernest Er, Urgent Ur and Irving Ir who each insist on a different spelling of their surnames.

There is no reason to withhold the surnames of the other Vowel Stealers until the timetable slots for teaching **or**, **er**, **ir** and **ur** in depth. The sooner the children become aware of these **r**-controlled units of sound, the more words will yield to phonic attack. For more information on **or**, see page 120 and for **er**, **ur**, **ir**, see pages 132-137.

A few words containing this 'ar' sound are spelt with **a** alone (see Yawning apples, page 169).

UNIT 8.1

ar (as in car)

Objectives

- To know that the letters **a** and **r** combine to make the 'ar' sound (**ar** as in **car**).
- To recognise and spell words containing **ar**.

What you need

- *Programme Two Picture Code Cards:* **ar** (40)
- *Programme One Picture Code Cards*
- *Programme Two Copymaster:* 28
- *Programme Two Word Bank Copymaster:* 11
- *Programme Two Songs Cassette*
- *Vowel Scenes Posters:* The Vowel Stealers

Preparation

- **Ar jars**
  Collect a l**ar**ge, old, coffee j**ar**. Put in: some b**ar**k, a toy sh**ar**k, a c**ar**, some st**ar**s and other objects not containing **ar**.
- **Arthur Ar's car**
  Prepare and copy Arthur Ar's car (without words) for each child (see page 95).
- **Go-carts**
  Collect some boxes, cotton reels, buttons and dowelling.

Introducing the sound

Display the *Vowel Stealers Poster.* Explain that the new robbers are all members of Robber Red's gang. They all have a bad habit of running away with vowel sounds! By challenging the children, as suggested on page 93, you may find interest high enough to merit introducing all these **r**-controlled phonemes earlier than planned.

Whenever Arthur Ar steals an apple he cries "Ar"

__Ar__thur __Ar__ is the robber who steals __a__pples. When he captures one, don't expect it to make its usual 'a…' sound. Instead, __Ar__thur __Ar__ reports back to Robber Red with a tiny walkie-talkie hidden inside his outstretched __ar__m. He calls in with just one word: his surname, "__Ar__!"

Write on the board the sentence **Arthur Ar parked his car in the dark by the barn** and ask the children to listen carefully as you read it out. How many times can they hear Arthur Ar saying "**Ar**!"?

Whole class word work

- Listen to and sing the Apple Stealer's song on the *Programme Two Songs Cassette.*
- Write the following sentences on the board and ask the children to help with picture coding **ar**.

  The dog was barking in the dark farmyard.
  Mark had a party in his back garden.
  Look at the stars in the dark, night sky.

- Live spell: **cat** → **car**, **had** → **hard**, **pat** → **part** → **party** → **partly** → **hardly** → **shark**.

The dog was barking in the dark farmyard.

Group word work

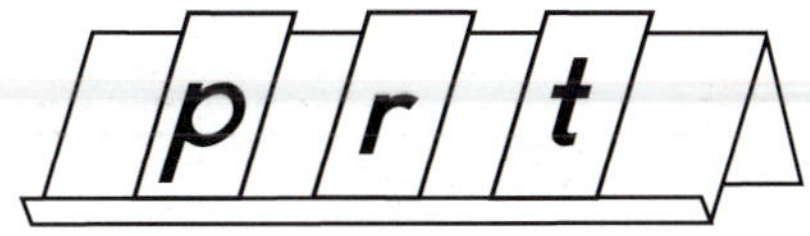

Robber Red says 'rrr'

Arthur Ar says 'ar'

- Use the *Picture Code Cards* to clarify any confusions between **r** ('rrr...') and the 'ar' sound by contrasting the two pictograms.
- Use *Programme Two Copymaster* 28 for further practice.
- Introduce *Word Bank Copymaster* 11. Ask the children to look for words containing **ar** in their books and to add them to their Word Banks.
- Take the objects out of your **Ar jar** (see Preparation) and with the children, sort them into objects containing the **ar** sound and objects that do not. Then put the **jar** and its contents away and ask the children to write a list of all the objects containing the **ar** sound that they can remember.
- Give each child in the group an A4 photocopy of the get-away c**ar** (see Preparation). Ask them to write **ar** words on the bodywork of the c**ar**. They can then cut out the c**ar**s, stick them on to an **Ar** wall display and compare the **ar** words on each others' cars.

Cross-curricular and other suggestions

- Ask the children to design and make their own small go-c**ar**ts from reclaimed items. Make some different textured hills and slopes of various inclines and ask the children to predict, on their own ch**ar**t, which go-c**ar**t they think will travel down which hill the fastest or the slowest. Then ask them to record their results on a ch**ar**t.

* High frequency words

Words containing ar

			Children's names	Challenge words
are*	dark*	pardon	Charles	barb
arm*	darling	part*	Charlie	barbed
art	far*	party*	Charlotte	barred
artist	farm*	scar	Darjit	larch
bar	farmer*	shark	Mark	lark
bark	garden*	sharp	Martin	regard
barn	hard*	star*	Parveet	remark
cart	hardly	start*		sparse
carve	jar	starving		varnish
charm	mark	target		
chart	market	yard		

References
For other **r**-controlled vowels, see p120 **or**; pp132-137 **er**, **ir**, **ur**. See also Unit 11: **air**, **are**, **ere**, **ear**; Unit 12: **oor**, **ore**; p123 **oar**, **our**; and p193 Magic **er**.

UNIT 9

UNIT 9.1

oy (as in toy)

UNIT 9.2

oi (as in boil)

The 'oy' sound

UNIT 9

Resources for Unit 9

- *Programme Two Picture Code Cards:* **oy** (34), **oi** (35)
- *Programme One Picture Code Cards*
- *Programme Two Copymasters:* 29-31
- *Programme Two Word Bank Copymaster:* 12
- *Programme Two Songs Cassette*

The number of words which need the **oy** spelling pattern is very limited. The examples listed in Unit 9.1 will cover most, if not all, of the children's reading and spelling needs.

The number of words needing the **oi** spelling pattern is also limited. By asking several children to retell the **oi** story in their own words, you will be helping them to remember both the **oy** and **oi** spelling patterns. Encourage the children to use the words **noisy** and **boisterous** when they retell the **oi** story to the class.

Typically the **oy** pattern appears at the ends of words and the **oi** pattern occurs inside words. However, the children will find **oy** occurring inside words wherever a new ending has been added to the original root **oy** word. For guidelines on when to use **oy** and when to use **oi,** see page 101.

To ensure that this sound lingers in the children's hearing memories and to bring the boy called Roy's 'oy game' to life, sing or chant the Roy and the Yo-yo Man song on the *Programme Two Songs Cassette.*

UNIT 9.1

oy (as in toy)

Objectives

- To know that the letters **o** and **y** combine to make the 'oy' sound (**oy** as in **toy**).
- To recognise and spell words containing **oy**.

What you need

- *Programme Two Picture Code Cards:* **oy** (34)
- *Programme One Picture Code Cards*
- *Programme Two Copymaster:* 29
- *Programme Two Word Bank Copymaster:* 12
- *Programme Two Songs Cassette*

Preparation

- **Flap books**
  Have ready some pieces of card and some smaller sheets of paper, a stapler or some tape.

Introducing the sound

Most children will be able to read the words **boy** and **toys** as sight words long before they need to study the 'oy' sound and its two spelling patterns **oy** and **oi**. The following story will reassure them that not only words which they *do* know, but also words which they *don't* know, have the same story explanations.

The boy called Roy's 'oy game'

*In Naughty Nick's class at school there is a b**oy** called R**oy**. At the **end** of words, this b**oy** called R**oy** enj**oy**s leap-frogging over an **o** and into the Yo-yo Man's sack. He calls this leap-frog game his '**oy** game' because he likes to shout "**oy**!" as he leaps. The Yo-yo Man shouts "**oy**!" too, every time R**oy** lands on him unexpectedly. The Yo-yo Man pretends to be ann**oy**ed with R**oy**, but really they both enj**oy** R**oy**'s '**oy** game' because they both enj**oy** shouting "**oy**!"*

You may like to explain to children at the outset that words which *end* in the 'oy' sound, always have the **oy** spelling.

Whole class word work

- Listen to the first verse of the Roy and the Yo-yo Man song on the *Programme Two Songs Cassette.* Then play it again so the children can join in, with one group taking the part of Roy and the other the part of the Yo-yo Man. Children could hold up the **oy** *Picture Code Card* each time the Roy group shouts "Oy, oy, oy!"
- Write these sentences on the board and ask the children to help with picture coding **oy**.

  They both enjoy playing Roy's 'OY game'.
  My Dad enjoyed employing the toyshop man.
  The Yo-yo Man is only pretending to be annoyed.

- Live spell or dictate: **boy** → **toy** → **joy** → **enjoy** → **employ** → **annoy**.

They both enjoy playing Roy's 'OY game'.

Group word work

- Use *Programme Two Copymaster* 29 for further practice.
- Introduce *Word Bank Copymaster* 12. Write a selection of examples from the **oy** word box below on the board and add a few distractors. Each child chooses six **oy** words to write in their Word Banks.
- Ask each child to draw his or her own picture-coded **oy** in the middle of a piece of card. Then tape or staple a series of flaps to both the left and right hand sides of the card so the child can write on them and turn the flaps up to make a series of **oy** words. The left-hand flaps can contain: **b**, **j**, **t**, **ann**, **enj**, **empl** and **destr**. The right-hand flaps can contain one blank flap and three others with: **s**, **ed** and **ing** on them.

Group book with a series of children's **oy** pictograms in the middle panel.

One child's **oy** book with her own coded pictogram in the middle panel.

Words containing oy

		Challenge words
annoy	enjoy*	buoy
boy*	joy	corduroy
convoy	Roy	coy
destroy	tomboy	decoy
employ	toy*	

Note: Where the **oy** spelling occurs *within* the words in the box below, this is because a new ending has been added to the root word. From the Yo-yo Man's point of view he is simply continuing to finish up the root word in his **y**-clothes.

Adding an ending to oy words

annoy	destroy	employ	enjoy*
annoyance	destroyed	employed	enjoys
annoyed	destroyer	employer	enjoyed*
annoying	destroying	employing	enjoying
annoys	destroys	employment	enjoyment

* High frequency words

References
For words with **oi**, see p100.

UNIT 9.2

oi (as in boil)

Objectives

- To know that the letters **o** and **i** combine to make the 'oy' sound (**oi** as in **boil**).
- To recognise and spell words containing **oi**.

What you need

- *Programme Two Picture Code Cards:* **oi** (35), **oy** (34)
- *Programme One Picture Code Cards*
- *Programme Two Copymaster:* 30
- *Programme Two Word Bank Copymaster:* 12
- *Programme Two Songs Cassette*

Introducing the sound

While the **oy** spelling occurs both at the *end* and *inside* words, the **oi** spelling only occurs *inside* words. Explain more about the job the Yo-yo Man does while he is playing Roy's game to help children to know whether to use **oy** or **oi** inside a word.

Roy and the Yo-yo Man play the 'oi game' inside words

*While the Yo-yo Man plays the game with Roy in a word, he also carries on doing his job. His job is to **finish** the '**oy**' word. He does this job in his usual working clothes.*

*Sometimes, however, the Yo-yo Man is not needed to finish up a word, so he does not need to stay in his working clothes. Then you will see him wearing his neat straight **i**-clothes while he plays the game with Roy. At that p**oi**nt, the '**oy** game' becomes the '**oi** game'. It is really the same game; it just looks different. It's also a little less n**oi**sy and b**oi**sterous when they play it inside the word.*

Whole class word work

- Listen to and sing the Roy and the Yo-yo Man song on the *Programme Two Songs Cassette.* Half the class can be Roy while the other half sings the Yo-yo Man's ann**oy**ed response. Ask a child to hold up the **oy** *Picture Code Card* as they sing "Oy, oy, oy!" Another child can hold up the **oi** *Picture Code Card* for the second version of the song. This time everyone sings it with less n**oi**sy and b**oi**sterous v**oi**ces.
- Write these sentences on the board and ask the children to help with picture coding **oi**. (They could also picture code **oy**.)

Roy has a noisy voice.

I was disappointed to lose that new coin.

Joyce has spoiled the point of my new pen.

- Live spell or dictate: **boil** ➜ **coil** ➜ **coin** ➜ **point** ➜ **moist** ➜ **noise** ➜ **noisy boy**.

Roy has a noisy voice.

Group word work

- ☆ Use *Programme Two Copymaster* 30 for further practice.
- ☆ Introduce *Word Bank Copymaster* 12. Write a selection of examples from the **oi** word box on the board and add a few distractors. Each child chooses six **oi** words to write in their Word Banks.
- ☆ Introduce group live spelling games where the children race to spell a given word. You could focus on spelling either **oy** words or **oi** words, or you could say words from either group. The children decide, with help as needed: **oy** or **oi**. You may like to write some guidelines on the board:

1. At the end of a word: use **oy**
2. At the end of a root word with a new ending after it: use **oy**.
3. Inside a word with no other root word in it: use **oi**.

n o i s e

boy but boil

coy but coin

joy but joint

toy but toil

Words containing oi

			Challenge words
appointment	join	point	boisterous
boil	joint	pointed	exploit
boisterous	jointed	pointless	hoist
coil	moist	poison	poise
coin	moisten	rejoice	recoil
disappointed	noise*	spoil	turmoil
embroider	noisy	toilet	
foil	oil*	turquoise	
invoice	ointment	voice	

* High frequency words

Adding an ending to 'oy' words

Where a fuller explanation of the second guideline above is needed, the following may be helpful (see also page 99):
When a final syllable such as **-s**, **-ed**, **-ing**, **-er**, **-ance**, **-ful** or **-ment** is added to a root word ending in **oy**, the **oy** spelling pattern remains unchanged. In Letterland terms, the Yo-yo Man doesn't stop to change into his neat, straight **i**-clothes, because he is still finishing the root word where he and Roy were already playing.

Revision

Revise the sounds covered so far using the *Picture Code Cards*. Aim for speed of response. This is a valuable exercise to include regularly.

References
For final **y** changing to **i** before a new ending, see p182.

UNIT 10

UNIT 10.1

ow (as in cow)

UNIT 10.2

ou (as in ouch!)

The 'ow' sound

UNIT 10

Resources for Unit 10

- *Programme Two Picture Code Cards:* **ow** (77), **ou** (75)
- *Programme One Picture Code Cards*
- *Programme Two Copymasters:* 32-34
- *Programme Two Word Bank Copymaster:* 13

The first sound of **ow** (as in **show**) was introduced in Unit 4.3, and featured the long **ō** spelling patterns. The story explaining the second sound of **ow** as in **cow** (see page 104) is another instance where Letterland's Witch tries to control the vowel, only to be foiled this time by her own greed and clumsiness. Summarising the two **ow** stories, one shows her surprise, 'Oh!', and the other her pain, 'Ow!'

Inconveniently, English orthography provides us with a second spelling pattern for the 'ow' (pain) sound: **ou** (as in **ouch**!). The Letterland story for **ou** helps children to organise these **ow** and **ou** alternatives in their minds by providing a logical link between them. In both cases the same story applies but with minor variations.

The best way to learn which words are spelt with which sound is to cluster them into phrases or sentences that are meaningful in their own right, e.g. **down in the town**, **shout out loud**. The children will also benefit by making some clusters of their own.

Another strategy is also suggested in each Unit: a Brown Owl display, where the children contribute **ow** words of their choice (either picture-coded or illustrated for whole word meaning or both), and a display of Cloud Words, where each **ou** word is displayed in its own little cloud within a bigger one. Again, the children can add their own picture coding or illustrations.

The Yellow Window display suggested for the long 'ō' sound of **ow** on page 65 together with the Brown Owl and the Cloud Words displays will function as visual organisers, supporting the children while they make these overlapping **ow**/**ou** sounds and spelling patterns their own.

UNIT 10.1

ow (as in cow)

Objectives

- To know that the letters **o** and **w** can combine to make the 'ow' sound (**ow** as in **cow**).
- To recognise and spell words containing **ow**.

Introducing the sound

This is the second **w**-controlled vowel and the alternative sound made by the letters **ow**. It is prevalent in a few much used words, such as **how**, **now**, **down** and **brown**. The Letterland story for this sound explains what happens to cause the Witch sometimes to cry out "Ow!" in pain instead of saying "Oh!" in surprise in **ow** words.

What you need

- *Programme Two Picture Code Cards:* **ow** (77)
- *Programme One Picture Code Cards*
- *Programme Two Copymaster:* 32
- *Programme Two Word Bank Copymaster:* 13

When the Witch tries to get the orange, she howls "Ow!"

*The Wicked Water Witch loves the big, round, ripe **o**ranges which Mr O imports from over the ocean. She knows these **o**ranges don't belong to her, but that doesn't stop her from wanting them! Every time she finds herself next to an **o**range in a word, she tries a wicked spell to get it out.*

*Luckily for the **o**range, the Witch is clumsy and foolish. When her spell doesn't work (and it never seems to), she gets so angry that she tries to break open the **o** with her broomstick. But she always falls and bumps her chin instead.*

*That is why, in lots of words where you see these two letters, all you can hear is the Wicked Water Witch h**ow**ling "**Ow**!"*

Preparation

- **Brown Owl display**
  Prepare a br**ow**n outline of an **owl** and clear wall space to collect words around it.

Whole class word work

- Write these sentences on the board and ask the children to help with picture coding **ow**.

  The Vowel Men heard the Witch howl "OW!"
  The clown with green eyebrows was frowning.
  How now, brown cow?
  There's a dry towel and powder in the shower.

- Live spell or dictate: **owl** → **howl** → **growl** → **brown** → **clown** → **flower** → **shower** → **power**.

  You may like to practise both sounds of **ow** using the following words: **owl** → **bowl** → **grow** → **growl** → **row** → **brown**.

The Vowel Men heard the Witch howl "OW!"

Group word work

- Use *Programme Two Copymaster* 32 for further practice.

- Introduce *Word Bank Copymaster* 13. Ask the children to find **ow** words for their Word Banks. Point out that they will also find some **ow** words (as in wind**ow**). These can be listed separately or added to the Yellow Window display suggested on page 65.

- Ask each child to select one of their Word Bank **ow** words, to write it very large, picture code it and illustrate its meaning (if convenient). Mount these words on and around the prepared brown owl and encourage the children to continue to add to it. The display then becomes an on-going spelling resource, helping to separate **ow** words from **ou** words which the children will meet in Unit 10.2 (see page 106).

- Tell the children some of the words in the word box below and ask them to add the appropriate *Picture Code Cards* to either side of the **ow** card to make **ow** words.

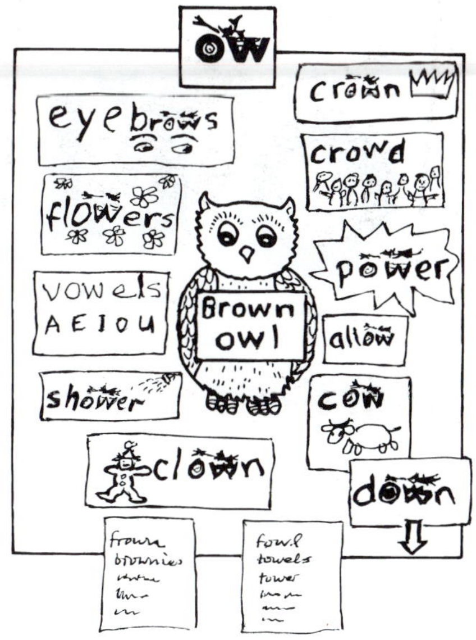

Words containing ow

allow	drown	growl	power*
brown*	drowsy	how*	shower
clown	eyebrow	however	somehow
cow*	flower*	howl	towel
crowd	fowl	owl	town*
down*	frown	powder	vowel

* High frequency words

Cross-curricular and other suggestions

- Help the children to write a list of instructions for h**ow** to gr**ow** a sunfl**ow**er from seed and h**ow** to look after it. This activity provides practice for both sounds of **ow**. Other children could see h**ow** many ways they can combine **ow** (surprise) and **ow** (pain) words, e.g. p**ow**er m**ow**er, foll**ow** the cr**ow**d, h**ow** l**ow**, **ow**l in the sn**ow**.

References
For **ow** as in **show**, see p64. For other **w**-controlled vowels, see p72 **ew** and p126 **aw**.

UNIT 10.2

ou (as in ouch!)

Objectives

- To know that the letters **o** and **u** combine to make the 'ow' sound (**ou** as in **ouch!**).
- To recognise and spell words containing **ou**.

What you need

- *Programme Two Picture Code Cards:* **ou** (75)
- *Programme One Picture Code Cards*
- *Programme Two Copymaster:* 33
- *Programme Two Word Bank Copymaster:* 13

Preparation

- **Cloud display**
  Prepare a cloud-shaped background for displaying children's picture-coded **ou** words.

Introducing the sound

The Witch tries an underwater spell and shouts "ou!"

*The Witch knows Mr O will stop her from trying to get his **o**ranges whenever he can. So she decides to hide inside a different letter where not even Mr O would expect to find her. Can you think of another letter which could hold water? The Witch can! The **u**mbrella letter! Her problem is that Uppy Umbrella is usually there protecting it from getting wet. So what does she do?*

*She uses her broomstick like a hose, shooting water at poor Uppy Umbrella. The water lifts Uppy up and sends her flying. While she is gone, the Witch quickly fills her letter full of water, dives down and tries an **u**nderwater spell to get the **o**range out. Silly witch! Her **u**nderwater spells don't work properly either! Again she tries to break into the **o** with her broomstick!*

*Can you imagine trying to hit anything hard when you are under water? It's not surprising that every time she tries she just fl**ou**nders, bumps her chin again and sh**ou**ts "**ou**!" That is why the only s**ou**nd you will hear is the Witch sh**ou**ting "**ou**!"*

Whole class word work

- Write these sentences on the board and ask the children to help with picture coding **ou**.

  She shouted out 'ouch!' very loudly.
  The pig had mud on his snout and mouth.
  My house is near the roundabout.
  Stop running around in the playground.

- Live spell or dictate: **loud** → **cloud** → **ground** → **pound** → **pouch** → **ouch**.

She shouted out 'ouch!' very loudly.

Group word work

- Use *Programme Two Copymaster* 33 for further practice.
- Introduce *Word Bank Copymaster* 13. Ask the children to look for words containing **ou** in their books, which they can add to their Word Banks. Help them to check the s**ou**nd in the words they find, so they do not enter ones which are exceptions, e.g. **soup**, **although**, **cough**, **four**.
- Each child draws his or her own picture-coded **ou** word, filling the whole page with it so it is easy to see at a distance. They cut **ou**t the word in a cl**ou**d shape and mount it on the cl**ou**d-shaped backgr**ou**nd.
- Ask the children to rec**ou**nt the **ou** story, or to write an acc**ou**nt of what happened.
- Working in pairs, the children make up sentences which contain at least three **ou** words.They can then take turns reading them **ou**t l**ou**d to the group.

Words containing ou

about*	ground*	our*	south*
around*	hound	out*	spout
blouse	hour*	pouch	sprout
bounce	house*	pound*	surround
cloud	loud	round*	thousand*
count	mouse	shout	trousers
flour	mouth*	sound	trout
found*	ouch	sour	voucher

* High frequency words

UNIT 11

UNIT 11.1

air (as in fair)

UNIT 11.2

are (as in scare)

UNIT 11.3

ere (as in there and as in here)

UNIT 11.4

ear (as in bear)

The 'air' sound

UNIT 11

Resources for Unit 11

- *Programme Two Picture Code Cards:* **air** (39), **are** (41), **ere** (56), **ear** (49)
- *Programme One Picture Code Cards*
- *Programme Two Copymasters:* 35-37
- *Programme Two Word Bank Copymasters:* 14, 15
- *Vowel Scenes Posters:* Vowels Out Walking

Four different spelling patterns for one phoneme, 'air', may seem excessive, but this is part of the heritage of the English language, coming as it does from many sources. To make matters worse, **-ere** has a second sound, 'ear' (compare **there** and **here**) and **-ear** can also represent either the 'air' or 'ear' sound (compare **bear** and **hear**).

Children who are getting to know what trouble-makers **r**obbers can be in Letterland will find once again that these bad characters are to blame for all these shifting sounds. They are controlling/destabilising two vowels behind their backs in **-air** and **-ear** and upsetting one on either side in **-are** and **-ere**! Fortunately there are relatively few words to learn in each of these groups.

Picture coding these varying spelling patterns is one valuable, concrete way for a child to get to know them. Drawing the robbers' sacks around the vowels very clearly illustrates each **r**'s control over the vowels, and an arrow pointing to the puff of air or the robber's ear illustrates whichever sound applies to a particular word.

hair care there bear

but hear

The 'air' stories are the subject of this Unit, but some teachers may wish to share the **-ear** story on page 148 as well, since 'ear' (as in **hear**) is the sound that is most commonly associated with the **-ear** spelling pattern. The panel at the bottom of the *Vowels Out Walking Poster* provides a useful on-going reference point for three of these 'air' and 'ear' spelling patterns: **-air**, **-ear** and **-eer**.

UNIT 11.1

air (as in fair)

Objectives

- To know that the letters **a, i** and **r** combine to make the 'air' sound (**air** as in **fair**).
- To recognise and spell words containing **air**.

What you need

- *Programme Two Picture Code Cards:* **air** (39)
- *Programme One Picture Code Cards*
- *Programme Two Copymaster:* 35
- *Programme Two Word Bank Copymaster:* 14
- *Vowel Scenes Posters:* Vowels Out Walking

Introducing the sound

Display the *Vowels Out Walking Poster* and ask the children to look for the robbers lurking in the scene. Draw their attention to the puffs of hot air coming from the robber's mouth in the **air** pictogram.

When two vowels out walking are captured, the robber does the talking

*Silent look-out men are not always able to spot a **r**obber in time to avoid being captured, so it is important to know what the wretched **r**obbers are up to. No Vowel Man can be expected to go on cheerfully saying his name when he has just been tossed into the **r**obber's sack! The **r**obbers usually shout out "**ear**" or "**air**" as they capture (except for Orvil Or, see page 120). Arthur Ar always puffs out "air" as he runs off with the p**air** of Vowel Men to his robber's l**air**.*

Whole class word work

- Write these sentences on the board and ask the children to help with picture coding **air**.

  He puffed out hot air as he ran to his lair.

  Claire had her hair cut fairly short.

  I found a pair of shoes on the stairs.

- Live spell or dictate: **aim** ➜ **air**, **fail** ➜ **fair**, **hail** ➜ **hair** ➜ **hairy**.

He puffed out hot air as he ran to his lair.

Group word work

- Use *Programme Two Copymaster* 35 for further practice.
- Introduce *Word Bank Copymaster* 14. Write a selection of examples from the **air** word box on the board and add a few distractors, e.g. **chain**, **faint**, **marry**, **fault**, **aimless**, **maintain**. The children then choose 12 **air** words which they consider most useful to them to write in their Word Banks.
- Underline the following words on the board: **stairs**, **repair**, **despair**, **unfair** and **chair**. Ask the children to work in pairs to think up stories based on these words and any others already on the board, and then exchange the results.

Words containing air

affair	hairless
air*	hairy
airy	lair
chair*	pair*
despair	repair
downstairs	stair*
eclair	staircase
fair*	unfair
fairies	unfairly
fairly	upstairs
fairy	
flair	
hair*	There are very few others.

* High frequency words

References
For other **r**-controlled vowel pairs, see p116 **ear**, p119 and p123 **oar**, **our**, p122 **oor**, p148 **ear**, p149 **eer**.

UNIT 11.2

are (as in scare)

Objectives

- To know that the letters **ar** and Magic **e** combine to make the '-air' sound (**are** as in **scare**).
- To recognise and spell words containing **-are**.
- To spell the word **are**.

What you need

- *Programme Two Picture Code Cards:* **-āre** (41) and the word **are** (42).
- *Programme One Picture Code Cards*
- *Programme Two Copymaster:* 36
- *Programme Two Word Bank Copymaster:* 14

Preparation

- **Look, say, cover, write, check**
  Make copies of the format on page 230.
- **Word slides**
  Have ready some A4 sheets of card or stiff paper for the children to make their own word slides.

Introducing the sound (and the word are)

Except in the word 'are' Arthur Ar puffs out air when he overpowers a and e

*In the single word **are**, Arthur **Ar** steals an **a**pple and reports "**Ar**!" as usual. But he also has to break Silent Magic **e**'s wand, so that its sparks won't shoot over his head and make his stolen **a**pple disappear!*

*In all other words where you see Arthur **Ar** plus a Magic **e**, he puts the **a**pple and the Silent Magic **e** into two sacks. Carrying both sacks is such hard work, that he breathes very heavily as he runs off, puffing out lots of **air**! So bew**are** and be prep**are**d! Unless you see these three letters in a word of their own, they will sound just like the word 'air'.*

Whole class word work

- Write these sentences on the board and ask the children to help with picture coding **-are**.

  Beware! Take care, when you are barefoot.
  Don't stare – you'll scare him.
  Can you compare a circle and a square?

- Live spell or dictate: **care** → **stare** → **square** → **aware** → **beware** → **prepare**. Strengthen the spelling/meaning link and ask the children to *stare* when they have made the word **stare**.

Beware! Take care, when you are barefoot.

Group word work

- Use *Programme Two Copymaster* 36 for further practice.
- Introduce *Word Bank Copymaster* 14. Write a selection of words from the word box below on the board. The children then choose 12 **-are** words which they consider most useful to them and enter them into their Word Banks.
- Ask the children to make up some sentences containing the word **are** and one or two words containing the '-are' phoneme, and to picture code both the word **are** and the **-are** words.
- Give the children some **ar** words (see page 95), together with **-are** words from the word box below and some words to revise from a previous Unit or Units. Ask them to complete the *look, say, cover, write, check* format.
- Write several short **-are** words on the board. Show your **-are** word slide to the children (see right). Then ask them to make their own word slides for **-are** words, putting the following letters on the sliding pieces: **c**, **d**, **aw**, **f**, **h**, **r**.

Words containing are

		Challenge words
aware	declare	fanfare
bare	fare	flare
barefoot	hare	glare
barely	prepare	nightmare
beware	rare	
care*	scared*	
careful	share	
careless	square	
compare	stare	
dare	unaware	

* High frequency words

UNIT 11.3
ere (as in there)

Objectives

- To know that the letters **e, r** and **e** can combine to make the 'air' sound (**ere** as in **there**).
- To know that **ere** can also represent an 'ear' sound (as in **here**).
- To recognise and spell words containing **ere**.

What you need

- *Programme Two Picture Code Cards:* **ere** (56)
- *Programme One Picture Code Cards*
- *Programme Two Copymaster:* 36
- *Programme Two Word Bank Copymaster:* 15

Introducing the sound

If it weren't for two much used words, **there** and **where**, there would be little justification in teaching this variant spelling pattern for the 'air' sound at this stage. It occurs rarely, apart from those words listed in the first word box on the opposite page. Given, however, the children's need to read and spell **there** and **where** correctly (singly and in compound words made from them) Letterland provides the following story.

Ernest Er puffs out hot air when he is surrounded by two e's

*What happens when Ernest Er is surrounded by **e**'s? In one word, **were**, he goes on saying 'er' as usual, breaking Magic **e**'s wand to stop its sparks.*

*But in two other much used words, **there** and **where**, Ernest Er is uncertain what to do. He is so nervous that he tries to overpower both **e**'s at once. Finally he does, but then he goes off puffing out hot 'air' probably because two vowel men are heavy to carry!*

The arrow on the **ere** *Picture Code Card* 56 pointing to the puff of air coming from the robber's mouth is the visual cue for the 'air' sound.

Whole class word work

- Write these sentences on the board and ask the children to help with picture coding **ere**.

  He said they were over there somewhere!
  We see there are footprints everywhere.
  Is there anywhere over there where we could go?

- Live spell or dictate: **there** → **where** → **elsewhere** → **nowhere** → **somewhere**. To live spell, the second **e** child points to the robber's mouth (as if pointing to the air).

He said they were over there somewhere!

These are the few words where **ere** represents the 'air' sound. The starred words are high priority to learn to spell correctly.

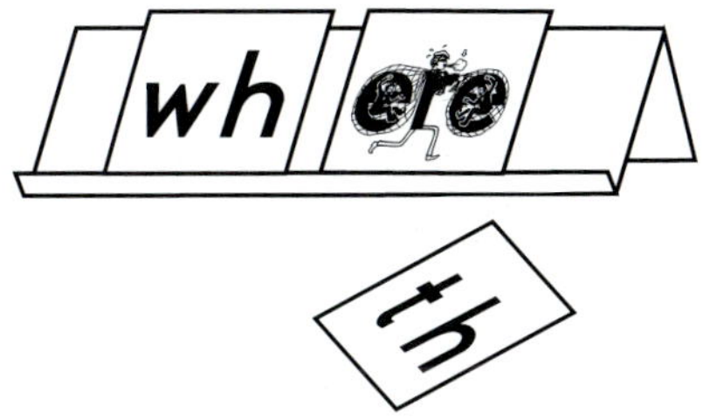

Words containing ere ('air')

anywhere	thereafter
elsewhere	therefore
everywhere	where*
nowhere	whereas
somewhere*	wherever
there*	

Exceptions

The next box contains the few words where **ere** represents the other sound of **ere**: 'ear' (as in **here**). The most important ones to know how to spell are **here** and **sincerely**. The arrow on *Picture Code Card* 56 pointing to the robber's swollen ear (the result of a scuffle) is the visual cue for this second sound of **ere**. Other words containing **ere** representing the 'ear' sound are rare. To live spell **here** the first **e** child points to the **r**obber's ear.

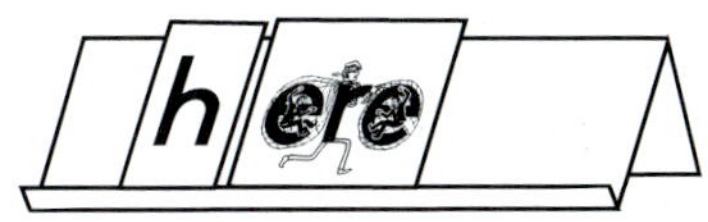

Words containing ere ('ear')

atmosphere	severe
hemisphere	sincere
here*	sincerely
interfere	sphere
mere	

* High frequency words

Group word work

- Use *Programme Two Copymaster* 36 for further practice.
- Introduce *Word Bank Copymaster* 15. Ask the children in the group to search in their books for the words **there** and **where**. But first, ask them to guess how many times they think they will find the words. After they have searched, compare their results with their guesses. You could make a chart showing their results. (The same activity can be widened to include **here** which, like **there** and **where**, is also within the 100 most used English words.)

UNIT 11.4
ear (as in bear)

Objectives

- To know that the letters **e, a** and **r** can combine to make the 'air' sound (**ear** as in **bear**).
- To recognise and spell words containing **ear** as in **bear**).

What you need

- *Programme Two Picture Code Cards:* **ear** (49)
- *Programme One Picture Code Cards*
- *Programme Two Copymaster:* 35
- *Programme Two Word Bank Copymaster:* 15
- *Vowel Scenes Posters:* Vowels Out Walking

Preparation

- **Look, say, cover, write, check**
  Make copies of the format on page 230.

Introducing the sound

Display the *Vowels Out Walking Poster* and ask the children to look for the robbers lurking in the scene. Draw their attention to the puffs of hot air coming from the robber's mouth in the **ear** pictogram. The story explanation below is the same as for Unit 11.1: **air**.

When two vowels out walking are captured, the robber does the talking

*Silent look-out men are not always able to spot a **r**obber in time to avoid being captured, so it is important to know what the wretched **r**obbers are up to. No Vowel Man can be expected to go on cheerfully saying his name when he has just been tossed into the **r**obber's sack! The **r**obbers usually shout out "**ear**" or "**air**" as they capture, except for Orvil Or.*

As the list in the box on the opposite page shows, this spelling pattern has a very limited application.

Whole class word work

- Write these sentences on the board and ask the children to help with picture coding **ear** saying 'air'.

  There is a tear in the T-shirt I was wearing.

  Do bears eat pears?

- Live spell or dictate: **beans** → **bear** → **pear** → **wear** → **wearing** → **team** → **tear** → **tearing**.

There is a tear in the T-shirt I was wearing.

Group word work

- Use *Programme Two Copymaster* 35 for further practice.
- Introduce *Word Bank Copymaster* 15. Write all the examples from the **ear** word box on the board and add a few distractors, e.g. **bean**, **hare**, **seal**, **leaves**. Each child writes the eight **ear** words in their Word Banks. Explain that it is unlikely that they will be able to fill the remaining lines, as there are not many more **ear** words to be found.
- Give the children some **ear** words from the word box and some words to revise from a previous Unit or Units. Ask them to complete the *look, say, cover, write, check* format.

Words containing ear saying 'air'

There are very few words sounding like 'air' but spelt with **ear**.

bear*
pear
sportswear
swear
tear
tearing
wear*
wearing*

* High frequency words

References
For other **r**-controlled vowel pairs, see p110 **air**, p119 and p123 **oar**, **our**, p122 **oor**, p148 **ear**, p149 **eer**.

UNIT 12

UNIT 12.1

or (as in sport)

UNIT 12.2

oor (as in floor)

UNIT 12.3

ore (as in sore)

UNIT 12.4

aw (as in awful)

UNIT 12.5

au (as in caught)

The 'or' sound

UNIT
12

Resources for Unit 12

- *Programme Two Picture Code Cards:* **or** (73), **oor** (72), **ore** (74), **aw** (43), **au** (44)
- *Programme One Picture Code Cards*
- *Programme Two Copymasters:* 38-42
- *Programme Two Word Bank Copymasters:* 16, 17
- *Programme Two Songs Cassette*
- *Vowel Scenes Posters:* The Vowel Stealers

The 'or' sound can be challenging because there are many alternative spelling patterns for this sound: **or**, **oar**, **oor**, **ore**, **our** (as in **four**), **aw**, **au** and **augh**. This group does not include **ough** (as in **thought**, see page 212), or words where the sound of **a** is altered beside **ll** or **l** (as in **all** and **almost**: see Giant All, page 163). In areas where regional accent causes a difference in pronunciation, those differences will help to guide the inexperienced speller.

Fortunately the **or** spelling dominates, and the rest of these spelling patterns are only used in a restricted number of words. This Unit focuses on **or**. It then covers **oor**, **ore**, **aw**, **au** (and **augh**), because although they are needed in fewer words, some of these words are high frequency ones, e.g. **door**, **more** and **saw**.

As usual, the villains of the English language are the **r**'s and **w**'s. Translated into Letterland terms, watch out for Orvil Or, the Orange Stealer, and the Wicked Water Witch. They will change vowel sounds wherever they can.

Orvil Or's boat by the sh**ore** and the **oar** he carries provide the *oral* and *visual* clues for this vowel stealer's sound, regardless of which spelling applies. Whether Orvil Or runs off with one vowel or two, as in **oor** and **ore**, he goes on saying 'or' as before. No *Picture Code Card* is provided for **oar** or **our** (as in **four**, **your** and **course**) as there are too few words which need the 'or' sound that are spelt that way. But the picture coding can easily be drawn on by hand to help a child to see and appreciate the **oar** and **our** spelling patterns as three-letter units of sound.

oar and our

The Witch's way of making apples taste **aw**ful (whenever she finds herself next to one in a word) is proof again that she is a trouble-maker. She has even developed an **u**nderwater spell so she can cause the same 'aw' sound in words with **au** (see page 128).

The trouble-makers in Letterland have one advantage in common for teachers. They always generate high interest among children, thereby making the **r**-controlled and **w**-controlled spelling patterns easier and more fun to learn.

UNIT 12.1

or (as in sport)

Objectives

- To know that the letters **o** and **r** can combine to make the 'or' sound (**or** as in **sport**).
- To recognise and spell words containing **or**.

What you need

- *Programme Two Picture Code Cards:* **or** (73)
- *Programme One Picture Code Cards*
- *Programme Two Copymaster:* 38
- *Programme Two Word Bank Copymaster:* 16
- *Programme Two Songs Cassette*
- *Vowel Scenes Posters:* The Vowel Stealers

Preparation

- **Look, say, cover, write, check**
  Make copies of the format on page 230.
- **'This morning' storyboard**
  Photocopy the storyboard format on page 232.
- **Passports**
  Bring in an old passport to show the children. Prepare some card and paper for them to make their own.

Introducing the sound

Display and talk about the *Vowel Stealers Poster* as you introduce this next phoneme. Robber Red is the ringleader and all the other robbers report back to him. They are all law-breakers and the challenge to the children is to become sharp-eyed detectives, catching them as they steal away the vowel sounds (see also page 92).

When Orvil Or steals an orange he reports back with his surname "Or!"

Orvil Or is the robber who steals oranges. When he does, don't expect the orange to say 'ŏ' anymore. All you will hear instead is the sound of Orvil Or reporting back to Robber Red, saying just his surname "Or!". Orvil Or keeps his get-away boat by the shore, and he makes sure no-one can take his boat by keeping his oar with him all the time.

The picture of the **oar** in Orvil's hand is the child's visual prompt for the oral information (the 'or' sound) across all the **r**-controlled ways to spell this sound.

Whole class word work

- Listen to and sing the Orange Stealer's song on the *Programme Two Songs Cassette.*
- Write these sentences on the board and ask the children to help with picture coding **or.**

  In one story Orvil Or rides a white horse.
  We are short of forks on our table.
  My report says I need to be better organised.

- Live spell or dictate: **pot** → **port** → **spot** → **sport** → **sort** → **born** → **storm** → **story** → **corn** → **corner**.

Group word work

- Use *Programme Two Copymaster* 38 for further practice.
- Introduce *Word Bank Copymaster* 16. Write a selection of words from the **or** word box on the board. The children then choose the six words which they consider most useful to them and enter them into their Word Banks.
- Ask the children to write a st**or**y containing several **or** words. These could include: **born**, **corner**, **fork**, **important**, **platform**, **report**, **resort**, **storm**, **torch**.
- Ask the children to *look, say, cover, write, check* some of the **or** words. Include some words to revise from a previous Unit or Units.

Cross-curricular and other suggestions

- Ask the children to draw pictures of all the things they did that m**or**ning before they came to school, using the st**or**y board f**or**mat (see Preparation). Then ask them to arrange their pictures into a sequence and write about each one.
- Show the children an old passp**or**t and discuss what inf**or**mation it contains. Give out some pieces of plain paper and card and help the children to make their own passp**or**ts.

Words containing or

border	important	report
born*	inform	reported
cord	lord	resort
corner*	morning*	short*
for*	normal	snort
force	north*	sort
forgiven	orchard	sport
fork*	order*	storm
forth	ordinary	story*
fortress	organise	support
forty*	ornament	thorn
glory	perform	torch
horse*	platform	unicorn
import	pork	worn

Challenge words

absorb
forlorn
portion
scornful
transform

Beware: In occupations, e.g. **actor**, **conductor**, **doctor**, **mayor**, **professor**, **sailor** the 'or' sound switches to 'er'.

* High frequency words

References
For the other Vowel Stealers, see p93 **ar**, pp132-137 **er**, **ur**, **ir**.

UNIT 12.2
oor (as in floor)

Objectives

- To know that the letters **o**, **o** and **r** can combine to make the 'or' sound (**oor** as in **floor**).
- To recognise and spell words containing **oor**.

What you need

- *Programme Two Picture Code Cards:* **oor** (72)
- *Programme One Picture Code Cards*
- *Programme Two Copymaster:* 39
- *Programme Two Word Bank Copymaster:* 16

Preparation

- **Look, say, cover, write, check**
  Make copies of the format on page 230.

Introducing the sound

When there is another vowel in between the **o** and **r**, it does not change the 'or' sound. Show children how you can picture code this **oor** spelling pattern by showing Orvil Or capturing the two vowels in his sack.

When Orvil Or captures two vowels, he still runs off saying his surname "Or!"

Whether Orvil Or captures one vowel or two, it is all the same to him! He just goes on reporting back with his surname "Or!" as he has always done before.

In spelling, a word will only need the **oor** spelling if it is **poor**, **door**, **floor** or **moor**, or a larger word made from any of these four root words.

Whole class word work

- Write the following sentences on the board and ask the children to help with picture coding **oor**.

  Let's keep that old chair outdoors, not indoors.

  There was a number on each of the doors.

  The floor was poorly painted.

- Live spell or dictate: **poor** → **door** → **floor** → **indoors** → **outdoors**.

Let's keep that old chair outdoors, not indoors.

Group word work

- Use *Programme Two Copymaster* 39 for further practice.

- Introduce *Word Bank Copymaster* 16. Write all the examples from the **oor** word box below on the board and add a few distractors, e.g. **boom**, **rooster**, **foolish**, **toothache**, **bedroom**. Each child chooses six **oor** words to write in their Word Banks.

- Put circles around some of the **oor** words already on the board and add some words to revise from a previous Unit or Units. Ask the children to complete the *look, say, cover, write, check* format.

Words containing oor

door*	moorhen
doorway	moorland
floor*	outdoors
indoors	poor*
moor	poorly

* High frequency words

Alternative spelling patterns for the 'or' sound: oar and our

The **oar** spelling is used in a few cases, e.g. **oars**, **board**, **hoarse**, **roar** and **soar**. The **our** spelling will be more familiar, because it occurs in the following seven high frequency words: **four**, **fourth**, **fourteen** (but not **forty**), **your**, **yours**, **yourself** and **course**, but not in many other words apart from **court, mourn, pour** and **source**. (Another small group of **our** words belongs in the **ou** (pain) category, e.g. **hour, flour**, see page 106.)

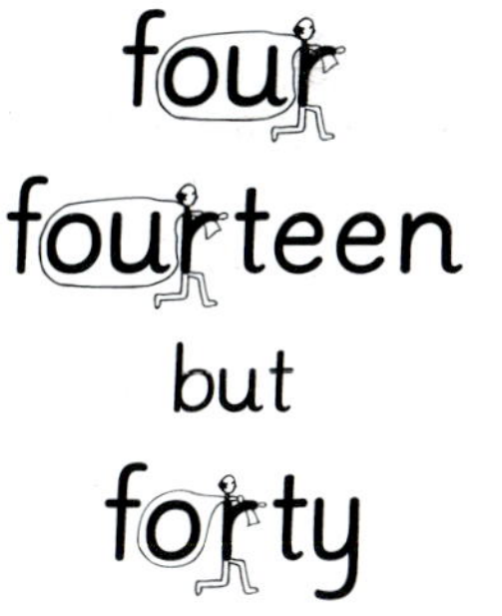

As mentioned on page 119, although there are no *Picture Code Cards* for these additional 'or' phoneme spelling patterns, they are easily coded by hand with a sack drawn around the two **r**-controlled vowels to illustrate their phonic structure and their sound.

References
For other **r**-controlled vowel pairs, see p110 **air**, p119 **oar**, **our**, p148 **ear**, p149 **eer**.

UNIT 12.3

ore (as in sore)

Objectives

- To know that the letters **o, r** and **e** can combine to make the 'or' sound (**ore** as in **sore**).
- To recognise and spell words containing **ore**.

What you need

- *Programme Two Picture Code Cards:* **ore** *(74)*
- *Programme One Picture Code Cards*
- *Programme Two Copymaster:* 39
- *Programme Two Word Bank Copymaster:* 16

Preparation

- **Look, say, cover, write, check**
  Make copies of the format on page 230.
- **Word tubes**
  Collect some pieces of card for the children to make into tubes which can be placed inside each other and turned to make words (see illustration page 125).

Introducing the sound

It would be reasonable to expect that the Magic **e** principle might apply to words ending in **ore**. It turns out, however, that the vowel-controlling **r** is more powerful than the Magic **e**.

Orvil Or never lets Magic e stop him stealing oranges

*Orvil **Or** can't afford to let a Magic **e** send its magic sparks over his head and make his stolen **o**range disappear. So he uses his oar in order to shorten the wand and stop the magic. Then he goes on saying "Or!" as he has done bef**ore**.*

Whole class word work

- Write these sentences on the board and ask the children to help with picture coding **ore**.

The first time he wore the jacket, he tore it.
Have you been to the seashore before?
Don't ignore reading that book's foreword.

- Live spell or dictate: **more** ➜ **sore** ➜ **snore** ➜ **before** ➜ **ignore** ➜ **explore**.

The first time he wore the jacket, he tore it.

Group word work

- Use *Programme Two Copymaster* 39 for further practice.

- Introduce *Word Bank Copymaster* 16. Write a selection of words from the **ore** word box on the board. The children then choose six words which they consider most useful to them and enter them into their Word Banks.

- Give the children some **ore** words from the word box and some words to revise from a previous Unit or Units. Ask them to complete the *look, say, cover, write, check* format.

- Make some word tubes with the children. Then ask each child to choose six different **ore** words. Ask them to write the first part of the word on the piece of card which is going to be the bigger tube. Then write the **ore** ending of the word on the card which is going to be the smaller tube which goes inside the other. Make sure that they write their letters towards the right hand side of the card. They can then exchange tubes and read each others' words.

Cross-curricular and other suggestions

- Ask the children to make up a poem about all the things that they may find at the seash**ore**, or make a collage of items found at the seash**ore**.

Words containing ore

			Challenge words
adore	foresee	shore	ashore
before*	foretell	snore	folklore
bored	foreword	sore*	foremost
boredom	ignore	store*	forethought
chore	more*	swore	galore
core	pore	therefore	spore
explore	restore	tore	
forecast	score	wore	
forehead	scored		
forerunner	seashore		

* High frequency words

UNIT 12.4

aw (as in awful)

Objectives

- To know that the letters **a** and **w** combine to make the 'or' sound (**aw** as in **awful**).
- To recognise and spell words containing **aw**.

What you need

- *Programme Two Picture Code Cards:* **aw** (43)
- *Programme One Picture Code Cards*
- *Programme Two Copymaster:* 40
- *Programme Two Word Bank Copymaster:* 17

Preparation

- **Word pieces**
  Have ready some strips of paper or card.

Introducing the sound

The Witch makes the apple taste awful

*When Annie Apple is next to the Wicked Water Witch in words, the Witch tries to get the apple out. But she can't make a spell powerful enough, so she does something wicked instead. She decides to splash nasty spell water on the **a**pple so that it tastes **aw**ful. So whenever you see these two letters together in a word, you will hear the 'aw' sound because the Witch has made the **a**pple taste **aw**ful.*

Whole class word work

- Write these sentences on the board and ask the children to help with picture coding **aw** and **a**.

  I saw the Witch crawl across the lawn at dawn.
  Can you draw a picture of the frog spawn?
  The boy sat on the seesaw and yawned.

- Live spell these words: **sat** ➜ **saw** ➜ **pat** ➜ **paw** ➜ **clap** ➜ **claw** ➜ **crawl** ➜ **draw** ➜ **awful** ➜ **shawl**.

I saw the Witch crawl across the lawn at dawn.

Group word work

- Use *Programme Two Copymaster* 40 for further practice.

- Introduce *Word Bank Copymaster* 17. Write some **aw** words on the board. Ask the children to select the words containing **aw** which they consider most useful to them and enter them in their Word Banks.

- Give out strips of paper or card to the children and ask them to write **aw** words on them. They could then cut up their words so that the **aw** parts are separate and ask a friend to put their words back together again (see illustration). Encourage the children to check their words in a dictionary.

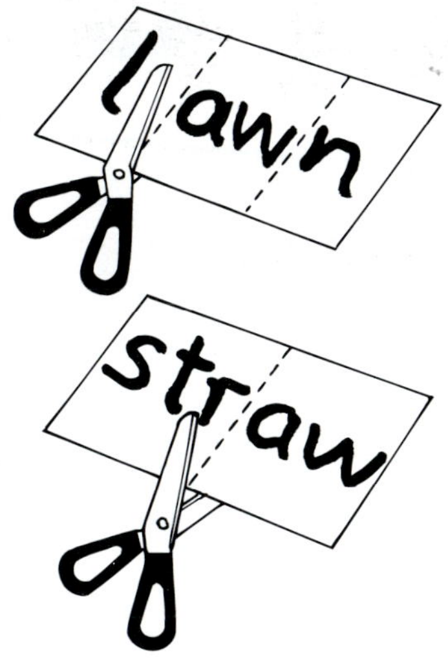

Cross-curricular and other suggestions

- Ask the children to write a recipe for an **aw**ful cake, using some of the words from the **aw** word box below.

More irregularities caused by w

This may be a good time to point out how the letter **w** can change the sound of many vowels found on either side of it. Look at the words **was**, **want**, **war**, **water**, **swan**, **woman**, **women** and **worm**, all proof that the Witch can make trouble for vowels, no matter which side they are on. Their new sounds are so unpredictable that there are no pictograms for them. The best strategy is: **Beware of the Witch wherever you find her!**

Words containing aw

			Challenge words
awful*	fawn	raw	awesome
awkward	gnaw	saw*	prawn
claw	hawk	seesaw	scrawl
crawl	hawthorn	squawk	trawler
dawn	jaw	straw	
draw*	law	thaw	
drawing	lawn*	yawn	
drawn	paw		

* High frequency words

References
For other **w**-controlled vowels, see p64 **ow**, p72 **ew**, p104 **ow**.

UNIT 12.5

au (as in caught)

Objectives

- To know that the letters **a** and **u** combine to make the 'or' sound (**au** as in **caught**).
- To recognise and spell words containing **au**.

What you need

- *Programme Two Picture Code Cards:* **au** (44)
- *Programme One Picture Code Cards*
- *Programme Two Copymaster:* 41
- *Programme Two Word Bank Copymaster:* 17

Preparation

- **Making words**
  Collect a set of *Picture Code Cards*, or magnetic letters, foam letters or letter tiles.
- **A haunted house**
  Get a large sheet of paper and some thick felt pens. Mark out some rectangular shapes to represent rooms in the house. Collect some large boxes to make a 3-D h**au**nted house and prepare some glue, scissors, and other suitable materials.

Introducing the sound

The Witch makes the apple taste awful from underwater

*We know that the Witch can't make any of her spells work, so when she wants to get an **a**pple out of its letter and eat it, she spitefully makes the **a**pple taste **aw**ful. Luckily the **aw**ful taste doesn't last long. But the old Witch has another idea – to try a new kind of spell to get an **a**pple out. She chases away Uppy Umbrella, fills her letter full of water, dives in and tries an **u**nderwater spell! Does it work any better? No! So once again she spitefully makes the **a**pple taste **aw**ful, just as she has done before.*

Whole class word work

- Write these sentences on the board and ask the children to help with picture coding each **au**.

  She caught a bad cold and felt exhausted.
  Put your dirty clothes in the laundry basket!
  Everyone applauded as the astronauts came out.
  The faulty switch could cause a fire.

- Live spell or dictate: **pause** ➜ **because** ➜ **sauce** ➜ **saucer** ➜ **laundry** ➜ **haunted**.

She caught a bad cold and felt exhausted.

Group word work

- Use *Programme Two Copymaster* 41 for further practice.
- Introduce *Word Bank Copymaster* 17. Write a selection of examples from the **au** word box below on the board and add a few distractors, e.g. **lunch**, **plant**, **animal**, **partly**, **squawk**, **drawer**. Each child chooses at least six words to write in their Word Banks.
- From the list of **au** words on the board, ask the children to work in pairs to make some of the **au** words using *Picture Code Cards*, magnetic letters, foam letters or letter tiles. Ask them to keep a list of the words they make, so they can read them out to you or each other later.

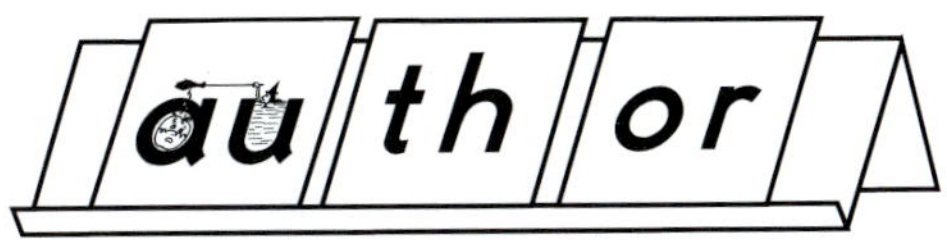

Cross-curricular and other suggestions

- Make a floorplan of a h**au**nted house with the children (see Preparation) and ask them to imagine what may be in each room. Then ask them to devise a route around the h**au**nted house in search of some hidden goodies!

lunch
but
launch

Words containing au

applaud
astronaut
audience
August*
author
automatic
autumn*
exhausted
fault

haunted
launch
launderette
laundry
pause
sauce
saucer

Children's names

Laura
Paul

augh words

caught*
daughter
naughty*
taught*

Challenge words

auburn
authority
daunting
haul

* High frequency words

References
For words spelt with **ough** (as in **thought**), see p212.

UNIT 13

UNIT 13.1

er (as in her)

UNIT 13.2

ir (as in bird)

UNIT 13.3

ur (as in fur)

The 'er' sound

UNIT 13

Resources for Unit 13

- *Programme Two Picture Code Cards:* **er** (54), **ir** (66), **ur** (82)
- *Programme One Picture Code Cards*
- *Programme Two Copymasters:* 43-46
- *Programme Two Word Bank Copymasters:* 18
- *Programme Two Songs Cassette*
- *Vowel Scenes Posters:* The Vowel Stealers

The fact that there are three alternative spellings for the 'er' sound (as in **her** and **were**) could be discon**cer**ting or int**er**esting. Letterland's law-breaking, vowel-stealing Er Brothers are attention keep**ers**, helping to make lessons on the three **er**, **ur** and **ir** digraphs popular.

As with **ar** and **or**, once again the challenge is on for the children to be sharp-eyed detectives. These vowel stealers will run riot in hundreds of words, unless the children learn the new 'er' sound that all three brothers make as they steal, and catch them in the act (i.e. spot the **er**, **ur** and **ir** spelling patterns) wherever they find them!

Keep *The Vowel Stealers Poster* on display while you teach this Unit. It contains a number of spelling cues: Ernest Er's legs are long**er** than all the oth**er** robb**er** broth**ers**. Urgent Ur wears boots of c**ur**ly p**ur**ple f**ur**, while Irving Ir comes th**ir**d in the sequence with spilt ink making his sh**ir**t all d**ir**ty.

The Er/Ur/Ir Brothers' song on the *Programme Two Songs Cassette* helps to strengthen the challenge as the three robber brothers brashly boast "Be al**er**t and obs**er**ve us, we are p**er**fect!" But the children will soon get to know their imp**er**fect ways.

Each of the three Robber Brothers has his own personality, as demonstrated in the three additional songs, Ernest Er in Person, Urgent Ur in Person and Irving Ir in Person, where each robber brother sings (or speaks) about himself in the first person. These three songs cluster **er**, **ur** and **ir** words around the relevant brothers, thereby acting as playful but highly effective spelling aids.

Revision of these sounds could be expanded to include all five Vowel Stealers, in a Space Explorers theme, or any other theme of your own choosing. The search for words containing the relevant spelling patterns within that theme will lead not only to a heightened attention to these particular digraphs anywhere, but also to an expansion in both written and spoken vocabulary.

UNIT 13.1

er (as in her)

Objectives

- To know that the letters **e** and **r** combine to make the 'er' sound (**er** as in **her** and **were**).
- To recognise and spell words containing **er**.

What you need

- *Programme Two Picture Code Cards:* **er** (54), **ir** (66), **ur** (82)
- *Programme One Picture Code Cards*
- *Programme Two Copymaster:* 43
- *Programme Two Word Bank Copymaster:* 18
- *Programme Two Songs Cassette*
- *Vowel Scenes Posters:* The Vowel Stealers

Preparation

- **Comparative charts**
  Collect some large sheets of paper for the children to use for their charts.

Introducing the sound

Of the three different spellings for the '**er**' phoneme (**er**, **ir** and **ur**), the **er** spelling is by far the most common. The **ur** and **ir** spellings occur in a much smaller, though still significant, number of words. Have *The Vowel Stealers Poster* on display so that you can point to it, or hold up the three **er**, **ur** and **ir** *Picture Code Cards.*

Ernest Er, the Elephant Stealer, says "Er!"

*Three of Robber Red's gang of Vowel Stealers are broth**er**s. They're known as the **Er** Broth**er**s because they all make the same sound. Like the other Vowel Stealers, they each say their own surname. The trouble is that they argue all the time about how to spell their surname: **er, ur** or **ir**?*

Show the **er** *Picture Code Card.*

*When you see Eddy Elephant's lett**er** behind a robber's back, don't expect that **e**lephant to be saying 'ĕ...' at that point, because **Er**nest **Er** will have captured it. Give **Er**nest **Er** a chance and he would capture a whole h**er**d of elephants! Luckily, he nev**er** mends his sack so a captured elephant soon breaks loose again. Howev**er**, in the meantime, keep a sharp look-out for **Er**nest **Er** the Elephant Steal**er** saying "er..." in many words.*

Now add the **ur** and **ir** *Picture Code Cards* under **er**.

*Now look closely at the three **Er** Broth**er**s cards. Can you notice something different about **Er**nest **Er**? Look closely at his legs. Yes, his legs are long**er** than eith**er** of the oth**er** robb**er** broth**er**s, so he can run fast**er** then they can. This is why you often hear him saying "er" at the end of a word. With those long**er** legs of course he gets to the **end** of a word before his slow**er** robb**er** broth**er**s.*

Whole class word work

- Listen to the Er/Ur/Ir Brothers' song and the Ernest Er in Person song on the *Programme Two Songs Cassette.*

This robber brother is a much faster runner.

- Write these sentences on the board and ask the children to help with picture coding **er**.

  This robber brother is a much faster runner.

  Is the weather colder in September or October?

  He was quicker at serving those customers.

- Live spell: **hen** ➜ **her** ➜ **ever** ➜ **never** ➜ **other** ➜ **mother** ➜ **brother** ➜ **father**.

other*	better*
mother*	letter*
brother*	met her
another*	wetter
older*	dinner*
colder	thinner
bolder	winner
smoulder	spinner
whiter	dimmer
lighter	glimmer
brighter	shimmer
tighter	swimmer
cleaner	flippers
greener	slippers
meaner	kippers

Group word work

- Use *Programme Two Copymaster* 43 for further practice.
- Introduce *Word Bank Copymaster* 18. Ask the children to look for words containing **er** in their books and to add them to their Word Banks. This search will produce words like **better**, **bigger**. (See page 185 for the reason for double letters.)
- Give the children a selection of rhyming **er** words from the word box on the right and ask them to write an **er** poem.

Cross-curricular and other suggestions

- Make some comparative charts on the board, e.g. items that are long**er** or short**er** than a rul**er**. Ask the children to make their own charts. (See photo on page 10.)

Words containing er

adverb	however	perfect	sister*
after*	insert	perform	sooner
alert	member	propeller	stern
butter*	modern	proper	summer*
customer	monster	property	term
danger	November	refer	transfer
December	number*	remember	under*
dessert	observe	reserve	universe
ever*	October	reserved	verb
expert	other*	river*	verse
father*	over*	September	weather*
fern	paper*	serve	were*
flower*	passenger	shelter	wherever
Germany	pattern	shepherd	winter*
hamburger	perch	silver	yesterday*

Plus hundreds of compartive words

bigger*
darker
harder
larger*
lighter
redder
shorter
smaller*
softer
thicker

Children's names

Jennifer
Oliver

Challenge words

confer
liberty
merchant

See also Magic **er** words, page 193.

* High frequency words

UNIT 13.2
ir (as in bird)

Objectives

- To know that the letters **i** and **r** combine to make the 'er' sound (**ir** as in **bird**).
- To recognise and spell words containing **ir**.

What you need

- *Programme Two Picture Code Cards:* **ir** (66)
- *Programme One Picture Code Cards*
- *Programme Two Copymaster:* 44
- *Programme Two Word Bank Copymaster:* 18
- *Programme Two Songs Cassette*
- *Vowel Scenes Posters:* The Vowel Stealers

Preparation

- **Birthday cards**
  Sort out a variety of different coloured card and some resource books showing artefacts from different periods in history.

Introducing the sound

Compare the three Er/Ur/Ir brothers on *The Vowel Scenes Poster.* Focus now on the third brother, **Ir**ving **Ir** the Ink Stealer. First write the word **return** on the board and explain that you will ret**ur**n to the second **Ur** brother later. Look now at their clothes, as you introduce **Ir**ving **Ir**.

Irving Ir, the Ink Stealer, says "Ir!"

Irving Ir is the third robber brother. He steals ink, then reports back to Robber Red with his surname "Ir!". But he turns up in far fewer words than either of his brothers. This is because he thinks most ink is not worth stealing. The kind of ink Irving Ir really wants to steal is gold ink or silver ink, but this is very difficult to find. So he has to make do with ordinary blue ink.

You might think that Irving Ir would check that the lid was tightly shut on any ink bottle he decided to steal. But no, the silly fellow never checks! This is why his shirt is always dirty. Virtually every shirt he owns has ink stains on it!

Whole class word work

- Listen to and sing the Irving Ir in Person and the Why Irving Ir Needs Ink songs on the *Programme Two Songs Cassette.*
- Write these sentences on the board and ask the children to help with picture coding each **i** and **ir**.

This is not Irving Ir's first dirty shirt.

My brother will be thirteen, on his next birthday.

At the circus two clowns squirted water at us.

- Live spell or dictate: **bid** → **bird** → **girl** → **fir** → **fist** → **first** → **skirt** → **shirt**.

This is not Irving Ir's first dirty shirt.

Group word work

- Use *Programme Two Copymaster* 44 for further practice.
- Introduce *Word Bank Copymaster* 18. Ask the children to look for words containing **ir** in their books and to add them to their Word Banks.
- Write this list of **ir** words on the board, and ask the children to write them in their own books in rhyming pairs. You may like to add a few distractors to the list.

bird	shirt	whir	girl	dirt	firm
third	skirt	fir	swirl	squirt	squirm

As an extension to this activity, the children could use their rhyming pairs to make up a nonsense poem.

Cross-curricular and other suggestions

- Ask the children to design and make a b**ir**thday card and write their own poem in it. They could be in a certain style, for example Victorian, or be decorated with Egyptian or Ancient Greek symbols and patterns.
- Ask the children to write a story about a b**ir**thday party, or what they think they might like to do on their th**ir**teenth or th**ir**ty-th**ir**d b**ir**thday.

Words containing ir

			Challenge words
birch	firm	swirl	confirm
bird*	first*	third*	quirk
birthday*	girl*	thirst	shirk
chirp	shirt	thirteen*	skirmish
circle	sir*	thirty*	smirk
circus	skirt	twirl	virtue
dirt	squirm	whir	
dirty	squirt	whirl	
fir	stir		

* High frequency words

UNIT 13.3
ur (as in fur)

Objectives

- To know that the letters **u** and **r** combine to make the 'er' sound (**ur** as in **fur**).
- To recognise and spell words containing **ur**.

What you need

- *Programme Two Picture Code Cards:* **ur** (82)
- *Programme One Picture Code Cards*
- *Programme Two Copymaster:* 45
- *Programme Two Word Bank Copymaster:* 18
- *Programme Two Songs Cassette*
- *Vowel Scenes Posters:* The Vowel Stealers

Preparation

- **Children's own ur picture code cards**
  Have ready some small pieces of card and some felt pens or crayons.
- **Purple book**
  Have ready some card and felt pens.

Introducing the sound

Explain that you are now ret**ur**ning to the second robber brother on *The Vowel Stealers Poster.* Point out that the three robber brothers are all dressed in the same colour (p**ur**ple). This is because they all make the same sound as in the word p**ur**ple. Notice, however, that only **U**rgent **Ur** has p**ur**ple boots.

Urgent Ur, the Umbrella Stealer, says "Ur!"

__U__rgent __Ur__ steals umbrellas to put in his sack. When he does, he reports back to Robber Red with his surname "__Ur__!". But he only works on cold and rainy days (have you noticed his thick boots of c__ur__ly p__ur__ple f__ur__?), so you don't see him as often as his brother Ernest Er. His shorter legs and thick boots make him slower, which means you hardly ever see him at the beginning or end of words.

Whole class word work

- Listen to and sing the Urgent Ur in Person song on the *Programme Two Songs Cassette.*
- Write these sentences on the board and ask the children to help with picture coding **ur**.

On Thursday and Saturday Urgent Ur returns.
The nurse had a purple purse.
They went to buy new curtains and furniture.
I like the boots with curly fur around the top.

- Live spell or dictate: **fun** ➜ **fur** ➜ **curl** ➜ **hut** ➜ **hurt** ➜ **turn** ➜ **bun** ➜ **burn** ➜ **burst** ➜ **disturb**.

On Thursday and Saturday Urgent Ur returns.

Group word work

- Use *Programme Two Copymaster* 45 for further practice.

- Introduce *Word Bank Copymaster* 18. Write a selection of examples from the **ur** word box on the board and add a few distractors e.g. **funny**, **worm**, **tumble**, **certain**. Each child chooses six **ur** words to write in their Word Banks.

- Add more **ur** words to your word list on the board. Ask the children to work in pairs. One child decides on an **ur** word that he or she is going to spell, but does not tell the other child what it is, while the second child writes and picture codes **ur** on a piece of card. The first child then writes or makes his or her **ur** word using magnetic letters or letter tiles, leaving out **ur**. The second child inserts his or her own **ur** card and reads the word. The first child says if it is correct. They then swop roles.

Cross-curricular and other suggestions

- Make a **Pur**ple Book of **ur** words to link them together in the children's minds. In it, they can illustrate, label and colour **ur** objects **pur**ple. Alternatively, they make sentence captions for as many **ur** things as they can bring together on a page. The fact that the number of things that the children can illustrate is limited reinforces the point that relatively few words are spelt with **ur**. Most other words will need **er** instead.

Words containing ur

burglar	furniture	purse*	turning*
burn	furry	return	turnip
burst	further	Saturday*	turtle
church*	hamburger	surface	urge
curl	hurt*	surprise*	urgent
curtain	injure	survive	
disturb	nurse*	Thursday*	
fur	purple	turkey	
furnish	purpose	turn*	

See also words with **-ture** (page 226)

* High frequency words

Revision

Mark the completion of this Unit with a quick revision of the sounds learned so far using the *Picture Code Cards* as cues. Any uncertain children can be paired with more confident ones so they can go through the sounds again together.

UNIT 14

UNIT 14.1

wh (as in when and who)

UNIT 14.2

ph (as in photograph)

UNIT 14.3

ch (as in school)

The 'wh', 'ph' and 'ch' sounds

UNIT 14

Resources for Unit 15

- *Programme Two Picture Code Cards:* **wh** (83), **wh** (84), **ph** (79), **ch** (46)
- *Programme One Picture Code Cards*
- *Programme Two Copymasters:* 47-48
- *Programme Two Word Bank Copymasters:* 19, 20
- *Programme Two Songs Cassette*
- *Programme One Songs Cassette*

Children at this stage will be well aware that English words often contain silent letters. Many children, however, have never really realised what is happening in terms of sound in the 'wh' phoneme. As a result, some confuse **who** ('hoo') and **how** in their spelling, or habitually leave the silent **h** out in **when**. The two **wh** stories can help, explaining the way sometimes **w** is silent and at other times **h** is silent. Even good spellers can find it satisfying to have explanations for otherwise arbitrary spelling patterns like these. As one child observed contentedly, "I always knew how to spell 'when', but I never knew 'why'!" Both sounds of 'wh' are supported by a song, in the knowledge that music and rhythm and the act of singing all reinforce the spelling patterns which the child will need to remember long after the relevant lesson is over.

The **ph** story is simple. Like all the other stories, it can be summarised in a sentence: Poor Peter and the Hat Man say 'ph...', as in **ph**otogra**ph**. Children often enjoy this story as their hearts have already gone out to Poor Peter. It is also an easy one to role play with an imaginary camera and a little click sound each time the children create a new **ph** word in live spelling. There is also a song on the *Programme Two Songs Cassette* which can be used to bring the **ph** story to life.

The **ch** Unit focuses on the second sound of **ch** ('c...'), found in, for example, the high frequency word **school**. Children who mispell this word as 'shcool' will soon see why they need to stop that habit, once they know the story. The story also provides a strategy for decoding unfamiliar words such as **mechanic** and **scheme** which 'don't work' when a child tries to apply the usual sneeze sound for **ch**.

Other digraphs with **h** are covered in Programme One: **sh**, **ch**, **tch**, **th** (voiced and unvoiced) and both sounds of **wh** (also revised here in Programme Two). For silent **gh** and **igh**, see page 54. See also pages 212 and 213 for **gh**, as in **bought** and in **laugh**.

UNIT 14.1

wh (as in when and who)

Objectives

- To know that the letters **w** and **h** can combine to make two distinct 'wh' sounds (**wh** as in **when** and **wh** as in **who**).
- To recognise and spell words containing **wh**.

What you need

- *Programme Two Picture Code Cards:* **wh** (83 as in **when**) **wh** (84 as in **who**)
- *Programme One Picture Code Cards*
- *Programme Two Copymaster:* 47
- *Programme Two Word Bank Copymaster:* 19
- *Programme One Songs Cassette*

Preparation

- **Wh word dials**
  Cut out some large card circles (about the size of a dinner plate) and some smaller inner card circles (see illustration). Collect paper fasteners to attach the circles together.

Introducing the two sounds

The two sounds of the 'wh' digraph were covered in Programme One. Shortened versions of the two stories are included below, which can be used as revision or to introduce the two sounds to children who are new to Letterland. These can be made more vivid with role play.

The Wicked Witch whacks off Hairy Hat Man's hat

*The Wicked Water Witch hates it **wh**en the Hairy Hat Man gets in her way so that she can't see ahead in the Reading Direction. Not only is he tall, but he wears a hat as well! So what does she do? She **wh**acks his hat off! This makes the poor Hat Man too startled to speak. That is **wh**y we can't hear him at all in words like **wh**en.*

*She **wh**acks most often in the five question words: **wh**en, **wh**ich, **wh**at, **wh**ere and **wh**y.*

The second story, which is an extension of the first, explains the few exceptions where the Hat Man gets angry and hits back in the words: **who**, **whose**, **whom** and **whole**.

The Hat Man gets angry with the Witch

*Every once in a while, the Hat Man shows that he has had enough by shouting at the Witch "**Who** do you think you are?" Then he grabs her broomstick and hits her hat off instead! Now **whose** turn is it to be too startled to speak? Yes, the Witch!*

Whole class word work

- Listen to and sing the Wicked Water Witch and the Hat Man song on the *Programme One Songs Cassette.*

When she whacks off his hat, he is silent.

✪ Write these sentences on the board and ask the children to help with picture coding **w**, **h** and both sounds of **wh**.

When she whacks off his hat, he is silent.
Where are you going?
What was that whispering noise?
Which way shall we go and with whom?
Why didn't you hear what he said?
Who do you think you are?

✪ Live spell or dictate: **when** ➜ **why** ➜ **wheel** ➜ **white** ➜ **who** ➜ **whole**. (The **o** as in **who** is explained on page 167.)

Group word work

✪ Use *Programme Two Copymaster* 47 for further practice.

✪ Introduce *Word Bank Copymaster* 19. Ask the children to look for words containing **wh** in their books and to add them to their Word Banks beside the correct **wh** pictograms.

✪ Write the five **wh** question words on the board. Ask the children to make their own word dials (see Preparation and illustration on the right). As they turn their dial, ask them to read their **wh** words to you or a partner.

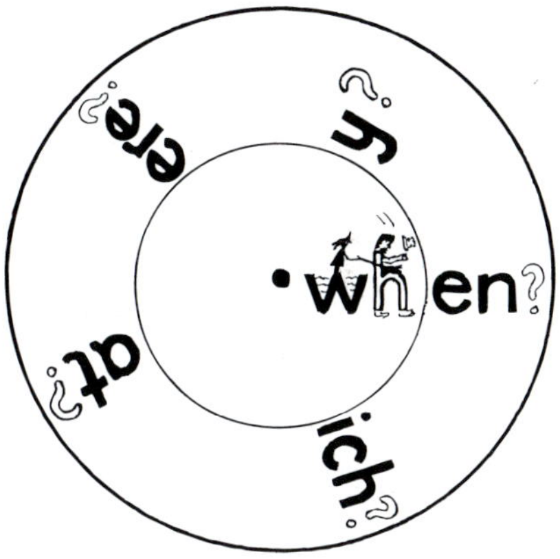

Words containing wh

wh (as in when)			wh (as in who)
anywhere	whenever	whip	who*
somewhere*	where*	whirlpool	whole
whack	wherever	whisk	whom
whale	whether	whiskers	whose
what*	which*	whisper	
wheat	whiff	whistle	
wheel	while*	white*	
when*	whimper	whizz	
	whine	why*	

* High frequency words

what

who

"Who do you think you are?"

UNIT 14.2

ph (as in photograph)

Objectives

- To know that the letters **p** and **h** combine to make the 'fff...' sound (**ph** as in **photograph**).
- To recognise and spell words containing **ph**.

What you need

- *Programme Two Picture Code Cards:* **ph** (79)
- *Programme One Picture Code Cards*
- *Programme Two Copymaster:* 48
- *Programme Two Word Bank Copymaster:* 20
- *Programme Two Songs Cassette*

Preparation

- **Making words**
  Collect a set of *Picture Code Cards*, or magnetic letters, foam letters or letter tiles.
- Bring in an old camera.

Introducing the sound

Hairy Hat Man is a kind fellow. Let's see what happens when he meets Poor Peter in a word.

Poor Peter and the Hat Man say "ph..." as in photograph

*Hairy Hat Man knows that Poor Peter is unhappy, because his ears droop. He also knows that Poor Peter loves having his **ph**otogra**ph** taken. So whenever he is next to Poor Peter in a word, he turns and takes Peter's **ph**otogra**ph** to cheer him up. That makes Poor Peter smile and Hairy Hat Man even laughs – quietly though – with his mouth half shut and his teeth on his lips. So his usual 'hhh...' sound becomes a 'fff...' sound, just like Fireman Fred. You can hear it twice in the word **photograph**!*

Write the word **photograph** on the board, and circle each **ph**.

Whole class word work

- Listen to and sing the Poor Peter and the Hat Man song on the *Programme Two Songs Cassette.*
- Write these sentences on the board and ask the children to help with picture coding **p**, **h** and **ph**.

  The Hat Man takes Poor Peter's photograph.
  Sophie's photo of Philip is by the phone.
  Joseph saw elephants and dolphins at the zoo.

- Live spell or dictate: **nephew** ➜ **phone** ➜ **trophy** ➜ **graph** ➜ **sphere**.

The Hat Man takes Poor Peter's photograph.

Group word work

- Use *Programme Two Copymaster* 48 for further practice.
- Introduce *Word Bank Copymaster* 20. Write a selection of examples from the **ph** wordbox on the board and add a few distractors e.g. **tough**, **high**, **apply**, **laugh**, **through**. Each child chooses six **ph** words to write in their Word Banks.
- From the list of **ph** words on the board, ask the children to make some of the **ph** words together using *Picture Code Cards*, magnetic letters, foam letters or letter tiles.

Cross-curricular and other suggestions

- Take in an old camera for the children to use and ask them to try taking their own **ph**otographs of the play-acting of the **ph** story, or **ph**otographs of the children forming whole **ph** words. The **ph**otographs could make a **ph** resource book.

photograph

Words containing ph

		Children's names	Challenge words
alphabet	phew	Joseph	decipher
apostrophe	phone	Philip	pamphlet
atmosphere	photo	Sophie	phosphorus
dolphin	photograph	Stephanie	prophesy
elephant*	phrase		prophet
geography	physical		sphinx
graph	physics		symphony
hyphen	sphere		
nephew	telegraph		
paragraph	telephone*		
phantom	trophy		
pheasant			

* High frequency words

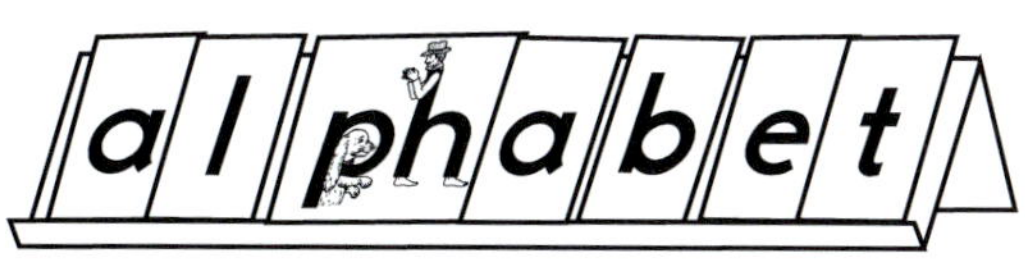

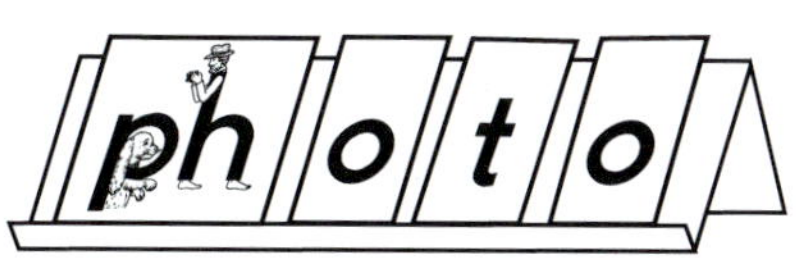

UNIT 14.3

ch (as in school)

Objectives

- To know that the letters **c** and **h** can combine to make the 'ch' sound (**ch** as in **school**).
- To recognise and spell words containing **ch**.

What you need

- *Programme Two Picture Code Cards:* **ch** (46)
- *Programme One Picture Code Cards*
- *Programme Two Copymaster:* 48
- *Programme Two Word Bank Copymaster:* 20

Introducing the sound

In Letterland lore the regular sound of **ch** is explained as follows. The Hairy Hat Man's hairy hat makes Clever Cat's nose tickle whenever she sits down beside him. This is why we hear a sneeze sound in words like **cheese** and **lunch** and two sneezes in the word **church**. This story was first introduced in the *Programme One Teacher's Guide* (see pages 145-147) as well as **tch** words and the hard 'c...' sound of **ch** (as in **school**). This hard 'c...' sound occurs in relatively few common words. The most common are **school** and **Christmas**, so they serve as good examples of this second sound of **ch**.

Clever Cat does not sneeze when the Hat Man's hat blows off

Sometimes the wind in Letterland blows the Hat Man's hairy hat off his head. When this happens, Clever Cat doesn't have to sneeze beside the Hat Man, because his hat has blown too far away to tickle her nose. Then Clever Cat is very pleased to go back to saying 'c...' for cat. But the Hat Man is too startled to speak, so he says nothing at all.

Whole class word work

- Write these sentences on the board and ask the children to help with picture coding **c** and both sounds of **ch**.

  We had chips at the school picnic.
  The choir joined in as the children sang the chorus.
  Richard and Christina's dad is an architect.

- Live spell: **ache** → **echo** → **school** → **chorus** → **anchor**. As the children come to the 'c...' sound in blending the sequence of sounds, ask one child to act as the wind and come along pretending to blow off the **h**-child's hat. The **h**-child should look suitably startled.

We had chips at the school picnic.

Group word work

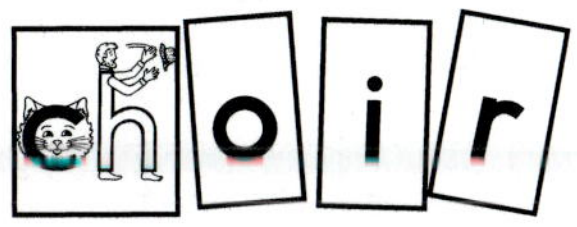

- ✩ Use *Programme Two Copymaster* 48 for further practice.

- ✩ Introduce *Word Bank Copymaster* 20. Write a selection of examples from the **ch** word box on the board and add a few distractors. Each child chooses up to 12 words containing **ch** (as in **school**) to write in their Word Banks.

Words containing ch (as in school)

			Challenge words
ache	choir	orchestra	chlorine
aching	chord	scheme	chrysalis
anchor	chorus	school*	dachsund
architect	Christmas*	stomach	ochre
character	chrome	technical	
chemist	chrysanthemum		
chemistry	echo		

* High frequency words

Exceptions

A few words derived from French have caused what may appear at first to be an odd way to spell the 'sh' sound, e.g. **machine**, **charades**, **parachute**, **moustache**, **Champagne**, **Cheryl**. The Letterland explanation is that *usually* Clever Cat only sneezes very softly beside the Hat Man, but every once in a while, she sneezes so loudly that he has to turn back and hush her up, exactly as he always does to Sammy Snake. That is why in a few words we hear a 'sh' sound from **ch**.

UNIT 15

UNIT 15.1

ear (as in hear)

The 'ear' sound

UNIT 15

Resources for Unit 15

- *Programme Two Picture Code Cards:* **ear** (48)
- *Programme One Picture Code Cards*
- *Programme Two Copymasters:* 49
- *Programme Two Word Bank Copymasters:* 21
- *Vowel Scenes Posters:* Vowels Out Walking

The **ear** spelling pattern (as in **hear**) provides an opportunity to revisit the major concept of Vowels Out Walking where 'the first one does the talking', unless of course both Vowel Men have fallen into the hands of a **r**obber!

In words where the two vowels are Mr E and Mr A, this is exactly what has happened. Both Vowel Men are under the **r**obber's control, and it is the **r**obber who does the talking. The 'air' sound (as in **bear)** was covered in Unit 11. This Unit deals with the alternative 'ear' sound and uses an arrow pointing to the robber's **ear** as the visual clue for this sound.

All the robbers (**r**'s) lurking in words with two vowels behind their backs, provide a special teaching opportunity. By challenging the children to be sharp-eyed detectives and to catch these **r**obbers in the act, you are motivating them to become alert, not only to single letters and digraphs, but also to longer phonemes like **ear** within words.

As with all the other **r**-controlled trigraphs (**air**, **eer**, **oar**, **oor**, **our**, **are**, **ere**, **ore**), the child's own picture coding (drawing the robbers' sacks around the vowels) consolidates their understanding that these particular letter strings must be processed as one unit of sound.

The **ere** spelling pattern is covered on page 115. The **eer** spelling pattern is touched on briefly in this Unit, but no *Picture Code Card* is provided as none of the words needing **eer** fall into the high frequency category. Once again, the best way for children to see that this is an **r**-controlled unit of sound is to picture code words in this group themselves.

UNIT 15.1

ear (as in hear)

Objectives

- To know that the letters **e**, **a** and **r** can combine to make the 'ear' sound (**ear** as in **hear**).
- To recognise and spell words containing **ear**.

What you need

- *Programme Two Picture Code Cards:* **ear** (48)
- *Programme One Picture Code Cards*
- *Programme Two Copymaster:* 49
- *Programme Two Word Bank Copymaster:* 21
- *Vowel Scenes Posters:* Vowels Out Walking

Preparation

- **Look, say, cover, write, check**
  Make copies of the format on page 230.

Introducing the sound

Display and talk about the *Vowel Out Walking Poster* as you introduce this next phoneme and point out **ear** in the panel at the bottom.

When two vowels out walking are captured, the robber does the talking

*Silent look-out men are not always able to spot a **r**obber in time to avoid being captured, so it is important to know what the **r**obbers are up to. No Vowel Man can be expected to go on cheerfully saying his name when he has just been tossed into the **r**obber's sack! The **r**obber usually shouts out "**ear**" or "**air**" as he captures Vowel Men. But now you may hear the **r**obber moaning "**ear**" because he bruised it in the scuffle with the Vowel Men.*

Whole class word work

- Write these sentences on the board and ask the children to help with picture coding **ea** and **ear**.

  She wore neat silver earrings in her ears.

  I can hear someone on the beach in tears.

- Live spell or dictate: **ear** → **hear** → **hears** → **near** → **tear** → **tears** → **fear** → **appear** → **appeared**.

She wore neat silver earrings in her ears.

Group word work

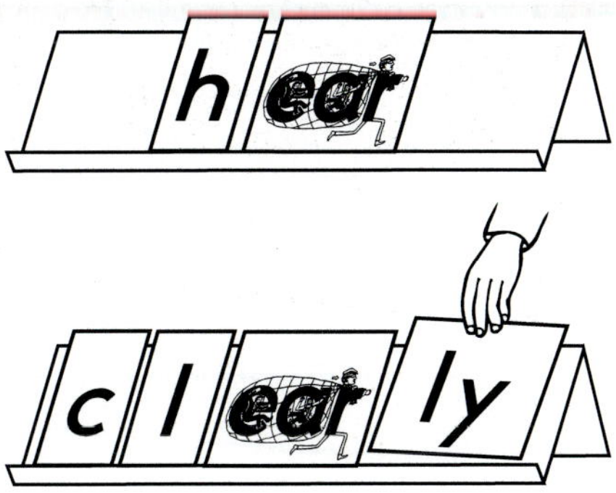

- Use *Programme Two Copymaster* 49 for further practice.
- Introduce *Word Bank Copymaster* 21. Write a selection of words from the **ear** word box on the board. The children then choose the six words they consider most useful to them and enter them into their Word Banks.
- Give the children some **ear** words from the word box and some words to revise from a previous Unit or Units. Ask them to complete the *look, say, cover, write, check* format.

Words containing ear

appear	dreary	hear*	spear
clear	ear*	near*	tear
clearly	earring	overhear	tears
dear*	fear	rear	weary
disappear	gear	smear	year*

* High frequency words

Note: A few words need the alternative **eer** spelling pattern for the 'ear' sound, shown in the panel at the bottom of the *Vowels Out Walking Poster*, e.g. **beer**, **deer**, **cheer**, **cheerful**, **sheer**, **sneer**, **peer**, **career**, **mountaineer**, **pioneer**, **engineer** and **volunteer**. The same **r**-controlled picture coding applies, i.e. both vowels shown in the sack behind the robber's back.

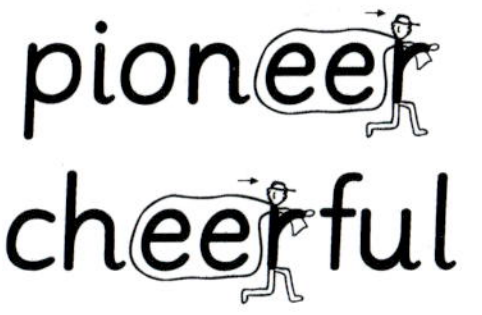

References
For the alternative spelling pattern for the 'ear' sound, see **ere** (as in **here**) p115. For the other sound of **ear** (as in **bear**) see p116.

UNIT 16

UNIT 16.1
ea (as in head)

The short ĕ sound

UNIT 16

Resources for Unit 16

- *Programme Two Picture Code Cards:* **ĕa** (23) **ēa** (22)
- *Programme One Picture Code Cards*
- *Programme Two Copymasters:* 50
- *Programme Two Word Bank Copymasters:* 21
- *Vowel Scenes Posters:* Vowels Out Walking

The children will have met Mr E and A out walking in many common words (e.g. **each**, **eat**, **ice cream**, **sea**) where Mr E clearly does the talking (see page 38). They may have also learned, in Unit 15.1, how a **r**obber can upset their walk, causing a new 'ear' sound as in **hear**.

There is one other variation which can happen as Mr E and Mr A go out walking. It is anticipated on the *Vowels Out Walking Poster* by showing Eddy Elephant out walking too, just behind Mr E. This pictogram points the way to teaching the second sound of **ea** whenever it crops up in either reading or spelling.

When Mr E and Mr A go out walking, Mr E may give his pet, Eddy Elephant, a turn with the talking. The result: words like **head** and **bread**. The rule 'the first one does the talking' still applies, in that the sound we hear comes from the **e**. The difference is that now, Eddy Elephant is doing the talking instead of Mr E. This means he makes his usual 'ĕ...' sound.

When trying to read an unknown word with **ea** in it, how can an inexperienced reader know which sound to expect: **ē** as in **seat,** or **ĕ** as in **head**? Look for context clues first. If that does not help, try the usual 'first man says his name' rule, because the majority of **ea** words do conform to the rule. Finally try **ĕ**, in case Eddy Elephant is having a turn at doing the talking.

The children should also get to know all the most common **ĕa** words well, e.g. **head**, **bread**, **heavy**, **weather**. This will increase the chances that in any *other* new words containing **ea**, Mr E will be saying his name as usual. However, beware of three exceptions: **great**, **break** and **steak**, where we actually hear neither Mr E nor Eddy, but Mr A saying his name instead! There are also the words **read** and **lead**, where either Mr E *or* Eddy Elephant could be talking and only context will tell us which one it will be.

UNIT 16.1

ea (as in head)

Objectives

- To know that the letters **e** and **a** can combine to make the 'ĕa' sound (**ea** as in **head**).
- To recognise and spell words containing **ĕa**.

What you need

- *Programme Two Picture Code Cards:* **ĕa** (23) **ēa** (22)
- *Programme One Picture Code Cards*
- *Programme Two Copymaster:* 50
- *Programme Two Word Bank Copymaster:* 21
- *Vowel Scenes Posters:* Vowels Out Walking

Preparation

- **Sorting ea words** Have ready A4 sheets of paper for each child and felt pens or crayons.

Introducing the sound

The most common sound of **ea** (as in **seat**) was presented in Unit 1.2, page 38, as one of the Vowels Out Walking pairs, where the first vowel did the talking and the second one was silent. Make sure your *Vowels Out Walking Poster* is on display as well as both **ea** *Picture Code Cards* so you can compare them. (The Poster uses one pictogram to represent both sounds of **ea**.) The story for this second sound of **ea** is as follows.

When Mr E and Mr A go out walking, the elephant may do the talking

*When Mr E goes out walking with Mr A, he sometimes gives his pet **e**lephant a turn with the talking. Then, instead of hearing Mr E say his name, expect **E**ddy **E**lephant to say "ĕ..." for **e**lephant inst**ea**d.*

Whole class word work

- Write these sentences on the board and ask the children to help with picture coding each **e** and **ea**.

Eddy is ready to lift his heavy head to say 'e'.
We love walking in this weather.
Let's have brown bread for breakfast instead.

- Live spell or dictate: **head** ➔ **ahead** ➔ **heavy** ➔ **heaven** ➔ **bread** ➔ **ready** ➔ **read**. Ask three children to come walking in from the left with the middle one miming Eddy saying "ĕ...". This child could wear an elephant h**ea**dband on his h**ea**d.

Eddy is ready to lift his heavy head to say 'e'.

Group word work

- Use *Programme Two Copymaster* 50 for further practice.

- Ask each child to draw both of the **ĕa** and **ēa** pictograms as headings on A4 paper. Select 12 words from the **ea** word box below and write them on the board mixed in with the following 12 **ēa** words.

appeal	clean	creamy	dream
eager	feast	greasy	heave
neatly	stream	teacher	yeast

The children sort the words out by analysing each **ea** sound and listing their words under the pictogram for that sound.

- Introduce *Word Bank Copymaster* 21. On the board write a selection of examples from the **ĕa** word box and add a few distractors from the word box on page 39. Each child chooses six **ea** words containing **ĕa** as in **head** to write in their Word Banks. Given the sorting practice they have just had, they will be better equipped to select only those words which say 'ĕa' as in **head**.

Words containing ĕa

			Challenge words
ahead	head*	pleasant	dread
bread*	healthy	ready*	heather
breakfast*	heaven	spread	jealous
breath	heavy*	steady	pheasant
dead*	instead*	thread	threat
deaf	lead	tread	wealth
dealt	leather	weather*	
death	meadow		
feather	meant		

* High frequency words

References
For the other sound of **ea** (as in **seat**), see p38.

UNIT 17

UNIT 17.1
–ful (as in restful)

UNIT 17.2
–ly (as in lovely)

The -ful and -ly suffixes

UNIT 17

Resources for Unit 17

- *Programme Two Picture Code Cards:* **full** (60), **-ful** (61), **ly** (33)
- *Programme One Picture Code Cards*
- *Programme Two Copymasters:* 51-52
- *Programme Two Word Bank Copymasters:* 22

Before the children study the **-ful** suffix, ask them who in Letterland sometimes p**u**shes and p**u**lls **u**mbrellas about rather roughly. Do they remember Giant Full (see page 88)?

The Giant Full story focuses on **full** and **-ful** for another reason. It is designed to bring life into the traditional rule 'drop one **l** when **full** becomes a suffix'. In Letterland lore, lazy old Giant Full often pulls up a word beside himself to lean on. Then, seen from the side, only one leg is in view. Knowing this bit of fiction-come-fact about Giant Full can be surprisingly help**ful** in preventing, or curing, typical spelling errors like 'carefull' and 'helpfull'. By picture coding Giant Full leaning on the root word the children will remember the rule.

Many teachers find it valuable to introduce Letterland's other giant, Giant All (see page 163), quite early in the school year in order to prevent or cure typical errors like 'allways' and 'allso'. The story line is virtually the same, except that it applies in this case to the prefix **al-**. Whatever your timing, you will find that the children enjoy learning about both of Letterland's Giants. They may even discover one more giant for themselves. He is Giant Till who only ever appears in two words: **till** and, when he turns sideways, **until**. The children can imagine and decide for themselves how he looks. Picture coding him will be the same as for Giant Full.

The second suffix in this Unit is **-ly**. This is an important suffix as shown by the number of words it can be attached to. Anyone who looks up words that end with **-ly** in a rhyming dictionary will be astonished to discover over 3500 **-ly** words listed (mostly adverbs).

In an effort to spell the suffix **-ly**, emergent writers often make the logical mistake of writing **le** instead of **ly** (e.g. 'badle' for 'badly') because the final **y** sounds like an **e**. In fact the Yo-yo Man is saying **ē**, a job he has agreed to do for Mr E. For the full story, explaining why **y** represents long **ē** in approximately 5000 words, including the 3500 **-ly** words, see page 172. With or without that story, the **-ly** pictogram already makes clear the function of **y** in this suffix by showing part of an **e** sticking out of the Yo-yo Man's sack.

UNIT 17.1

-ful (as in restful)

Objectives

- To know that when **full** becomes a suffix it drops one **l** (**-ful** as in **restful**).
- To recognise and spell words ending in **-ful**.

What you need

- *Programme Two Picture Code Cards:* **full** (60), **ful** (61)
- *Programme One Picture Code Cards*
- *Programme Two Copymaster:* 51
- *Programme Two Word Bank Copymaster:* 22

Preparation

- Have materials ready for making a Lazy Giants display, leaving space on the left for a second giant, Giant All display.

Introducing the suffix

Mention of Giant Full has been made on page 88 as the Letterland Giant who tries to help Mr U by filling his **u**'s **full** of umbrellas for him. Giant Full's rough handling, however, causes the irregular 'o͝o' sound coming from the **u**mbrellas as he p**u**shes and p**u**lls them about. The only times we see Giant Full's two long legs is beside some of these irregular **u**'s and in the word **full**. (Otherwise we use the Lamp Ladies coding as usual.)

Introducing the 'ful' spelling

The following story provides a way to bring to life the rule: drop one **l** when **full** becomes a suffix. The two places where Giant Full does a very careful job of filling a **u** really full are in the word **full** and the suffix **-ful**. But why can't we see Giant Full's second leg in this **-ful** ending?

Giant Full leans on other words whenever he can

*It seems that, apart from helping Mr U, Giant **Full** is even lazier than Letterland's other lazy giant, Giant All. Giant **Full** leans on so many words that he hardly ever stands on his own two feet, apart from in the word **full**. When he leans on another word you won't see his second leg because one leg is behind the other.*

(The words he leans on are usually nouns or verbs, but the moment Giant Full leans back on them, he turns them into adjectives.)

Will Giant Full be harmful or helpful?

Whole class word work

- Write the following sentences on the board and ask the children to help with picture coding **ful** and **full**.

  Will Giant Full be harmful or helpful?

  Be careful of those full baskets.

  He was grateful for a handful of pennies.

- Live spell these words: **full ➜ restful ➜ helpful ➜ handful ➜ thankful**. One child hides the **ful** *Picture Code Card* behind the **full** Card. He or she stands alone in the word **full**, but as soon as children forming **rest** join the child, he or she shows the **ful** card and mimes leaning on the word **rest**. Between forming each new word the child stands alone holding the **full** card in front again.

Group word work

- Use *Programme Two Copymasters* 51 for further practice.

- Introduce the *Word Bank Copymaster* 22. Write a selection of examples from the **-ful** word box on the board. The children then choose the six words which they consider most useful to them and enter them into their Word Banks.

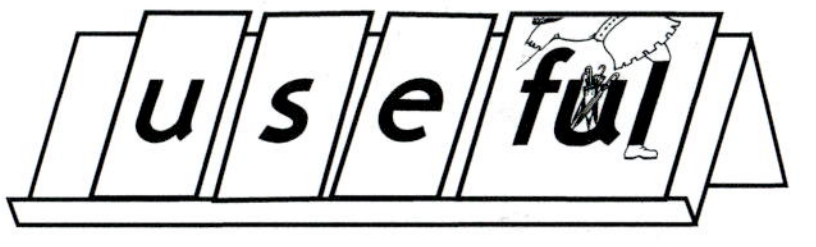

* High frequency words

Words ending in -ful

armful	eventful	helpful	spoonful
awful*	fearful	hopeful	successful
beautiful*	forgetful	mouthful	thankful
careful	grateful	painful	thoughtful
cupful	handful	peaceful	useful
delightful	harmful	skilful	wonderful*

This is only a small selection of words which end in **-ful**.

Activities combining al- and -ful

- If the children have not already met Giant All they soon will (on page 163). The opportunity will then arise to create a 'Lazy Giants' display showing both giants leaning lazily on other words. You can begin with the display for either giant, depending which one the children have learned about first. See page 164 for the Giant All display.

References
For the irregular sound of **u** in **put**, **push**, **pull** and **full**, **-ful**, see page 88.

UNIT 17.2

-ly (as in lovely)

Objectives

- To know that the letters **l** and **y** combine to make the 'lee' sound (**-ly** as in **lovely**) at the end of words.
- To know that the final 'ē' sound in the **-ly** suffix is represented by the letter **y**.
- To recognise and spell words ending in **-ly** (as in **lovely**).

What you need

- *Programme Two Picture Code Cards:* **ly** (33)
- *Programme One Picture Code Cards*
- *Programme Two Copymaster:* 52
- *Programme Two Word Bank Copymaster:* 22

Introducing the suffix

Inexperienced spellers often write **-le** when they should be writing **-ly**, because they hear a 'lee' sound as they pronounce this suffix slowly. The following story explains why most English words which *sound* as if they end in **ē**, in fact end in **y**. For a fuller version of this story, see page 172.

How the Yo-yo Man came to work for Mr E

Much as the Yo-yo Man enjoys working for Mr I, he needs more work than Mr I can give him. Luckily, the Yo-yo Man has another friend who needs help. It is Mr E.

*Do you remember Mr E's special invention for the ends of words, his Silent Magic **e**? Well, he quite forgot that in many, many words people just don't want an **e** to become silent at the end.*

*There was nothing Mr E could do to change his Silent **e**'s back into **e**'s which could still say **ē**. In fact, his magic had worked so well that now nearly any **e** that anyone puts at the end of a word automatically turns into a Silent **e**! What could Mr E do?*

*It was very luck**y** that the Yo-yo Man was looking for a second job and came by just as Mr E realised he had a problem. It didn't take the Yo-yo Man long to learn to say **ē** for Mr E. And so they agreed that Mr E would pay him to do the job, not just in a few words, but in thousands of them! Mr E has even given the Yo-yo Man a tin**y** little **e** to carr**y** in his sack instead of his yo-yo's to show everybod**y** just how man**y** words he finishes for Mr E.*

Picture code the **y**'s in this sentence for the children:

The Yo-yo Man likes to carry the tiny **e**.

Lucy Lamp Lady and Yo-yo Man together say "lee"

*Luck**ily** a great many words end in **-ly**. This makes Lucy Lamp Lady and the Yo-yo Man very happy indeed, because she loves lighting up words and he is very pleased to work for Mr E. So they appear together most willing**ly** at the end of thousands of words.*

It's lovely that the Yo-yo Man helps so willingly.

Whole class word work

- Write the following sentences on the board and ask the children to help with picture coding each **y** working for **i** (see page 56) and **y** working for **e** as in **-ly**.

It is lovely that the Yo-yo Man helps so willingly.
We are trying to talk softly and quietly.
Exactly why did Tommy suddenly feel shy?

- Live spell or dictate: **lovely** ➜ **badly** ➜ **flatly** ➜ **quickly** ➜ **exactly** ➜ **softly**.

Words ending in -ly

			Challenge words
abruptly	ghostly	rapidly	
badly	gladly	sadly	
bluntly	invisibly	sensibly	absurdly
clearly	madly	shockingly	currently
exactly	oddly	softly	distinctly
flatly	promptly	splendidly	frequently
fondly	quickly*	willingly	vastly

These are only a few of the 3500 English words ending in -ly.

* High frequency words

Group word work

- Use *Programme Two Copymaster* 52 for further practice.

- Introduce *Word Bank Copymaster* 22. Ask the children to look for words ending in **-ly** in their books and to add them to their Word Banks.

- Write the sentences below on the board. Ask the children to copy them into their own writing book and then to add a word ending in **-ly** which will give more meaning to the verb.

I eat crisps .... I sing ....
I run .... I whisper ....
I walk ....

- Write these six **-ly** words on the board for the children to choose from:

beautifully quickly slowly
noisily quietly happily

☆ Write words from the following list on the board. Then ask the children to copy them into their writing book and add **-ly** to them.

clever	clear	glad
sad	slow	sudden

Then play this game emphasising the '-lee' phoneme as you speak. The group sits in a circle and takes it in turns to think of **-ly** words to describe the way in which they do various actions. For example, the first person says '**I breathe deeply**'. The next person then has to think of a way in which *they* breathe, for example '**I breathe quickly**'. Other useful verbs are: talk, eat, run, get dressed, go shopping, think, listen, dance, skate.

Don't mistake -le for -ly

Children who continue to confuse **-ly** with **-le** (spelling, for example, **badly** as 'badle') will be helped if they are shown the Candle Magic **le** pictogram (see *Programme Two Picture Code Card* 32 and page 197). Remind them that an **e** at the end of a word will almost always be silent. That is why Mr E pays the Yo-yo Man to say **ē** for him in literally thousands of words that end in **-ly**!

Don't drop Silent Magic e before -ly

Here is a suggestion for children who write 'likly' or 'latly'. There is no magic in the **-ly** ending, so don't drop a Magic **e** before you add **-ly** or your Vowel Man will disappear! Instead, keep your Magic **e** so that it can go on shooting its sparks. The Lamp Lady will enjoy watching the sparks fly.

likly

likely

Don't even drop a Burnt-Out Magic **e** before **-ly**, e.g. not 'lovly', 'surly', 'activly' but **lovely**, **surely** and **actively**.

> **References**
> For the few words ending in **-ley** instead of **-ly**, see page 175.

Snow has looked extremely likely lately.

SECTION 3

Other important spelling patterns

Some spelling patterns are not specified by the National Literacy Strategy Key Stage 1 word level objectives. Letterland strategies, however, easily bring these spelling patterns within reach of Key Stage 1 attainment. They are valuable because they give children access to thousands of words much sooner than they could acquire them as sight vocabulary.

This section pays attention to frequently mis-spelled words and provides strategies for preventing or curing these errors.

all and al

High priority is given to the rule 'When **all** becomes a prefix, drop one **l**', to preclude all too predictable errors, e.g. 'allso', 'allways', 'allmost' before they become engrained (see page 163).

o (irregular)

Since the words **one** and **once** are among the 30 most used words, there is a Letterland story to preclude typical errors like 'wun' or 'won' (see pages 165–167).

Silent Magic e exceptions

Letterland introduces the idea of power failures to prepare children to handle common exceptions to the Magic **e** principle (see page 171) since these occur in many high frequency words.

y (as in body)

The Letterland story of the Yo-yo Man's business deal with Mr E gives children a reason why over 5000 English words, e.g. **very**, sound as though they end with a long **e** sound, but need to be spelled with a final **y** instead (see pages 172–174).

Double consonants before Magic Endings (-ed, -ing, -en, -est and others)

When to double the consonant before adding a suffix like **-ed**, **-ing**, **-en** or **-est** is made clear by showing the children how to picture code the sound of the preceding vowel. A strategy is given (see pages 185–186) for understanding the function of the second consonant.

Soft c and g

Children discover Letterland story reasons why **c** and **g** become 'soft' before **e**, **i** and **y**, thereby adding many new words to their reading vocabulary (see pages 200–207).

The tion ending

The **tion** story provides a strategy for accessing over 1500 multi-syllabic words ending in **tion** (from **action** to **telecommunication**). Once children have heard the story (which deliberately repeats **tion** 15 times) and have learned to picture code **tion** words with a Vowel Man at Mr 'Tion's door, they can see how easy it is to read hundreds of words ending in **tion** (see pages 220–222).

Other spelling strategies for high usage words

- when to use **-c**, **-k**, **-ck** or **-ke** to spell the final 'k' sound (see pages 178–181),
- why **k** is silent before **n** (see pages 208–209),
- why **w** is silent before **r** (see pages 210–211),
- why **o** is silent before **us** in over 230 adjectives ending in **-ous** (see pages 218–219).

The strategies within this section are presented in one possible order, though it is the needs of the particular children you teach which will determine your teaching order.

all (as in call)
al (as in almost)

Objectives

- To know that the letters **a**, **l** and **l** combine to make the 'all' sound (**all** as in **call**).
- To know that when **all** becomes a prefix it drops one **l** (as in **almost**).
- To recognise and spell words containing **all** and **al**.

What you need

- *Programme Two Picture Code Cards:* **all** (37), **al** (38)
- *Programme One Picture Code Cards*
- *Programme Two Copymaster:* 53
- *Programme Two Word Bank Copymaster:* 23
- *Programme Two Songs Cassette*

Preparation

- **Giant All murals**
  Prepare display spaces for murals (see page 164).
- **Look, say, cover, write, check**
  Make copies of the format on page 230.

The earlier that children learn about Giant All the better. The two murals suggested on the following page provide an excellent reference to help avoid typical mistakes like 'allso' and 'allmost'.

The first Giant All story explains why the letter **a** seldom makes its usual 'a' sound beside **ll**, and the second one provides a reason for the 'drop one **l**' rule.

Giant All eats almost all the apples he can find

*Giant **All** is so t**all** that **all** you can see of him in words is his two **l**ong **l**egs. In fact his legs alone are as long as the Lamp Lady is t**all**! How can you tell when he appears in a word?*

*The secret lies in knowing Giant **All**'s one great weakness. He has a passion for **a**pples! He is so fond of Letterland **a**pples that he just strides into words and takes them without asking.*

*So if you see a word with an **a**pple in it and then two straight lines right beside it, the chances are that you have spotted the two **l**ong **l**egs of Giant **All**. When you do, don't expect the **a**pple to be saying 'a...', because Giant **All** will be eating that **a**pple!*

- Listen to and sing the Giant All song on the *Programme Two Songs Cassette*. This is a good song to accompany with miming.
- Write these sentences on the board and ask the children to help with picture coding **all**.

The tallest man of all is Giant All.

The ball fell from the tall wall.

Nearly all the small apples
that had fallen were bruised.

- Live spell or dictate: **ball** ➜ **hall** ➜ **call** ➜ **fall** ➜ **fallen**.
- Use *Programme Two Copymaster* 53 for further practice.

The tallest man of all is Giant All.

☆ Introduce *Word Bank Copymaster* 23. Write a selection of examples from the **all** word list on the board. The children choose the six **all** words which they consider most useful to them and add them to their Word Banks.

☆ Help the children to create a Giant All display based on words which they picture code, cut out and stick around the Giant. Add some sm**all** apple trees to show how much t**all**er than the trees he is.

Words containing all

			Exceptions
all*	fallen	snowball	Allan
ball*	hall*	stall	alley
call*	holdall	tall*	alligator
called*	rainfall	tallest	challenge
calling*	recall	wall*	Hallowe'en
eyeball	small*	waterfall	Sally
fall*	smallest*		valley

* High frequency words

al (as in almost)

Giant All leans on other words because he is lazy

*Giant **All** really is a lazy old giant. If he can find another word to lean on while he eats, he will. Being so t**all** he just reaches over, pulls up a word, and leans right back on it.*

*When Giant **All** is leaning on a word you will only see one of his legs because the second one is just behind the other. But don't let that fool you. It is still Giant **All**. Most of **all**, Giant **All** likes to lean on the words **most**, **so** and **ways**. His next favourite words are **ready** and **though**.*

* High frequency words

Words containing al

almost*	altogether
already*	always*
also*	walnut
although*	

☆ Help the children to create a Lazy Giant display featuring Giant All leaning on words, or a bigger display including Giant Full as well, as suggested on page 157.

He has already eaten almost all the apples.

o (as in love, one and who)

Objectives

- To know that the letter **o** can sometimes represent an 'uh' sound (as in **love**).
- To know that the letter **o** can sound like 'wuh' (as in **one** and **once**).
- To know that the letter **o** can sound like 'oo' (**o** as in **who**).
- To recognise and spell words containing these irregular **o** sounds.

What you need

- *Programme One Picture Code Card:* **Oscar's Little Brother** (26)
- *Programme Two Copymasters:* 54-55
- *Programme Two Word Bank Copymaster:* 24

Choose the timing for teaching any of these irregular **o** sounds to meet the needs of your class or of particular individuals.

The 'uh' sound of o (as in love)

The reason for the irregular **o** (in words like **love**) dates back to the days when monks used italic handwriting and found the **u** to be a problem whenever one occurred next to an **m**, **n**, **r** or **v**. The words became very hard to read, (e.g. *ammg* for **among**), so they closed the **u** and made the join at the top. Known as a 'scribal **o**', this letter continues to sound like a short **u** and can be a source of confusion for children in their early writing.

Unfortunately, there are over 130 relatively common words in the English language or roughly one in every 23 of the 3000 most used words, which contain this scribal **o**. To solve the resulting spelling problem, Letterland represents this irregular **o** as Oscar Orange's Bothersome Little Brother, introduced briefly in Programme One.

Oscar's Bothersome Little Brother just says 'uh'

Oscar's Bothersome Little Brother is too little to say 'ŏ...' properly, so he just says 'uh'. He knows no other sound, even though his mother and brother and everybody else have tried to teach him the proper 'ŏ...' sound. If only somebody could ... but never mind! They all love him just as he is!

- Write these sentences on the board and ask the children to help with picture coding each regular **o** and irregular **o**.

  Some mothers have bothersome sons.

  On Monday my big brother is coming home.

  In October we will go on a wonderful trip.

- Use *Programme Two Copymaster* 54 for further practice.
- Introduce *Word Bank Copymaster* 24. Write on the board a mixture of words containing both regular **o** and **o** saying 'uh' (see page 166). Ask the children to find the Little Brother words and enter them in their Word Banks.

Some mothers have bothersome sons.

Words containing o saying uh

above*	company*	honey	monkey*	some*
among*	cover*	London*	month*	somebody*
another*	does*	love*	mother*	son*
become*	done*	lovely*	none	ton*
brother*	dove	loving*	nothing*	won*
come*	front*	Monday*	other*	wonder
coming*	glove	money*	others*	wonderful*

* High frequency words

o (as in one and once)

The pictogram for the irregular **o** in **one** and **once** is provided here and on *Word Bank Copymaster* 24, but not on a *Programme Two Picture Code Card.*

once

one

Tell the following story to any children in the habit of trying to spell **one** or **once** starting with **w**.

Why o makes a 'www...' sound in one and once

__Once__ upon a time, long ago, the Wild West Wind blew the Wicked Water Witch into a letter __o__ – and, as luck would have it, the Witch got stuck! She could neither come nor go. "Help, help!" she cried. "Help, everyone!" but everyone said "No!". It's lucky for her that (like all the other letters in Letterland) she can be in more than __one__ place at a time, because she is still stuck in __one__. Even adding a __c__ to make the word into __once__ doesn't get her out. So now you know the reason for the Witch's sound inside that annoying __o__!

Ask the children to picture code **one** and **once** with the Witch's hat on the **o** in these sentences.

'Once upon a time' is one way to start a story.

Everyone had seen the film once, one year ago.

These sentences contain both of the irregular **o**'s introduced above:

It was wonderful when I won one race.

Somebody once took Oscar's Little Brother to London.

Words containing o (as in one)

anyone*
everyone*
no-one
once*
someone*

* High frequency words

'Once upon a time' is one way to start a story.

o (as in who)

Section 2, Unit 5.1 introduces the Boot and Foot Twins as they make a long 'oo' sound (as in **boot**). For children who notice the 'oo' sound in a word like **who** and ask what has happened to the second Boot and Foot twin, explain with the following story.

Sometimes while the Boot Twin says 'oo', his brother hides behind him

*In a few words like **do, to, into** and **lose**, you can only see one of the Boot and Foot Twins, even though people in Letterland know that both twins are there. There are two reasons. Sometimes the Foot Twin just likes to play a hiding game behind his brother while the Boot Twin says '**oo**' as usual.*

*In little words like **who, whose** and **whom**, the Foot Twin hides behind his brother for a different reason: he's scared of the Wicked Water Witch. But the Boot Twin isn't scared, so he goes on saying '**oo**' as usual.*

- Write these sentences on the board and ask the children to help with picture coding the varying sounds of **o** and **oo**.

  What are those two children doing?

  The twin moved to and fro.

  Who will be the first one to lose a loose tooth?

  (To keep **lose** and **loose** separate in children's minds, use this reminder: 'You **lose** one twin in **lose**'. It also helps to link **loose** to **tooth**, since every child soon has a loose tooth!)

- Use *Programme Two Copymaster* 55 for further practice.

- Introduce *Word Bank Copymaster* 24. Write several words on the board, some containing regular **o** and some containing **o** pronounced 'oo'. Ask the children to write only words containing **o** saying 'oo' in their Word Banks.

Words containing o saying oo

approve	prove
disapprove	remove
do*	to*
doing*	two*
into*	undo*
lasso	who*
lose	whose
move*	whom
overdo	

Exceptions

group*
route
soup
troupe
you*

* High frequency words

References
For words spelt with **oo** as in **boot**, see page 69.

What are those two children doing?

a (as in umbrella, America)

Objectives

- To know that the letter **a** may be pronounced 'uh' (frequently at the end of words).
- To recognise and spell words containing **a** sounding like 'uh'.

What you need

- *Programme Two Picture Code Cards*: **a** with umbrella (6)
- *Programme One Picture Code Cards*
- *Programme Two Copymaster*: 56
- *Programme Two Word Bank Copymaster*: 25

When the letter **a** is in an unaccented syllable, we tend to pronounce it rather like a short **u**, best shown by the word **umbrella** and the names of many countries (see the word box below). In Letterland these **a**'s are called Parachuted Apples.

Parachuted Apples say 'uh'

*Many names of far away countries end with an **a** – but these apples make an 'uh' sound, as in umbrell**a**! Why? Well, these **a**pples need to be transported to those far-**a**way countries by air. Since Mr A has no plane, he's solved the problem by par**a**chuting each of them in with the help of one of Mr U's umbrell**a**s. As the **a**pple lands it tries to say 'ă' as usual, but the only sound that comes out is 'uh' because it lands with such a thud! Mr A also uses Par**a**chuted Apples for some jobs closer to home.*

- Write these sentences on the board and ask the children to help with picture coding each **ă** and Parachuted Apple.

These apples have umbrellas for parachutes.

We ate lots of bananas in Malaysia.

The gorilla found a camera in the caravan.

Note: In the *Programme Two Word Book* this **a** is coded with a wiggly line to show it is an exception.

- Use *Programme Two Copymaster* 56 and *Word Bank Copymaster* 25 for further practice.

References
For words where an irregular **o** represents this 'uh' sound, see p166.

Words containing Parachuted a

		Countries	
alike	canvas		Canada
alive	caravan	Algeria	China
along*	catapult	America	India
aloud	gorilla	Arabia	Malaysia
banana*	parachute	Australia	Russia
camera	umbrella	Austria	Tunisia

* High frequency words

These apples have umbrellas for parachutes.

a (as in father)

Objectives

- To know that the letter **a** can sometimes be pronounced as 'ah'.
- To recognise and spell words containing **a** pronounced as 'ah'.

What you need

- *Programme Two Picture Code Cards:* **Yawning Apple** (7)
- *Programme One Picture Code Cards*
- *Programme Two Copymaster:* 56
- *Programme Two Word Bank Copymaster:* 25

The change in sound of the letter **a** in a word like **father** is rare in some regions and frequent in others, depending on accent. How can we explain this change? In Letterland the question becomes "What's happened to the apple?" and the answer is "You've discovered a Yawning Apple!"

Yawning Apples say 'ah'

Most apples say 'ă...' for apple in words (unless they are unlucky enough to be stolen by a ***r****obber). But in some words* ***a****pples get sleepy. Just as they are about to say 'ă...' they start to yawn – and with their mouths so wide open, their usual 'ă...' sound comes out as 'ah'.*

- Write these sentences on the board and ask the children to help with picture coding each **ă** and Yawning Apple.

  Look at the glass on the grass!

  The calf ran after my father.

  Ask her for the answer at half past nine.

  Note: In the *Programme Two Word Book* this **a** is coded with a wiggly line to show it is an exception.

- Use *Programme Two Copymaster* 56 and *Word Bank Copymaster* 25 for further practice with the Yawning Apple sound.

f | a | th | er

father

References
For the similar sounding **ar** phoneme, see p94.

Words containing Yawning a

			Challenge words
after*	dance*	mast	pasture
answer*	father*	master*	plaster cast
ask*	France	nasty	prance
basket*	glass*	past*	
blast	grant	plant*	
brass	grass*	rather*	
calf	half*	slant	
class*	headmaster	tomato	
daft	last*		

* High frequency words

Look at the glass on the grass!

e–e (as in these)

Objectives

- To know that when the letter **e** is next to a single consonant plus final **e**, the **e** is usually long.
- To recognise and spell words containing **e–e**.

What you need

- *Programme Two Picture Code Cards:* **Magic e** (9), **Mr E** (2)
- *Programme One Picture Code Cards*
- *Programme Two Copymaster:* 22
- *Programme Two Songs Cassette*
- *Vowel Scenes Posters*: Silent Magic **e**

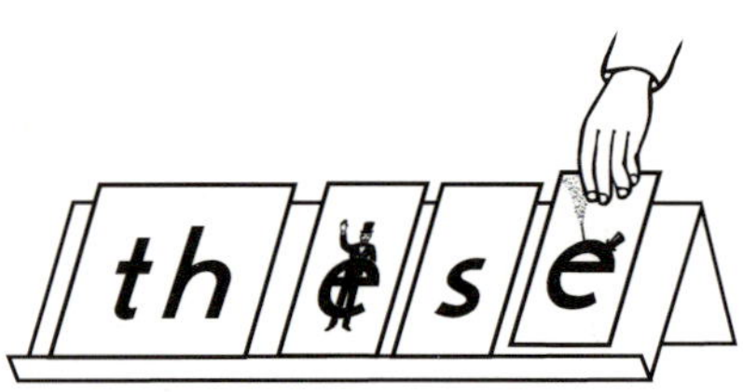

To complete the teaching of Silent Magic **e** as capable of making any Vowel Man appear and say his name, one more group of words needs attention, those with **e–e**. Now Mr E causes his very own Magic **e** to make himself appear and say his name, loud and clear!

Compare them with these and take note of a word that all computer-literate children need to know early on: **delete**. This is a small but interesting group of words, as the examples in the word box below show.

- You may like to refer to the *Silent Magic* **e** *Poster* and sing the Magic **e** song on the *Programme Two Songs Cassette* as a final revision of the Magic **e** principle.
- Write these sentences on the board and ask the children to help with picture coding **e–e**.

These athletes are extremely fit.

We watched a centipede run after a millipede.

The scene was serene until Steve shouted, 'Stampede!'.

Words containing e–e

		Exceptions (r–controlled)
athlete	Japanese	here*
centipede	millipede	there*
Chinese	scene	were*
complete	serene	where*
concrete	stampede	
delete	Steve	
eve	supreme	
extreme	these*	
interfere		

* High frequency words

These athletes are extremely fit.

Silent e (Magic e exceptions)

Objectives

- To know that a final Silent **e** may sometimes not function as a Magic **e**.
- To recognise and spell irregular words with final Silent **e**'s.

What you need

- *Programme Two Picture Code Cards:* **Burnt-out Magic e** (10)
- *Programme One Picture Code Card:* **Oscar's Little Brother** (26)
- *Programme Two Copymaster:* 57
- *Programme Two Word Bank Copymaster:* 26

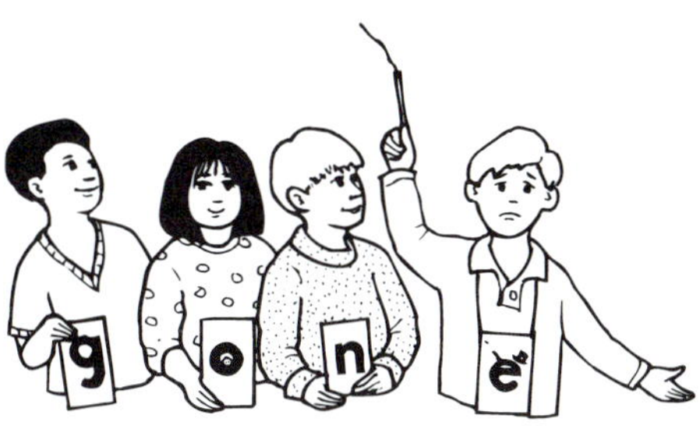

* High frequency words

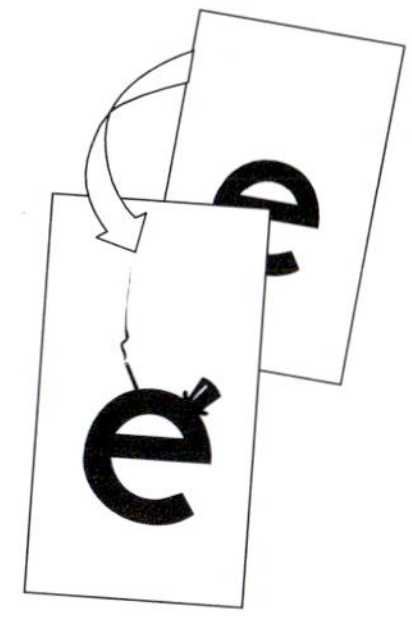

As soon as we try to teach the Magic **e** principle, exceptions seem to turn up everywhere! This is because 20 out of the 60 most common Silent **e** words do not obey the rule. They are **one**, **gone**, **done**, **come**, **some**, **minute**, **have**, **give**, **love**, **live**, **above**, and the **r**-controlled words **care**, **more**, **before**, **here**, **where**, **there**, **were**, **store** and **sure**. Nearly all are among the 200 most used words in the English language. Consequently they abound in most books and in children's free writing.

To deal with the exceptions as well as the rule, explain that, as with all kinds of power, occasionally Magic **e**'s power runs out. The children illustrate the power failure by drawing a wisp of smoke coming from the wand.

bone but gone and done

The vowel in Burnt-out Magic **e** words may keep its original sound (as in **gone**) or it may become irregular. These irregular vowel words are particularly difficult to spell. Each child should make a collection of them, especially the starred ones in the box below.

- Write these sentences on the board and ask the children to help with picture coding each Magic **e** and Burnt-out Magic **e**.

  I promise the work will be done on time.

  Come home this minute!

  The police notice says that this land is private.

- Live spell or dictate: **one** → **gone** → **shone** → **love** → **notice.**
- Use *Programme Two Copymaster* 57 for further practice.
- Introduce *Word Bank Copymaster* 26. Ask the children to look for Burnt-Out Magic **e** words and to add them to their Word Banks.

Words ending in Burnt-Out Magic e

above*	done*	have*	love*	one*	purchase
college	engine	lettuce	machine	private	notice
come*	gone*	live*	minute*	promise	some*

I promise the work will be done on time.

y (as in very) (as in bicycle)

Objectives

- To know that the letter **y** can represent a long **ē** sound at the end of a word (as in **very**).
- To recognise and spell words ending **y**.

What you need

- *Programme Two Picture Code Cards:* **y** (with **e** in sack - 15), **y** (with ink bottle - 14)
- *Programme One Picture Code Cards*
- *Programme Two Copymaster:* 58
- *Programme Two Word Bank Copymaster:* 27

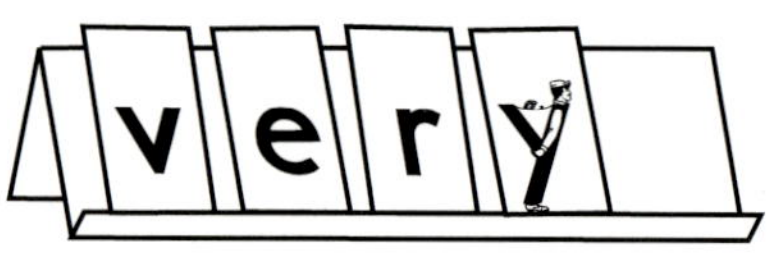

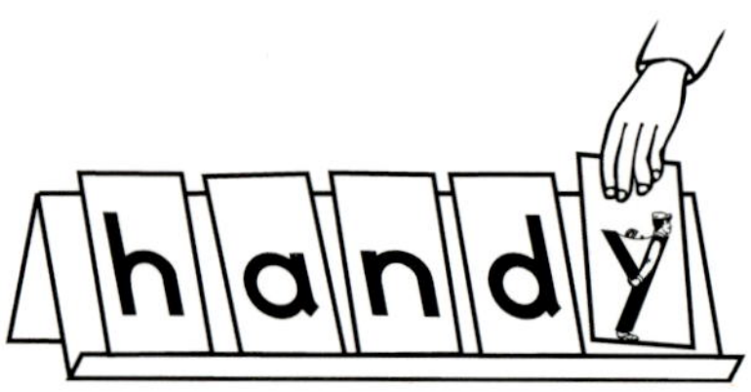

Work on this spelling pattern will be very important for any children who, in their earliest efforts to spell words ending in **y**, regularly choose **e** (e.g. 'cose' and 'softle' for **cosy** and **softly**) because this is the final sound they hear. It will also be helpful in clearing up the other common mis-spelling of **-ey**: 'softley'. Show any child who has an **-ey** habit the list on page 175 containing most of the very few words that really do end in **-ey**. By contrast, there are over 5000 words which end in **y** sounding like an **ē**. Picture coding will help: the child simply writes **y** and draws a tiny **e** in the Yo-yo Man's sack instead of mis-spelling the word.

The following story has been introduced briefly in Unit 17.2 before the **-ly** story. This fuller version features the Yo-yo Man's biggest and best business deal.

Yo-yo Man's business deal with Mr E

Yo-yo Man's says ē in over 5000 words for Mr E

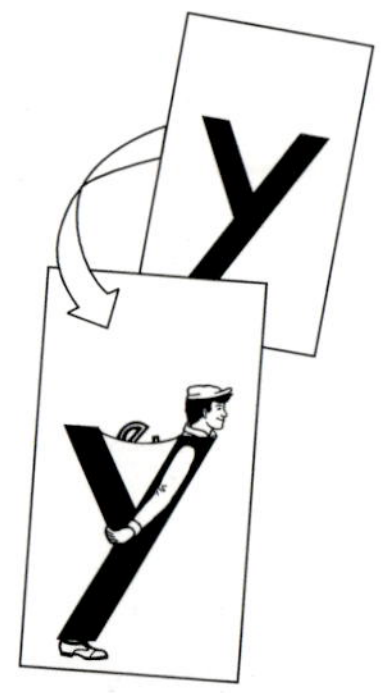

Much as the Yo-yo Man enjoys working for Mr I, he needs more work than Mr I can give him. Luckily, the Yo-yo Man has another friend who needs help. It's Mr E. Do you remember Mr E's special invention for the end of words, his Silent Magic ***e****? Well, he quite forgot that in many, many words people just do not want an* ***e*** *to become silent at the end.*

There was nothing Mr E could do to change his Silent ***e****'s back into* ***e****'s which could still say* ***e****. In fact, his magic had worked so well that now nearly every* ***ē*** *that anyone puts at the end of a word automatically turns into a Silent* ***e****! What could Mr E do? He was rushing about in a terrible state until he saw the Yo-yo Man.*

"Can you say ***ē*** *for me?", he cried desperately.*

*"I don't know," said the Yo-yo Man slowly. He put down his yo-yos and took a deep breath. Then he said "****ē****" quite easily!*

Mr E was ever so pleased, and immediately gave the Yo-yo Man the job of saying ***e*** *for him in nearly every word which sounds as though it ends in* ***e****. So now the Yo-yo Man earns a very good living indeed, because there are not just hundreds but thousands of words where he can say* ***e*** *for Mr E. And Mr E has given him a tiny little* ***e*** *which he can carry in his sack, to show everybody just how many words he finishes for Mr E.*

He went to the party with Harry and Emily.

☆ Write these sentences on the board and ask the children to help with picture coding final **-y** saying **ē**.

He went to the party with Harry and Emily.

In assembly we heard a story about a lucky pony.

These next sentences revise **y** working for Mr E and for Mr I.

My granny gave me a shiny, juicy apple.

Unfortunately nobody has a magnifying glass.

Our supply of juicy grapes comes from Italy.

☆ Live spell or dictate: **history** → **story** → **body** → **copy** → **reply** → **magnify** → **enemy** → **envy** → **empty**.

☆ Ask each child to choose and picture code in colour a word with **-y** saying **ī** or **-y** saying **ē**. Leave room on the wall to display a collection which can be extended later.

☆ Ask children to retell in their own words the story about the Yo-yo Man's deals with Mr I or Mr E, or both.

☆ Use *Programme Two Copymaster* 58 for further practice.

☆ Introduce *Word Bank Copymaster* 27. Ask the children to find words containing final **y** working for Mr E and to add them to their Word Banks. Ensure that they sift out any words with **y** working for Mr I, e.g. **multiply** (see page 56) or Mr E out walking with the Yo-yo Man (see page 175).

☆ Write a selection of the **-y** words on the board (see page 174), including the word **story**. Discuss with the children some ideas for a story which could be built around these words. Some children could write their story.

☆ Show the children an example of a family tree. Discuss how a family tree is drawn, and write a family tree with the children for the Yo-yo Man. Since no information is given, they can decide for themselves how big his family is, and invent names for them – all starting with his usual 'y...' sound or ending with **y** saying '**ē**'. Alternatively, you could work through a family tree relating to a topic that you are covering in history during the current term.

The Yo-yo Man's Other Jobs

y	y	y	ey	y
my	mummy	cosy	key	gym
try	funny	baby	money	
fly	very			
	lazy			
	slowly			
	quickly			
	(over 5000 words)		(only 24 words)	(Add after page 174)

References
For long **ī** sound made by **y**, see p56.

My granny gave me a shiny, juicy apple.

Words ending in –y saying ē

already*
any*
anybody*
balcony
berry
body*
busy*
carry*
city*
clumsy
company*
copy
country*
Daddy*
dirty
dusty
easy*
empty

enemy
envy
every*
family*
February*
fifty*
filthy
frosty
Germany
handy
heavy*
history
Hungary
hungry*
hurry*
Italy
January
juicy*

marry*
melody
merry*
milky
misty
Mummy*
monopoly
nearly*
only*
party*
plenty*
pretty*
ready*
rocky
scratchy
seventy*
sixty*
sorry*

sticky
story*
study
tricky
truly
ugly
very*
windy*
(and thousands more)

Children's names

Harry
Holly
Emily
Sally

Challenge words

anatomy
astronomy
calamity
cavity
monarchy
primary
query
remedy

Exceptions

Words ending in
-key
-ley
-ney
(see page 175)

* High frequency words

A smaller business deal with Mr I

Yo-yo Man carries ink into words for Mr I

The Yo-yo Man has found another way to help a Vowel Man. He helps Mr I by carrying ink bottles into a few words which need an ĭ sound in them. That way he earns a little more money and some free ink from Mr I as well.

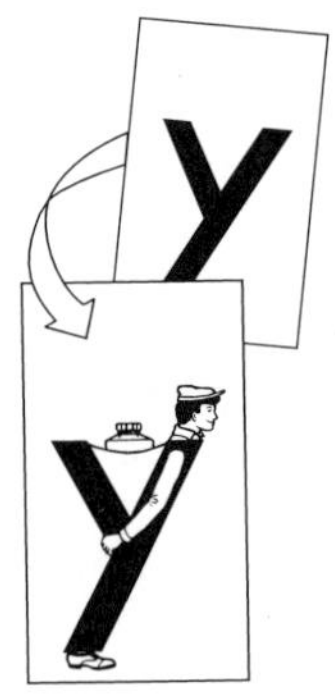

This story is a quick way to draw children's attention to a small but important group of words where **y** represents short **ĭ**, picture coded by drawing an ink bottle in **y**'s sack. The most useful words to know in this group are in the word box below. (See page 56 for the Yo-yo Man's first deal with Mr I.)

bicycle
pyramid

Words containing y saying ĭ

bicycle	cymbals	mystery	rhythm
cygnet	gymnast	oxygen	symbol
cylinder	hymn	pyramid	typical

References
For **y** as a Magic Ending, see p195.

This cylinder has oxygen in it.

ey (as in donkey)

Objectives

- To know that the letters **e** and **y** combine to represent long **e** (**ey** as in **donkey**).
- To recognise and spell words ending in **-ey**.

What you need

- *Programme Two Picture Code Cards:* **Mr E** (2), **ay** (45)
- *Programme One Picture Code Cards:* plain side of **y** card (21 or 22)
- *Programme Two Copymaster: 59*
- *Programme Two Word Bank Copymaster: 27*

The majority of words that sound like long **ē** at the end are spelt with **-y**. However, a small group of useful words end, not in **-y** alone, but in **-ey**. All but one of these words (**storey**) ends in **-key**, **-ley** or **-ney**.

When Mr E and the Yo-yo Man walk, Mr E talks

*As everyone in Letterland knows, Mr E has given the Yo-yo Man the job of saying **ē** at the ends of most words – more than 5000 words, in fact! But in about 20 words, instead of paying the Yo-yo Man to do work for him, Mr E takes the Yo-yo Man on a journ**ey**. As they walk, Mr E does the talking and the Yo-yo Man acts as the look-out man.*

- Write these sentences on the board and ask the children to help with picture coding Mr E and the Yo-yo Man.

  We took our donkey and plenty of money.

  On the journey we saw a beautiful valley.

  Who let that turkey loose in the field of barley?

- Live spell: **honey** → **money** → **monkey** → **donkey** → **hockey** → **holey** → **trolley**. Since there is no **ey** *Picture Code Card*, the children can hold the long **e** and a **y** card (from the *Programme One Picture Code Cards*) with the plain black side showing. Both children can make the arm gestures as for Vowels Out Walking.
- Use *Programme Two Copymaster* 59 for further practice.
- Use the Mr E *Picture Code Card* placed over the **ay** card for building words on a table.

Words ending in -ey

-key	-ley	-ney	Children's names
donkey	alley	chimney	Hayley
hockey	barley	honey	Wesley
jockey	holey	journey	
key	parsley	money*	
monkey*	pulley		
turkey	trolley	**-rey**	
	valley	storey	
	volley		

Exceptions

A few words ending in **-ey** sound like **ay** (see page 176).

* High frequency words

We took our donkey and plenty of money.

e (as in they)

Objectives

- ☆ To know that, in a few words, the letters **ey** sound like long **ā**.
- ☆ To recognise and spell these irregular words.

What you need

- ☆ *Programme Two Picture Code Cards:* **Mr Mean-E** (11), **ay** (45)
- ☆ *Programme One Picture Code Cards*
- ☆ *Programme Two Copymaster:* 60
- ☆ *Programme Two Word Bank Copymaster:* 28

* High frequency words

Words containing ey sounding like ā

disobey	obey
grey*	prey
hey	survey
they*	

If any child starts to spell **they** as 'thay', it is worth tackling the problem immediately, before it becomes habitual. Mr Mean-E, the grey-haired old scrooge in Letterland who likes to make spelling difficult, can motivate all the children in the school to spell **they** correctly. This rhyme sums him up:

*Mr Mean-E, he looks like an **e**,*
*But he tricks us all by saying **ā**.*
He's too mean to be seen very often in words,
*But you **can** see him in the word **they**!*

The challenge is to ensure that Mr Mean-E doesn't manage to fool anyone into spelling **they** incorrectly. There are a few other words in this group, but the top priority is to master the high frequency word **they**.

In Programme One just the irregular **e** was picture coded, as the children had not yet been introduced to the Vowels Out Walking concept. At this stage, their picture coding can include the Yo-yo Man acting as the silent look-out man for grouchy old Mr Mean-E. There are so few words where **ey** sounds like **ā** (see the word box on the left) that there is no *Picture Code Card*, but the Mr Mean-E card can be laid over the **a** in the **ay** card.

- ☆ Write these sentences on the board and ask the children to help with picture coding **ey** saying **ā**.

  "Hey! I bet you can't spell they!"

  That grey dog obeys its master, but it disobeys me.

- ☆ Use the top half of *Programme Two Copymaster* 60 for further practice.
- ☆ Introduce *Word Bank Copymaster* 28. Write the words from the word box on the board and ask the children to write all the **ey** words in their Word Banks. They are not likely to come across any others, proving that Mr Mean-E is too mean to be seen very often in words!

Note: *Programme One Copymaster* 69 features **they** and will be useful for those children who need more focus on this high frequency word. Consider setting a school-wide challenge to outwit Mr Mean-E. The goal: no child ever mis-spells **they** again!

Hey! I bet you can't spell they!

ei (as in eight)

Objectives

- To know that, in a few words, the letters **ei** sound like long **ā**.
- To recognise and spell these words.

What you need

- *Programme Two Picture Code Cards:* **Mr Mean E** (11), **ai** (18)
- *Programme One Picture Code Cards*
- *Programme Two Copymaster:* 60
- *Programme Two Word Bank Copymaster:* 28

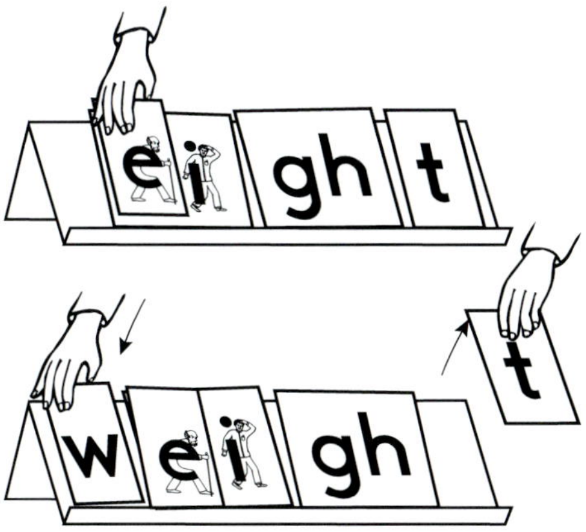

References
For more common spelling patterns for long **ā**, see p40.

When Mr Mean-E walks with Mr I, Mr Mean-E talks

Although he is very old and grey, in just a few words Mr Mean-E goes out walking with Mr I! Kind Mr I acts as his silent look-out man even though Mr Mean-E is such an old grouch that he doesn't even smile. How old do you think Mr Mean-E might be? Golden Girl, who usually comes next in these words, has quietly decided that …

*… he must be **e**ighty-**e**ight!*

There is no *Picture Code Card* for this rare spelling pattern, but the Mr Mean-E card can be laid over the **a** in the **ai** card.

- Write these sentences on the board and ask the children to help with picture coding **ei** saying **ā**.

  Is Mr Mean-E eighty or eighty-eight?
  The fur on the reindeer's necks was beige.
  Do you know how much your neighbour weighs?

- Use the bottom half of *Programme Two Copymaster* 60 for further practice.
- Introduce *Word Bank Copymaster* 28. Write the words from the word box below on the board and ask the children to select the six words which they consider most useful to write in their Word Banks.

Words containing ei saying ā

beige	feint	sleigh
eight*	neigh	weigh
eighteen*	neighbour	weight
eighty*	reindeer	weightless

* High frequency words

Is Mr Mean-E eighty or eighty-eight?

Spelling the 'k' sound

Objectives

- To know whether to spell a 'k' sound with **-ck**, **-ke**, **-k** or **-c**.

What you need

- *Programme Two Picture Code Cards:* **ck** (47), **ke** (67), **oo** (70), **oo** (71)
- *Programme One Picture Code Cards:* **c**, **k**
- *Programme Two Copymaster:* 61
- *Programme Two Word Bank Copymaster:* 29
- *Vowel Scene Posters:* The Vowels, Silent Magic **e** and Vowels Out Walking.

Four guidelines can help children who are not sure how to spell a word containing a 'k' sound:

1. After a short vowel, use **-ck**.
2. After a long vowel, use **-ke**.
3. After two vowels, use **-k** alone.
4. In most other words, if in doubt choose **c**, (except beside **n**, **r** and **l**).

Select as needed any of the following three brief 'k' stories to help uncertain spellers to see specific spelling patterns emerging. Fuller understanding will come as they picture code the vowel(s) before **k** themselves.

Use any of the examples in the **-ck** word box below to explain what a 'short, quick' word is: one with a short vowel in it (e.g. Annie Apple), and one that it is quick to say because it is a one syllable word. Over 85 one syllable words end in **-ck**.

Clever Cat and Kicking King end short, quick words

Clever Cat loves watching Kicking King practise his kicks at the end of short, quick words, where he does most of his really big kicks.

- Live spell or dictate: **crack** → **check** → **chick** → **clock** → **cluck**.

Words containing a short vowel plus -ck

sack	peck	stick	lock	stuck
back*	check	brick	block	buck
black*	deck	chick	clock	duck*
crack	fleck	pick*	dock	luck
pack	neck*	thick	flock	suck
track	speck	trick	sock	truck

* High frequency words

The King alone says 'k' in Magic e words

When you hear a Vowel Man saying his name just before a 'k' sound, the chances are that magic sparks are landing on him from a Magic ***e****. These sparks jump back over only one letter, the Kicking King alone.*

☆ Live spell or dictate: **back** ➜ **bake**, **lick** ➜ **like**, **duck** ➜ **duke**, **smoke** ➜ **stroke**.

Words containing a long vowel plus -ke

ake		ike		oke		uke
awake	mistake	alike	pike	awoke	poke	duke
bake*	quake	bike	spike	broke*	smoke*	fluke
lake*	shake	dislike	strike	choke	stroke	
make*	take*	like*		joke		

* High frequency words

Spelling tip for children who write '-cke'

Why is **-cke** wrong? Explain that Clever Cat is afraid the magic sparks might land on her instead of the vowel. So she hides whenever a Magic **e** is placed beside the Kicking King, e.g. ba**ck** but ba**ke**, li**ck** but li**ke**, du**ck** but du**ke**.

After two vowels the King alone says 'k'

Clever Cat stays away from the Boot and Foot Twins and from Vowel Men Out Walking because she is frightened of being stepped on. So don't expect to see her in her usual place beside Kicking King.

☆ Live spell or dictate: **week** ➜ **weak** ➜ **oak** ➜ **croak** ➜ **soak** ➜ **shook**.

Words ending in -k after two vowels

shook	weak	steak	cheek	soak
book*	beak	break*	Greek	cloak
cook*	leak		leek	croak
hook	peak		meek	oak
look*	speak		peek	
spook	streak		seek	
took*			week*	

(There are very few others.)

* High frequency words

In all other words, if in doubt choose Clever Cat

Clever Cat is proud to ***begin*** *far more words than Kicking King because the King finds kicking too cramped at the start of words.*
(For proof compare the size of the ***c*** *and* ***k*** *sections of any dictionary.)*

Clever Cat also turns up far more often than the King ***inside*** *words.*

Clever Cat proudly ***finishes*** *many longer words all by herself.*
(Words of two or more syllables)

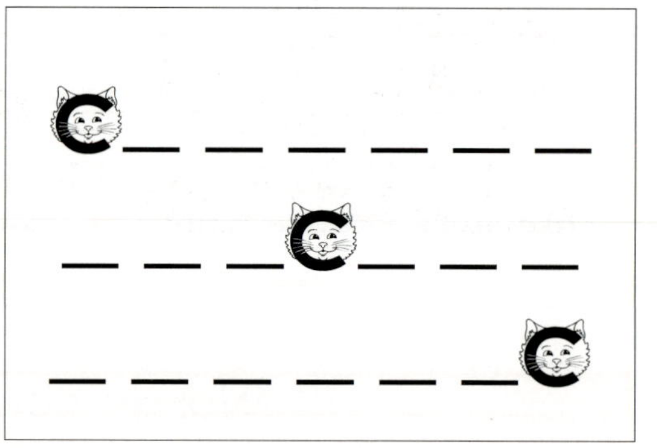

Words ending in –c

			Challenge words	
acrobatic	cubic	metric	basic	hectic
athletic	elastic	pathetic	domestic	lilac
attic	electric*	picnic*	fabric	prehistoric
clinic	fantastic	realistic	havoc	septic
comic*	historic	romantic		
cosmic	magnetic			

* High frequency words

☆ Write these sentences on the board and ask the children to help with picture coding **ck**, **ke**, **k** and **c**, plus the preceding vowels.

The duck pecked at the black and white clock.
The truck put the bricks and blocks on the track.

The duck pecked at the black and white clock.

Thick smoke can make you choke.
They had amazing luck to strike gold so quickly.

Thick smoke can make you choke.

Did he speak to the spook?
Last week I felt too weak to cook steak for our Greek friend.

Did he speak to the spook?

- Live spell or dictate: **back → bake, lick → like, duck → duke → book → week → weak → oak → soak → shook**.

- Follow up work on **-ck** and **-ke** by selecting several words from the **-ck** and **-ke** word boxes to say out loud. The children listen for a short or long vowel. If it is a short vowel, they tell you the word will end with **-ck**. If it is a long vowel, they tell you **-ke** because the vowel is saying its name. It must be, because magic sparks from a Silent Magic **e** have made a Vowel Man appear. Display *The Vowels Poster* and *Silent Magic* ***e*** *Poster* for reference.

- Do the same again after going over words with two vowels plus **-k**, selecting now from the **–ck**, **-ke** and **-k** word boxes. The children will still be listening for a short or long vowel (in this case a pair of Vowel Men Out Walking) or for the Boot and Foot Twins. Have the *Vowels Out Walking Poster* and the Boot and Foot Twin *Picture Code Cards* on display for reference.

- Use *Programme Two Copymaster* 61 for further practice.

- Introduce *Word Bank Copymaster* 29. Ask the children to look for words ending with a 'k' sound and to enter them into their Word Banks in the appropriate places.

Words ending in -nk, -rk or -lk

A few words end in **-k** alone because instead of a vowel there is a consonant behind the King's back, usually Nick (**n**) or a robber (**r**). Examples include **think**, **thank**, **park**, **fork**. Explain to children who add **ck** instead of **k** alone (e.g. 'thinck') that Clever Cat runs away from these words because she is afraid that Nick or a **r**obber might step on her! The only other consonant that turns up beside the King in just a few words is Lucy Lamp Lady in words such as **walk**, **talk**, **chalk**, **milk** and **silk**.

y changing to i (as in cries, ponies)

Objectives

- To know that the letter **y** changes to **i** before a new ending (as in **cry → cries**).
- To recognise and spell words containing **y** changed to **i**.

What you need

- *Programme Two Picture Code Cards:* **i** (with hut - 17), **y** (with ice cream - 13), **y** (with with tiny **e** - 15)
- *Programme One Picture Code Cards*
- *Programme Two Copymasters:* 62-64
- *Programme Two Word Bank Copymasters:* 30-31

Preparation

- **Look, say, cover, write, check**
  Make copies of the format on page 230.
- **Word posters**
  Have ready some large pieces of card or paper.
- **Changing box**
  To make Yo-yo Man's changing hut, paint stripes on a cereal box. Cut out a door big enough for the **y** *Picture Code Card* to fit inside. Make a 'secret' panel at the back for storing the **i** card, ready to pull out as needed (see illustration page 183).

Children are slow to learn when they can see no reason for a shift in spelling patterns. Since they are accustomed to adding an **s** (correctly) to high frequency words ending in **-ay** and **-oy** (e.g. **days** and **boys**), they will often add **s** to high frequency words where **y** should be changed to **i**. This leads to typical errors such as 'carrys' 'citys', 'crys' 'partys', 'ponys', 'storys'. Ideally, teach the Letterland story below *before* any such errors become habitual. If left unchecked, the errors begin to 'look right' and can become very difficult to eradicate.

Yellow Yo-yo Man changes into his i-clothes before new endings

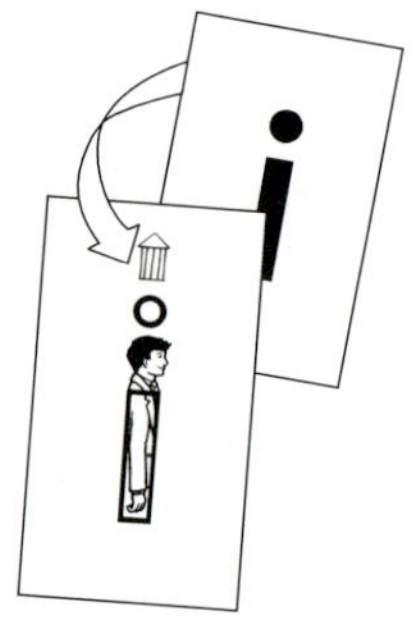

*Yellow Yo-yo Man really enjoys the work he does, finishing some words for Mr I and a great many words for Mr E. In fact, he has become a very familiar sight at the end of words. However, if **-ed**, **-er**, **-est** or any other ending except **-ing** comes along to finish the word for him, he stops work right away and changes out of his working clothes into some neat, straight **i**-clothes which Mr I has kindly given to him.*

*The trousers of his **i**-clothes are invisible, however, so that when the Yo-yo Man is working for Mr I he can even look like Mr I as well.*

*Anyone who looks carefully will see that the Yo-yo Man regularly disappears into his changing-hut to slip into his **i**-clothes in hundreds of words!*

- Practise this picture coding first by writing **fly →** large on the board. Ask a child to write **flies** after the arrow, then picture code the **y** and draw a little changing hut above the **i**. You can emphasise this shift by using the cereal box changing hut (see Preparation). Put *Picture Code Card* **y** (13) into the hut, pause (while he changes), then produce the Yo-yo Man in his **i**-clothes (card 17) from the other side (see illustration page 183). Use the same approach but put in the **y** (with **e**) *Picture Code Card* 15 for words like **pony → ponies**. (In both cases, keep the **y** card hidden in the hut when taking out card 17.)

Note: The Yo-yo Man has no **e**-clothes so he always changes into his **i**-clothes.

Now write any of these sentences on the board. The children decide which **i**'s need changing huts (to show where there used to be a **y**) and draw huts over them.

-ies I like stories about puppies and ponies.
Babies often cry at parties.

-ied They tried looking at the fly magnified.
She carried white roses when she got married.

-ier A picnic on a sunnier day will be easier.
When she's happier she will look prettier.

-iest The shaggiest dog has the bushiest tail.
The friskiest pony has the silkiest coat.

-iness A busy business can bring happiness.

-iful Her beauty lies in her beautiful eyes.

Live spell or dictate: **try** → **tries** → **dry** → **dried** → **drier** → **driest** → **baby** → **babies** → **lady** → **ladies**. The child holding the **y** *Picture Code Card* should also hold the changing hut **i** card just behind it. When a new ending is added to the word, he swaps the cards round so the changing hut **i** card is in front. (You could increase the effect by making a large picture of the hut to put in front of **y** as the Yo-yo Man changes.)

Use *Programme Two Copymasters* 62-64 for further practice.

Introduce *Word Bank Copymasters* 30 and 31. Ask the children to look for words containing **y** changed to **i** in their books and to add them to their Word Banks.

Give the children the following examples to study. They are the ten most frequently used words with **y** changed to **i**.

babies	countries	flies	replies
carries	cries	parties	tries
cities	families	puppies	stories

Build up a display of children's picture coded words with the Yo-yo Man and his changing hut in the middle.

Exceptions
In the following two instances, the Yo-yo Man does not change out of his working clothes:

- before **-ing**, e.g. **flying**, **carrying**.
- when he is out walking (**ay**, **ey**) or playing the **oy** game with Roy, e.g. **played**, **journeys**, **employer**.

I like stories about puppies and ponies.

Words containing y changed to i

y → i

cry → cries → cried

allies	allied
amplifies	amplified
applies	applied
cries*	cried*
defies	defied
denies	denied
dries*	dried*
fries	fried
horrifies	horrified
magnifies	magnified
multiplies	multiplied
occupies	occupied
replies	replied
satisfies	satisfied
signifies	signified
spies	spied
supplies	supplied
tries*	tried*

babies*	accompanied
berries	buried
bodies*	carried*
centuries	emptied
cherries	hurried*
cities*	married
countries*	steadied
daisies	studied
discoveries	tidied
enemies	worried
fairies	
families*	
jellies	
ladies*	
memories	
parties*	
ponies	
puppies*	
stories*	

Challenge words

amplifier
categories
enquiries
spiciest

y → i

empty → emptier → emptiest

angrier	angriest
busier	busiest
cloudier	cloudiest
dirtier	dirtiest
dustier	dustiest
easier	easiest
emptier	emptiest
funnier	funniest
greedier	greediest
happier	happiest
heavier	heaviest
lazier	laziest
lonelier	loneliest
merrier	merriest
moodier	moodiest
muddier	muddiest
prettier	prettiest
steadier	steadiest
sunnier	sunniest
uglier	ugliest

Words containing y changed to i before other endings

-iness	-iless	-iful	-ily	-ihood	-iment	-ious
business	merciless	beautiful*	busily	likelihood	embodiment	envious
happiness	penniless	merciful	easily	livelihood	merriment	melodious
loneliness		plentiful	happily			
tidiness						

* High frequency words

Double consonants before Magic Endings: ed, ing

The concept of shared sounds, to describe double consonants, was introduced in Programme One. Letterland uses the term 'shared sounds' to indicate that both consonants are of equal importance and share a common purpose. The other useful term is 'Best Friend' to refer to the second letter in any consonant pair.

The specific double consonants *Picture Code Cards*❖ included in Programme One are **ff**, **ll** and **ss** — three pairs which are permanent features at the end of many one-syllable, short-vowel words. There are, of course, a few other words ending in other consonant pairs, notably **add**, **egg** and a small number of words ending in **-zz** (as in **fizz**). Adding a prefix like **ac-**, **ir-** or **im-** can also cause double consonants in words like **account**, **irregular** and **immobile**.

These words apart, however, the chief reason for doubling a consonant is to protect a short vowel before particular suffixes. The aim is to help children to understand that *they can predict when to double a consonant* and so avoid innumerable spelling errors. To alert young spellers to those final syllables which have the same impact on the previous vowel as Magic **e**, Letterland identifies them all as Magic Endings.The children learn to predict when to add a second consonant by seeing it as performing a rescue act, saving the short vowel from disappearing in a shower of magic sparks. Role playing this sort of act is a very effective way of ensuring that the children understand the second consonant's function.

The following Units will draw on and reinforce this understanding, as they explain how Best Friends come to the rescue before Magic **-ed** and **-ing** (already covered as Magic Endings in Section 2, Unit 6), Magic **-en** and **-est**, and the part-time Magic Endings **-er** and **-y**. The most important ones are **-ed** and **-ing**, since the need to add these endings arises most often.

❖ Footnote

*Because the **ff**, **ll** and **ss** pairs are usually permanent features in words, their pictograms show both letters on one Programme One Picture Code Card. The other letters are provided on separate Programme One cards so that later on the children can learn by doing – by physically adding the 'Best Friend' before a Magic Ending. The second card in some of the pairs (**b**, **d**, **m**, **p** and **z**) is almost identical to the first. (Spot the differences: eyelashes or mouth details.)*

References
The principle Magic Endings are **-ed** (p78), **-ing** (p82), **-en** and **-est** (p190). See also Part-time Magic Endings: **-er** (p193) and **-y** (p195) and Candle Magic **le** (p197).

The Letterland Best Friends' names that follow provide identification for the second consonant in any word (double or separate singles, e.g. **bulb**, **tent**, **nests**). They can also serve as a stimulus to spur on free writing, where the children create their own stories about these Letterland Best Friends. (They can choose other alliterative names for these consonants if they prefer, as long as the initial sound is the same.)

Letterland's Best Friends

Bouncy Ben's best friend is a bright-eyed little brown bunny called Bouncy Barbara.

Clever Cat's best friend is her country cousin called Clever Carol.

Dippy Duck's best friend is a dear little duck called Diana Duck.

Fireman Fred's best friend is his fellow fireman – Fireman Frank.

Golden Girl's best friend is her very own grandmother, Golden Granny, who, although she is old is still full of 'go'.

Lucy Lamp Lady's best friend is Lamp Lady Linda, who helps her light up lots of little words.

Munching Mike's best friend is a merry little monster called Munching Maria.

Naughty Nick's best friend is his next door neighbour, Naughty Nicola, who loves hammering nails just as much as Nick.

Poor Peter's best friend is a pretty little puppy called Poor Patsy, whose ears droop just like Poor Peter's!

Sammy Snake's best friend is his sister Sally. They both love to hiss at the end of short words.

Ticking Tess's best friend is her team-mate, Ticking Tom, who knows all about telephones, tape recorders, etc. just like Tess.

Zig Zag Zebra's best friend is Zoe Zebra. She is just as shy as Zig Zag and also just as fast at zipping in and out of words.

In the following Units, it is the all-important *function* of Best Friends which comes to the fore. Described as Best Friends to the Rescue, this is the Letterland way of making it clear to children why they need to add a second consonant to so many words before they add a suffix. The second consonant blocks the effect that any Magic Ending could otherwise have had on the previous vowel (see pages 187-189).

Blocking Magic ed and Magic ing

Objectives

- To know when to double the consonant before Magic **ed** and Magic **ing**.
- To recognise and spell these double consonant words correctly.

What you need

- *Programme Two Picture Code Cards:* **ed** (50-52), **ing** (65)
- *Programme One Picture Code Cards*
- *Programme Two Copymasters:* 67-68
- *Programme Two Word Bank Copymasters:* 35-36
- *Programme Two Songs Cassette*
- *Vowel Scene Posters:* The Vowels

Silent Magic **e** was introduced in Programme One, where it was recommended that children play-act the Magic **e**'s function in **tap** and **tape**. In the same way, let the children now act out the wand waving and vowel change caused by Magic **ed** in **tap**, **taped** and **hop**, **hoped**. Congratulate the Mr A and Mr O children for making these new words with the help of Magic **ed**. Then present everyone with the problem: what should they do if they don't want **tap** (or **hop**) to be changed into a completely different word? What if they *want* to write **tapped** (or **hopped**)? Some children may know that two **p**'s are needed. Your aim is to see that not only these children but every child has grasped the second consonant's vital function of preventing the Magic Ending from causing a Vowel Man to displace the short vowel. The following story is the Letterland answer to the problem.

Point to *The Vowels Poster* (top row of short vowels) to support your teaching of both the problem and the solution.

Best Friends to the Rescue

Mr E, the Easy Magic Man, found it very ***eee****asy to invent his Magic* ***e****'s with their beautiful jumping yellow sparks. He also found it very* ***eee****asy to teach Eddy Elephant to shoot the sparks back over exactly one letter in endings like* ***ed****. It was* ***eee****asy, too, for him to make magic sparks fly from* ***ing****, once the magician had made* ***ing*** *into a Magic Ending as well.*

But … had it all been a bit ***too*** *easy? The idea had perhaps been too good. Suddenly Letterland was having problems. With so many Magic Endings showering sparks on to* ***a****pples,* ***o****ranges,* ***i****nk bottles and* ***u****mbrellas, they were all disappearing from words! Even worse, whenever one of them disappeared, a Vowel Man* ***had*** *to appear and say his name – even when he didn't* ***want*** *to play the Naming Game! "Help!" cried Mr E. "What shall I do? I can't undo magic. Once I make an ending magic, it stays magic!" For once he could see no* ***eee****asy way out.*

In the end it was Mr O (who is very old and wise) who solved the problem, simply by asking Mr E one question, "Can magic sparks ever jump back over more than one letter?" "No!" cried Mr E.

"Then all we need," said Mr O slowly, "is to bring in a Best Friend to the Rescue!"

Discuss what Mr O might mean. Lead the children to discover that the doubled letter puts the short vowel out of reach. The magic sparks are not strong enough to reach over two letters – only over one. So, to stop the magic, put another letter in between: not just any letter, because the word does not need a new sound. Another letter of the same kind is the perfect answer, sharing the sound and keeping off the sparks: in fact, a Best Friend.

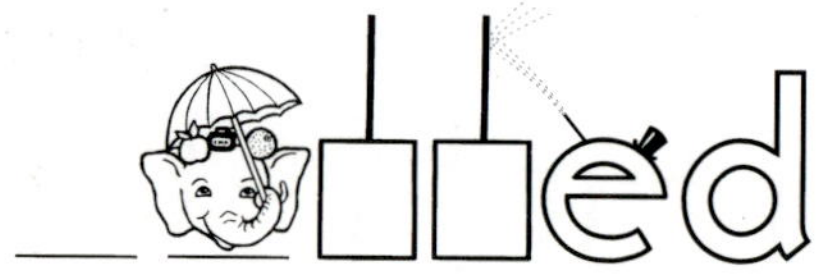

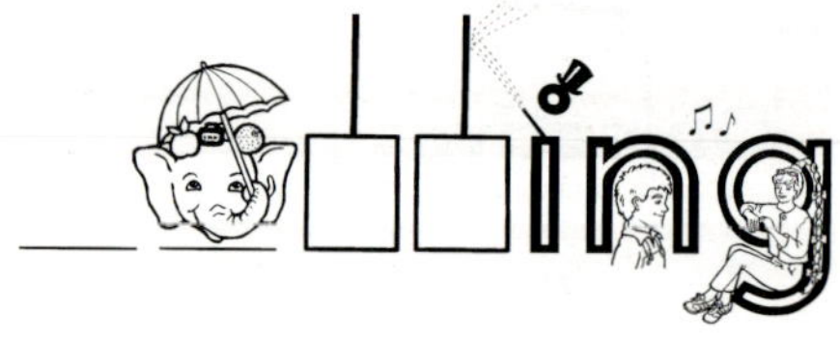

- The Best Friends to the Rescue song on the *Programme Two Songs Cassette* is ideal to support play-acting the role of the Best Friend. The time taken to act out the song, using the words **clap** and **clapping**, may make all the difference for some children in helping them really understand the reason for adding that second consonant.

- Write these sentences on the board and ask the children to help with picture coding the vowels before the double consonants, the Best Friends and the Magic Ending.

  He stopped clapping as the ball hit the netting.

  She pinned the flower on to her wedding dress.

  I slipped on the sitting room floor.

- Live spell: **rub → rubbed, drum → drumming, wag → wagged, fit → fitting, shred → shredded → pop → popped**.

- Use *Programme Two Copymasters* 67-68 for further practice.

- Introduce *Word Bank Copymasters* 35 and 36. Ask the children to look for words containing double consonants followed by Magic Endings in their books. Before adding them to their Word Banks, they need to check the vowel sound. Is it short? If so, now they know why!

- Play the thumbs up, thumbs down game. Dictate the following words where the magic has and hasn't affected the letters. Ask the children to put their thumbs up if they think that they can hear that the Vowel Men have appeared, and down if they think that the double consonants have blocked the magic.

waded	decided	mopping	rubbing	wedding
wagging	fitted	voted	confused	completed

He stopped clapping as the ball hit the netting.

Short vowel verbs need protection from Magic ed and Magic ing

clap	beg	chip	nod	drum
clapped	begged	chipped	nodded	drummed
clapping	begging	chipping	nodding	drumming

clip	flop	prod	stop*	top*
dip	jog	rob	strap	trim
drip	net	rub	strip	trip*
drop	pad	scan	tag	trot
fit	peg	skip*	tan	wag*
flag	pin	slip	tap	wrap

* High frequency words

BEWARE!

Look out for the following issues which commonly arise after studying double consonants.

1 Magic sparks already out of reach
As soon as we ask children to focus on double consonants there is a risk that they will start doubling consonants everywhere. Point out that there is no need to double up when two consonants are already in the way, e.g. e**nd**ed, re**st**ing, thi**nk**ing. The sparks from the Magic Ending will never reach the vowel.

2 Do not protect Vowel Men
There is also a risk that the magic sparks will be blocked by mistake. Play-act some *long vowel* words to make it clear that hearing a Vowel Name in a word is a clear indication *not* to double the consonant. Otherwise the Vowel Man will disappear, whether we like it or not! Act out the result: **scraped** would become **scrapped**, **filed** would become **filled**, **sloping** would become **slopping**.

scraped my knee

scrapped my knee

☆ Go over *Programme Two Copymaster* 68 in detail with any children who need more help in understanding when to double the consonant and equally important when not to.

3 Exception: Not cc but ck
The hard **c** is seldom doubled. Instead of calling in Clever Cat's country cousin to form **cc**, the King helps Clever Cat to keep the short vowel safely two letters away from any Magic Ending that might be added. So the short vowel is already protected, e.g. **cracked**, **cracking**, **picked**, **picking**.

Magic en and Magic est

Objectives

- To know that the suffixes **-en** and **-est** can function as Magic Endings (as in **ēven** and **lātest**).
- To recognise and spell words containing **-en** and **-est**.

What you need

- *Programme Two Picture Code Cards:* **en** (53), **est** (57), Magic **e** (9)
- *Programme One Picture Code Cards*
- *Programme Two Copymaster:* 65
- *Programme Two Word Bank Copymaster:* 33

The following story introduces two more Magic Endings, **en** and **est**. Both are cases where a Silent Magic **e** ceases to be silent, taking on Eddy Elephant's sound instead as it becomes part of a new suffix.

The -en and -est endings shoot magic sparks

We know that Mr E has taught Eddy Elephant to shoot the magic sparks for him in Magic ***ed****. Eddy has learnt to aim the wand just right, so that the magic sparks jump back over exactly one letter to make a Vowel Man appear and say his name. Now Mr E has asked Eddy Elephant to make another Magic Ending with Naughty Nick. This new ending is just as powerful as a Silent Magic* ***e****. It can even make Mr E himself appear and say his name in one or two words.*

even Steven

Mr E, in turn, is so pleased and proud of his pet elephant that he has put him in charge of a third Elephant Ending: Magic ***est****. All three Elephant Endings – Magic* ***ed****, Magic* ***en*** *and Magic* ***est*** *– give the Vowel Men many more chances to appear in words and say their names.*

- Write these sentences on the board and ask the children to help with picture coding **en** and **est**.

  Even Steven likes apples when they ripen.

  I think my mum is the bravest, finest, wisest person in the world.

  Eddy is the tamest and wisest elephant.

- Live spell or dictate: **eve** → **even** → **wide** → **widen** → **frozen** → **late** → **latest** → **white** → **whitest**.
- Use *Programme Two Copymaster* 65 for further practice.

Even Steven likes apples when they ripen.

☆ Introduce *Word Bank Copymaster* 33. Write on the board some words ending with Magic **en** and **est**. The children choose the four which they judge to be most useful to add to the first column in their Word Banks. Warn them to expect a few exceptions, e.g. **Steven** but **seven** and **eleven**. They should wait before adding examples in the second column until you have explained about blocking Magic Endings.

☆ To show that the Magic **e** has now become part of a new Magic Ending, write some Magic **e** words from the word box on the board. Ask one child to pretend to be the teacher and cover the final **e** with either the **en** or **est** *Picture Code Card*. He or she can then choose another child to try and read the new word. The other children in the group can help if necessary.

awaken

Magic en makes Vowel Men appear

awaken	mistaken	stolen
broken*	open*	taken*
enliven	outspoken	token
even*	raven	widen
frozen	ripen	whiten
laden	shaken	woven
liken	siren	

Magic est makes Vowel Men appear

bravest	latest*	safest
closest	nicest	tamest
finest	palest	widest
lamest	ripest	wisest

Adding Magic en and Magic est

en	est
broke* ➜ broken*	cute ➜ cutest
froze ➜ frozen	late* ➜ latest*
mistake ➜ mistaken	nice* ➜ nicest
wide* ➜ widen	ripe ➜ ripest

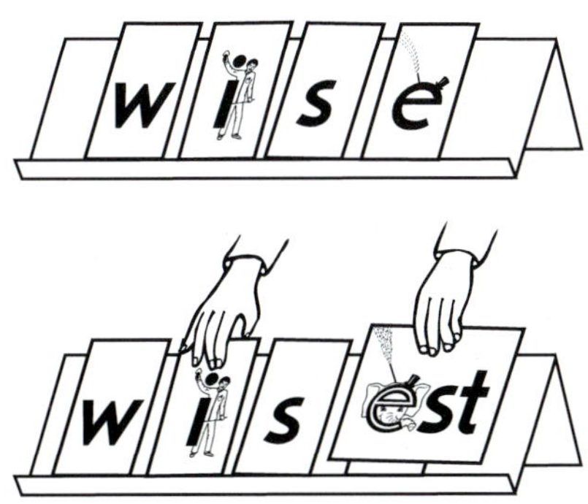

* High frequency words

Eddy is the tamest and wisest elephant.

Blocking Magic en and Magic est

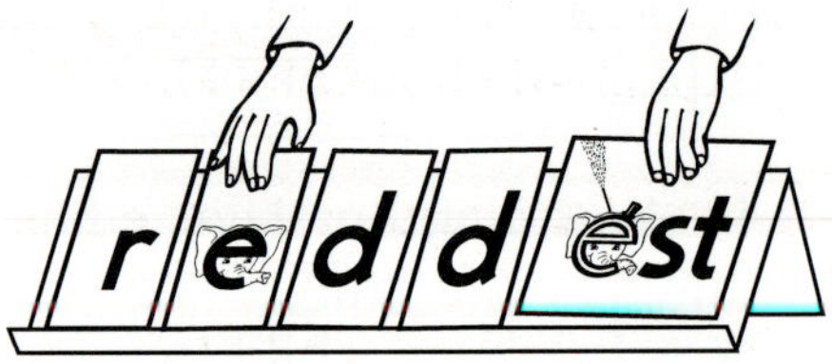

As the children found with Magic **ed** and Magic **ing**, in words with short vowels the vowel needs protection before Magic **en** and Magic **est**. Once again it's a case of Best Friend to the Rescue! (See the story explanation on page 187.)

- Write these sentences on the board and ask the children to help with the picture coding of the vowels, double consonants and Magic Endings.

  Write down all the words written on that note.

  With the sudden cold weather we put on mittens.

- Choose any of the words below for Live Spelling. The children raise their arms to block the wand's sparks and to emphasise that now there are *two* consonants in the way to protect the short vowel.

- Use *Programme Two Word Bank Copymaster* 33 (second column), as collecting places for examples of Magic **en** and **est** being blocked by Best Friends to the Rescue.

* High frequency words

Magic en's sparks are blocked

bitten	happen*	madden	rotten	sudden*
fatten	hidden	mitten	sadden	sullen
forbidden	kitten*	pollen	smitten	trodden
forgotten	lessen	redden	stiffen	written*

Magic est's sparks are blocked

biggest*	fattest	flattest	reddest	thinnest
dimmest	fittest	maddest	slimmest	wettest

Which to use: est or ist?

est = the most
ist = one who

We all tend to pronounce **est** and **ist** alike, e.g. **smartest** and **artist**, so children can easily confuse the spellings. Explain that Magic **est** is used to spell words which mean 'the most' (e.g. the most hot, the most smart).

The **ist** ending, on the other hand, is used to describe a person who does a particular thing, (e.g. art**ist**, chem**ist**, dent**ist**, flor**ist**, pian**ist**, novel**ist**, motor**ist**). So if children stop to think about the meaning of the word, it will help them to spell it correctly.

Sometimes Magic: er

Objectives

- ☆ To know that final **er** can function as a Magic Ending.
- ☆ To recognise and spell words containing **er** as a Magic Ending.

What you need

- ☆ *Programme Two Picture Code Cards:* **Magic er** (55)
- ☆ *Programme Two Copymaster:* 66
- ☆ *Programme Two Word Bank Copymaster:* 34

Remind the children first of the story of Ernest Er, the elephant stealer (see page 132).

The er ending can shoot magic sparks

*When **Er**nest **Er** is feeling especially daring, instead of stealing an **e**lephant he steals a Magic **e**. As he grabs the Magic **e** he runs off so fast that he doesn't even notice that he has left the top hat and wand in place. So the magic sparks keep on firing away while **Er**nest **Er** says "**er**!". He thinks he is very clev**er**, but he nev**er** discov**er**s that the magic sparks are still getting ov**er**. So he can't be that clev**er**, can he?! But, **you** can be clever!*

*If you can't read a word with **Er**nest **Er** in it, check the previous vowel. **Er**nest **Er** may have stolen a Magic **e** and let the sparks get ov**er** to make a Vowel Man appear and say his name.*

☆ Write these sentences on the board and ask the children to help with picture coding Magic **er.**

It is safer to rescue the Magic **e** later.

I made a paper tiger and a paper skyscraper.

I need a piece of paper to stick on this parking meter.

☆ Live spell or dictate: **paper** ➜ **dive** ➜ **diver** ➜ **driver** ➜ **over** ➜ **clove** ➜ **clover** ➜ **computer**.

* High frequency words

Words containing Magic er

				Exceptions
admirer	diver	maker	safer	clever
baker	driver	meter	skyscraper	cover
braver	glider	miner	striker	ever
cater	grocer	nicer	tiger	hover
clover	invader	October	user	liver
composer	joker	over*	voter	proper
computer	later*	paper*	whiter	river*
consumer	lifesaver	producer	wiper	
crater	liner	ruler	writer	

It is safer to rescue the Magic e later.

Best Friends to the Rescue

*Since Ernest Er steals Magic **e**'s so often, if the vowel before Magic **er** is short, it will need to be protected so that it is not replaced by a Vowel Man. Once again, a Best Friend must come to the rescue (double the consonant)!*

Give the children some practice in picture coding the magic sparks blocked, in words like **supper** and **summer**. Explore the effect of removing the second consonant so that the magic sparks can and do reach the previous vowel. **Supper** becomes **super** and **summer** would have to be pronounced as in **consumer**.

☆ Write these sentences on the board and ask the children to help with picture coding the **double consonants** and Magic **er**.

This robber should know better.

Eating so much butter with supper makes you fatter!

☆ Introduce *Word Bank Copymaster* 34. Write Magic **er** words on the board for children to choose from and to add to their Word Banks. They can then look for examples in their books of words where Magic **er** is blocked by double consonants and add them to their Word Banks.

Magic er's sparks are blocked

banner	differ	matter	summer*
better*	fatter	mutter	supper
bitter	flatter	otter	slimmer
butter*	flipper	pepper	slipper
clatter	flutter	planner	soccer
clutter	glimmer	redder	splutter
copper	gutter	robber	stagger
cutter	hotter	rubber*	thinner
dagger	letter*	runner	trigger
dimmer	litter	scatter	twitter
dinner*	madder	shutter	upper
dipper	manners	suffer	wetter

* High frequency words

References
For the introduction to double consonants, see p185.

This robber should know better.

Sometimes Magic: y

Objectives

- To know that a final **y** sounding like long **ē** (as in **tiny** and **hurry**) can be a Magic Ending.
- To recognise and spell words ending with a Magic **y**.

What you need

- *Programme Two Picture Code Cards:* **y** (16)
- *Programme One Picture Code Cards*
- *Programme Two Copymaster:* 66
- *Programme Two Word Bank Copymaster:* 34

There is no way to predict exactly when this final **y** will 'shoot the magic sparks', i.e. make the preceding vowel say its name. It is worth knowing, however, that it happens quite often. The evidence lies not only in words like **bony**, **tiny**, but also in the many words where double consonants are needed to protect short vowels from Magic **y**'s sparks, e.g. **bonny**, **tinny**. Once again a Best Friend has come to the rescue. For the story explaining the function of double consonants before Magic Endings, see page 187.

Yellow Yo-yo Man can shoot magic sparks for Mr E

The Yo-yo Man is very glad to work for Mr E, saying 'ē' for him at the ends of many words. But he is especially proud when the magician asks him to shoot magic sparks, as well as saying Mr E's name for him. In fact, he manages the magic sparks so well that roughly half of the times he appears in short words for Mr E, he shoots the sparks for Mr E.

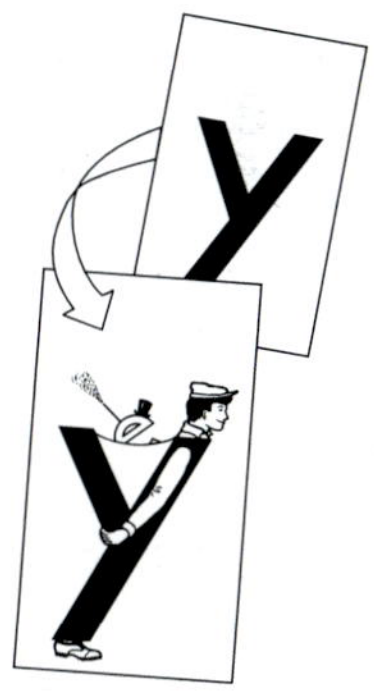

- Write these sentences on the board and ask the children to help with picture coding **y**'s magic sparks reaching the previous vowel.

  Yo-yo Man has a tiny **e** and shiny sparks.
  Some shady parts of the road are still icy.
  The rosy cheeked baby looked cosy in its soft blanket.

- Live spell or dictate: **baby** ➜ **rub** ➜ **ruby** ➜ **lad** ➜ **lady** ➜ **bony** ➜ **pony** ➜ **stony** ➜ **shin** ➜ **shiny**.
- Use *Programme Two Copymaster* 66 (lower half) for further practice.
- Introduce *Word Bank Copymaster* 34. Ask the children to look for short words ending in Magic **y** in their books. Some children may need help in analysing the sound value of the vowel to ensure they only enter correct examples in the first column of their Word Banks. Ask the children to save any examples they find of the Yo-yo Man's sparks being blocked until you have looked together at the sentences on page 196.

Yo-yo Man has a tiny e and shiny sparks.

- Write these sentences on the board and ask the children to help with picture coding **y**'s magic sparks blocked to protect the short vowel when he is carrying a Magic **e**.

I like slippy, sloppy cherry jelly!

What nice fluffy ears that bunny has.

It gets very stuffy and muggy, if it's hot and sunny.

- Use the second column of *Word Bank Copymaster* 34 for entering words with Magic **y**'s sparks blocked and *Programme Two Copymaster* 66 for further practice.
- Write on the board a number of the final **y** words with double consonants from the word box on the right. Ask the children to make up stories about them, e.g. The frizzy puppy, The fluffy bunny, A silly hobby, Yummy cherry jelly, A sunny day, Sorry I was silly, Billy is funny.

Words ending in Magic y

baby*
bony
cosy
crazy
dozy
duty
gravy
hazy
holy
icy
ivy
lady*
lazy

navy
pony*
rosy
ruby
shady
shaky
shiny
slimy
stony
tidy
tiny
wavy

Children's names

Tony
Tracy

Challenge words

puny
wily

See page172-173 for other words ending in **y**.

* High frequency words

Magic y's sparks blocked

baggy
berry
bunny
carry*
cherry
Daddy*
dizzy
flabby
floppy
fluffy
foggy
frizzy
funny*
fuzzy
giddy
hobby
hurry*
jelly*
jolly
marry*
merry*
muddy
Mummy*
nutty
penny

poppy
puppy*
silly
sloppy
sorry
spotty
stuffy
sunny
witty

Children's names

Holly
Jenny
Sally
Tommy

Challenge words

groggy
muggy
shabby
soggy

References
p199 for **-al** as a word ending.

I like slippy, sloppy cherry jelly!

le (as in table)
al (as in medical)

Objectives

- To know that the letters **l** and **e** can combine to make the 'ul' sound (**le** as in **table**) and that this is a Magic Ending.
- To recognise and spell words ending in **le**.
- To recognise and spell words ending in **al**.

What you need

- *Programme Two Picture Code Cards:* **le** (32)
- *Programme One Picture Code Cards*
- *Programme Two Copymaster:* 72
- *Programme Two Word Bank Copymaster:* 37
- *Programme Two Songs Cassette*

Since **l** and **e** together are usually pronounced 'le' as in **letter**, children are often surprised that the same two letters make an 'ul' sound at the end of words. Make sure that the children who spell by ear identify this final 'ul' sound so they can avoid endlessly spelling it **ul** or **el**. Explain that, unless the word ends in **ful**, their safest choice is the **le** spelling, since over 270 useful words end in **le**.

The second important point about **le** is that it is a Magic Ending! However, this new Magic Ending is a little bit different, and is called Candle Magic (stress the **le** sound) to point out that difference.

Candle Magic with e for a handle

Candle Magic works like this. First of all yellow sparks shoot up from Magic ***e*** *and transform Lucy Lamp Lady into a big, magic cand****le*** *– quite a trick in itself! The* ***e****'s magic sparks then light the cand****le*** *so that the cand****le*** *has more magic than Magic* ***e*** *itself. The* ***e*** *simply becomes the candlestick hand****le****. If there is a single vowel within firing range, the magic cand****le*** *will shoot sparks up and over one letter, just as the jumping yellow sparks usually do, but these sparks always jump back from the top of the cand****le*** *instead of from the Magic* ***e****. That is why this ending is called 'Cand****le*** *Magic'.*

- Listen to and sing the Candle Magic song on the *Programme Two Songs Cassette.*
- Write these sentences on the board and ask the children to help with picture coding single **l** and **le**. Make sure they count back one letter from the top of the **l**.

  The lovely candle is on the table.

  'If you look carefully in the stable, you will be able to see the baby in the cradle,' said the King.

- Live spell: **map → maple, bug → bugle, is → isle, stab → stable**. Two children hold the Magic **le** card and the **e** child holds a longer wand than usual and shoots the sparks. They make a short vowel disappear and a Vowel Man appear in its place.

The lovely candle is on the table.

✩ Use *Programme Two Copymaster* 72 for further practice.

✩ Introduce *Word Bank Copymaster* 37. Write a selection of words ending with Magic **le** on the board and ask the children to choose the ones they judge to be most useful to write in their Word Banks.

Words ending in Magic le

able*	cable	idle	noble	table*
bible	cradle	isle	rifle	title
bridle	disciple	ladle	stable	trifle
bugle	fable	maple	stifle	

* High frequency words

Candle Magic blocked by two consonants

There are relatively few words where Candle Magic **le** causes a preceding vowel to be long. However, proof that **le** is a Magic Ending does turn up in the large number of words which contain double consonants to protect short vowels from the cand**le**'s magic sparks. Otherwise, words like **little** would become 'litle' as in **title**, and words like **paddle** and **saddle** would have to rhyme with **ladle**. Encourage children to pronounce any mistakes just as their spelling indicates (e.g, drop the 'botle', go into the 'midle') so that they can learn from their mistakes in a fun way and then add the Best Friend. (See story on page 197.)

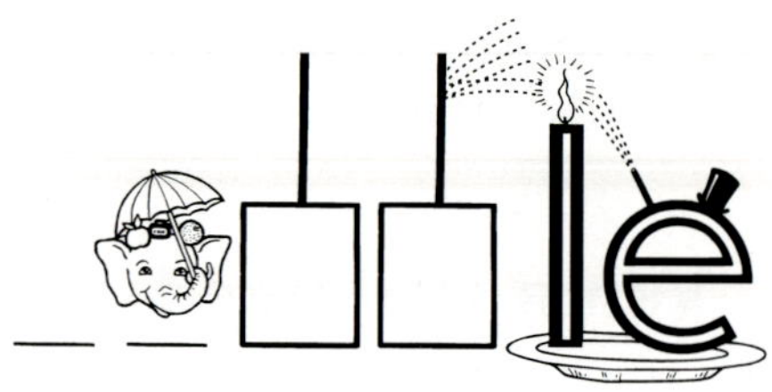

✩ Write these sentences on the board and ask the children to help with picture coding the short vowels, double consonants and Candle Magic.

This little pony wants to nibble my apple.

I like to cuddle the baby except when she dribbles.

Don't wobble while you paddle the canoe.

* High frequency words

Magic le's sparks are blocked to protect the short vowel

apple*	dazzle	little*	nuzzle	ripple	squabble
babble	dribble	meddle	paddle	ruffle	struggle
battle	drizzle	middle*	pebble	scribble	throttle
bottle	giggle	muddle	puddle	scuffle	tussle
brittle	guzzle	muzzle	puzzle	settle	wiggle
bubble	huddle	nettle	quibble	shuffle	wobble
cattle	juggle	nibble	rattle	sizzle	wriggle
cuddle	kettle	nobble	riddle	smuggle	

This little pony wants to nibble my apple.

al saying 'ul' (as in medical)

Most words which end with a final 'ul' sound are spelt **le** or end with **ful** (see page 156). The two other possibilities are **al** and **el**. Many of the words ending with **al** are predictable, once children know that **al** means 'to do with'. The irregular 'uh' sound coming from the **a** can be picture coded as a Parachuted Apple or with a wiggly line.

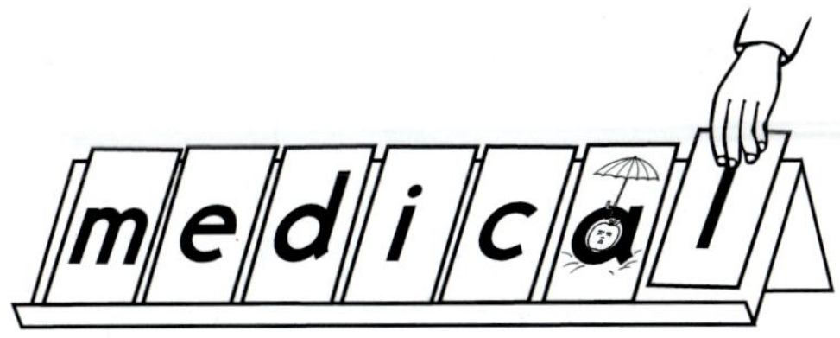

to do with medicine

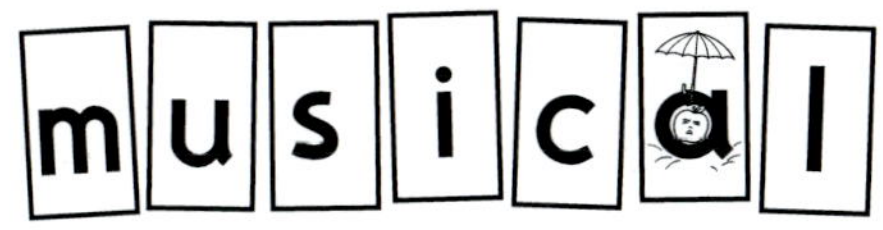

to do with music

☆ Use *Programme Two Copymaster* 73 and *Word Bank Copymaster* 37 for further practice with the **al** ending.

hospital

national

Words ending in al

accidental	horizontal	postal
chemical	hospital*	removal
classical	liberal	rental
continental	logical	reversal
critical	magical	sensational
emotional	medical	structural
experimental	musical	survival
external	national	universal
factual	natural	
historical	personal	

* High frequency word

el saying 'ul' (as in angel)

There are about 18 common words ending in **el** sounding like 'ul'. They are best learnt as they are needed. The children might enjoy trying to group them into phrases or sentences (e.g. What a marv**el** to trav**el** through the Chann**el** Tunn**el** on a cam**el**) and then illustrate them. The picture coding for **e** is a wiggly line (see right).

angel

travel

Words ending in el

angel	label	satchel
barrel	marvel	shovel
camel	model	squirrel
channel	novel	towel
chapel	parcel*	travel
kennel	quarrel	tunnel

* High frequency word

References
For help with **-le**/**-ly** confusions, see p156.

ce, ci, cy

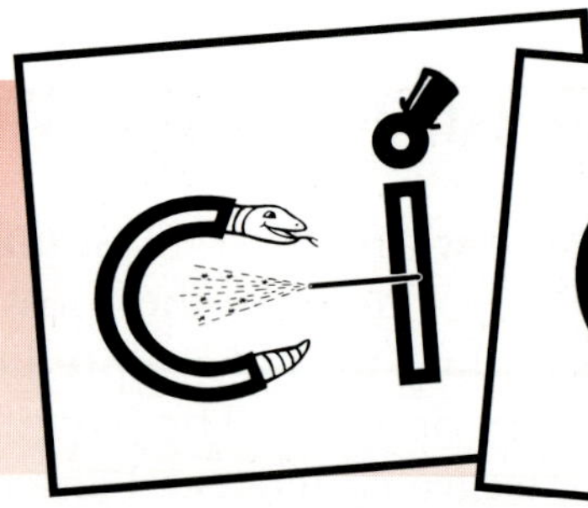

Objectives

- To know that the letter **c** changes from its hard sound to its soft sound beside **e**, **i** or **y** (as in **nice**, **city** and **fancy**).
- To recognise and spell words containing **ce**, **ci** and **cy**.

What you need

- *Programme Two Picture Code Cards:* **ce** (19), **ci** (20), **cy** (21).
- *Programme One Picture Code Cards*
- *Programme Two Copymasters:* 74-75
- *Programme Two Word Bank Copymaster:* 38

Preparation

- **Cat or snake?** Have ready some different coloured white board markers or coloured chalks.

Most children know that **c** sometimes sounds like **s**. However, to read new words, they also need to know exactly *when* this is so. In fact, the 'soft' sound is entirely predictable, it is the next letter in the word which provides the clue. The Letterland story which explains the soft **c** before **e**, **i** and **y** is similar in each case: that the **e**, **i** or **y** shoots back *blue* magic sparks to change Clever Cat into a little hissing snake. In picture coding, the children confirm the signalling power by drawing a top hat on the **e** or **i**, and going right between the **c** and subsequent letter to draw the wand and blue sparks shooting into **c**'s open side (Blue Magic can only affect the letter behind it.) The only other letter affected by Blue Magic is **g**, see page 204.

Introducing soft c in ce

Clever Cat turns into a hissing snake beside e

*Cats and snakes don't usually like each other – but the Hairy Hat Man has both a **c**at and a **s**nake for pets (**ch** and **sh**) and they don't always get on with each other. How can he help them to get on better? Mr E has a bright idea. "It's eeeasy," he says. "If I turn Clever Cat into a snake they can enjoy playing together!" So he makes a new kind of silent Magic **e**.*

*The **e**'s sparks are blue. They aren't powerful enough to jump back over one letter to make a Vowel Man appear, like the jumping yellow sparks. The blue sparks are only strong enough to change Clever Cat into a snake if she is right next to Blue Magic **e**. Then hey presto! Beside the **e**, she becomes a little blue snake and Clever Cat and Sammy Snake can have a fine time both hissing in words – until the magic wears off. Then Clever Cat becomes a **c**at again and goes back to making her little 'c...' sound in words, as usual.*

- Write these sentences on the board and ask the children to help with picture coding **c**, **s** and **ce**.

  Can you spot the sparks once or twice?

  Carly wrote a sentence about a race in a spaceship.

- Live spell or dictate: **ace** → **face** → **dance** → **cancel** → **price**.

Can you spot the sparks once or twice?

Words containing ce

absence
accept
ace
advice
ambulance
balance
cancel
celery
cement
centipede
central
century
cereal
certain
certificate
chance
choice
concern
convince
dance*
dice
difference
eccentric
entrance

evidence
excellence
except*
exception
face*
fence*
force
glance
grace
grocer
ice
importance
lace
lice
mince
nice*
niece
office*
once*
pace
peace
pence*
piece*
place*

price
prince*
princess*
process
race*
recent
rice
romance
scene
scent
sentence
since*
slice
spice
surface
terrace
trace
twice
voice

In words with **cc** + **e**, the second **c** is soft.

Children's names

Alice
Laurence

Challenge words

admittance
allowance
ancestor
cease
ceremony
conceal

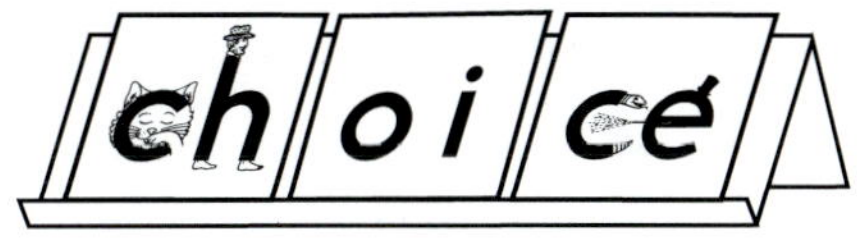

conceal
excellence
peace
process

* High frequency words

Introducing soft c in ci

Clever Cat turns into a hissing snake before i

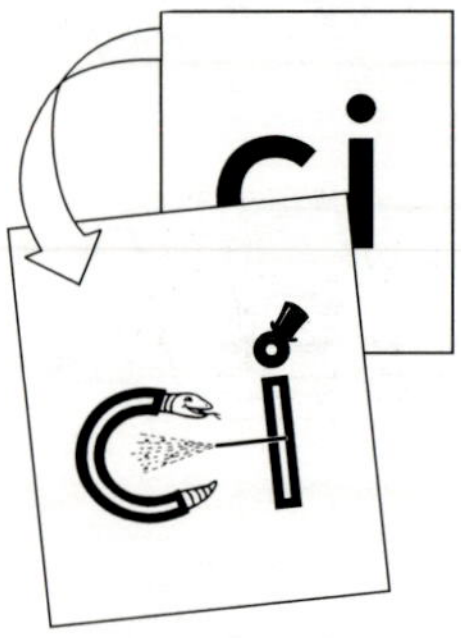

*Clever Cat loves to hiss like Sammy – but Mr E is a very busy man, so he looks for another letter he can trust to shoot Blue Magic for him. He chooses **i**. Mr E just leaves his top hat on the **i**-dot and a spare wand to shoot the blue sparks. Hey presto! Once again Clever Cat becomes a snake so she can hiss just like Sammy.*

scissors

circus

☆ Write these sentences on the board and ask the children to help with picture coding hard **c** and **ci**.

Come to the exciting circus in the city.

Eric decided to go by car to the Science Museum.

☆ Live spell or dictate: **decide** → **pencil** → **city** → **electricity**.

Words containing ci

accident	city*	electricity	scissors
acid	civil	fascinate	society
calcium	civilisation	incident	specific
capacity	concise	medicine	
Cinderella	council	Pacific	
circle	criticise	pencil*	**Exception:** when **ci** sounds like **sh**, as in **special**.
circus	decide*	precise	
citizen	decimal*	scientist	

* High frequency words

Come to the exciting circus in the city.

Introducing soft c in cy

Clever Cat turns into a hissing snake before y

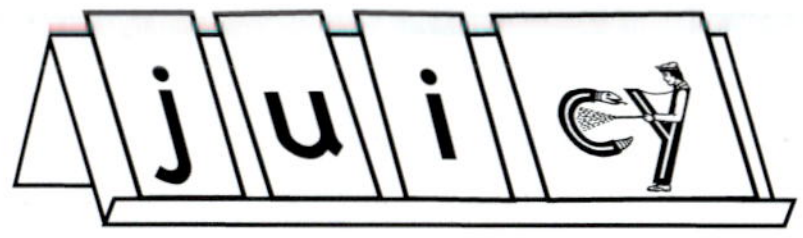

The only other letter which Mr E trusts to handle Blue Magic for him is the Yo-yo Man. So the only other time Clever Cat has a chance to be transformed into a hissing snake is when she is next to the Yo-yo Man. Then once again she can hiss just like Sammy Snake.

- Write these sentences on the board and ask the children to help with picture coding hard **c** and **cy**.

  Lucy likes spicy curries.
  Can you cycle in Cyprus?

- Live spell: **fancy** ➜ **lacy** ➜ **icy** ➜ **bicycle**.

- Use *Programme Two Copymasters* 74-75 for further practice.

- Introduce *Word Bank Copymaster* 38. Ask the children to look for words containing **ce**, **ci** and **cy** in their books and to add them to their Word Banks in the appropriate places.

- Choose several **ce**, **ci**, **cy** words which are outside the children's sight vocabulary. Write them large on the board or on paper. Explain that you do not want anyone to try to read the words, only to picture code them. Then ask "cat or snake?" at each **c**. They should spot each **c**, **ce**, **ci** or **cy** sequence, answer "cat" or "snake" and use a light blue felt pen to overwrite both letters, add a top hat, wand and sparks. Let them go back and work out the words, confident that they know exactly how to pronounce each **c**. Later they can try the same group of words without picture coding support. It only takes a few exercises like this to help most children be able to predict every hard or soft **c** in virtually any word.

Words containing cy

agency	cypress	lacy	**Children's names**
bicycle	decency	pharmacy	Lucy
currency	delicacy	privacy	Nancy
cyclone	emergency	secrecy	
cygnet	encyclopedia	tendency	
cylinder	fancy	urgency	
cymbal	frequency	vacancy	

Lucy likes spicy curries.

ge, gi, gy and dge

Objectives

- To know that the letter **g** will make its soft 'g' sound in the **ge**, **gi** and **gy** spelling patterns (as in **gentle**, **ginger** and **gym**).
- To recognise and spell words containing **ge**, **gi** and **gy**.
- To know that **d** before **ge** will be silent (as in **bridge**).

What you need

- *Programme Two Picture Code Cards:* **ge** (25), **gi** (27), **gy** (28), **silent d** (8)
- *Programme One Picture Code Cards*
- *Programme Two Copymasters:* 76-78
- *Programme Two Word Bank Copymasters:* 39-40
- *Programme Two Songs Cassette*

The children have met Golden Girl and Golden Granny (see page 186). Both characters symbolise the hard **g** sound. Golden Girl's friend Gentle Ginger symbolises **g**'s soft sound. The signal for Gentle Ginger to appear and make this soft sound is the same as for soft **c**: when the next letter is an **e**, **i** or **y**.

Gentle Ginger is just as athletic as Jumping Jim, whose sound is identical to hers. But she is far less shy. She loves people watching her as she practises her gymnastic tricks in words which is why she turns up in more words than Jumping Jim.

You may choose to teach only the story for **ge** to start with, as it includes the majority of soft **g** words. Alternatively, your class may be ready to learn **ge**, **gi** and **gy** together.

Introducing soft g in ge

Gentle Ginger the gymnast says 'g...' before e

*Golden Girl always says that her Granny is her best friend, but she has a special friend at school, too. She is **Ge**ntle **Gi**nger, the **gy**mnast. Golden Girl admires **Ge**ntle **Gi**nger because **Gi**nger is so good at **gy**mnastics. Somersaults, cartwheels, balancing acts – she can do them all! Golden Girl thinks everyone should notice **Ge**ntle **Gi**nger's **gy**mnastic tricks in words, so she asks Mr E if he could use some of his new Blue Magic **e**'s to light her up with sparkling blue light as she does her somersaults. "**Eee**asily!" cries Mr E.*

__Ge__ntle __Gi__nger is so pleased to be in the limelight that she does her best somersaults every time she is next to a Blue Magic __e__. She also starts to say her name like this, 'ge…' for '__Ge__ntle Gin__ge__r'.

- Write these sentences on the board and ask the children to help with picture coding **ge**.

Gentle Ginger's somersaults are gorgeous.
Danger! Stop! Help needed urgently!
All passengers must change trains here.

Gentle Ginger's somersaults are gorgeous.

Words containing ge

age	gems	legend	surge	**Children's names**
agent	general	messenger	surgeon	Angela
angel	generous	orange*	tangerine	George
cage*	genie	outrageous	twinge	
change	genius	page	urge	**Countries**
charge	gentle	passenger	vegetables*	Argentina
courageous	gentlemen	pigeon	verge	Germany
danger	germs	plunge		
detergent	ginger	range		
digest	gorge	revenge		
dungeon	hinge	sponge		
emerge	huge	stage		
energetic	indulge	strange		
fringe	large*	suggest		

Exceptions

These include **get**, **geese**, **target**, **tiger**, **together** and some words with **gg:** **biggest**, **wagged**, and **ng: longer**, **finger**.

* High frequency words

Introducing silent d before ge

Silent Duck beside Gentle Ginger

*Normally when you see Dippy Duck in a word you will hear her making her usual little 'd...' sound. But not when the next letters are **Gentle Ginger** and a Blue Magic **e**! Then she is too dazzled by **Gentle Ginger's gymnastics** to speak!*

☆ Write these sentences on the board and ask the children to help with picture coding **dge**.

"Let's give Ginger a badge," said the judge.

Ed sat on the edge of the bridge.

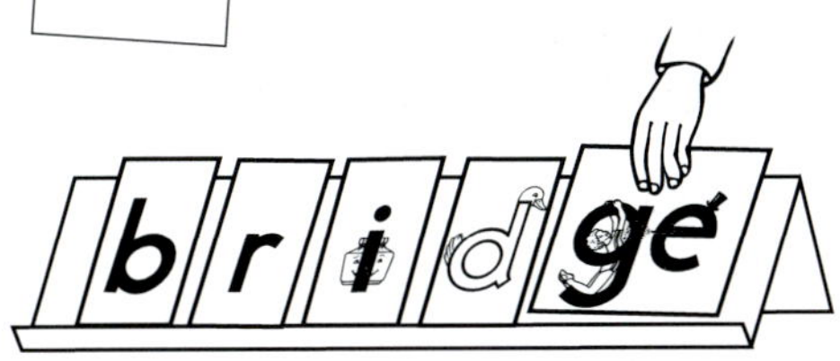

Words containing dge

–adge	–edge	–idge		–odge	–udge
badge	edge	abridge	midge	dislodge	budge
badger	hedge*	bridge*	partridge	dodge	fudge
cadge	knowledge	cartridge	porridge	lodge	judge
gadget	sledge	fridge		stodge	smudge

* High frequency words

"Let's give Ginger a badge," said the judge.

Sound alikes: -idge and -age

Only nine words end in **i-d-g-e**. They all contain the word **ridge** except for the last two: **abridge**, **bridge**, **cartridge**, **fridge**, **partridge**, **porridge**, **ridge**, **midge**, **midget**. There are, however, many **a-g-e** words. Longer **a-g-e** and *all* **i-d-g-e** words are pronounced 'ige'. Since **bridge** is the only frequently used word ending in **-idge**, a rough generalisation for all other 'ige' words is: unless the word is **bridge**, spell it **a-g-e**.

bridge

bandage

Words ending in -age

advantage	encourage	luggage	percentage	usage	**Note:** The only word actually spelt as it sounds is **vestige**.
average	haulage	manage	postage	vicarage	
bandage	heritage	marriage	salvage	voltage	
courage	image	mileage	savage	voyage	
disadvantage	language	mortgage	shortage		
drainage	leakage	package	storage		

* High frequency words

Double consonants before seven -age words

Strangely, there are seven words in which the short vowels before **-age** need protecting. They can be learnt in these two sentences:

I saw his luggage in the Baggage Room passage, so I left him this message.

Come and eat cabbage at our cottage in the village.

Introducing soft g in gi

Gentle Ginger says 'g…' for Ginger before i

*When Mr E is too busy elsewhere to shoot Blue Magic Sparks to light up **Ge**ntle **Gi**nger the **Gy**mnast, he **ge**nerously gives the job to **i**. So the blue sparks shoot straight from **i** to **Gi**nger to light her up. Once again **Ge**ntle **Gi**nger is so pleased that she starts to say her name, 'gi…' for **Gi**nger.*

☆ Write these sentences on the board and ask the children to help with picture coding **gi**.

See Ginger in blue magic light!

Do giraffes live in that grassy region?

Can you imagine a giant as gigantic as a skyscraper?

gigantic

engine

See Ginger in blue magic light!

Words containing gi

			Also **ge** words on p205 which drop **e** before **ing**	Exceptions	
agitate	ginger	regiment	arranging	begging	girl*
engine	giraffe	region	bulging	begin*	giggle
engineer	imagine	register	engaging	beginning*	jogging
fragile	logical	religion	judging	gift	
geologist	magic*	surgical		give*	
giant	margin	tragic		giving*	
gigantic	original	Virginia			

* High frequency words

Introducing soft g in gy

Gentle Ginger says 'g...' for Ginger before y

*In some words Mr E generously gives the Yo-yo Man some of his Blue Magic too. The Yo-yo Man is pleased to do the job of lighting up **Gi**nger's **gy**mnastics for him. Then **Gi**nger smiles and says 'gy...' for **gy**mnast.*

- Listen to and sing the Gentle Ginger song on the *Programme Two Songs Cassette.*
- Write these sentences on the board and ask the children to help with picture coding **gy**.

  I bought my spongy gym shoes in Egypt.

  The gymnasts were full of energy.

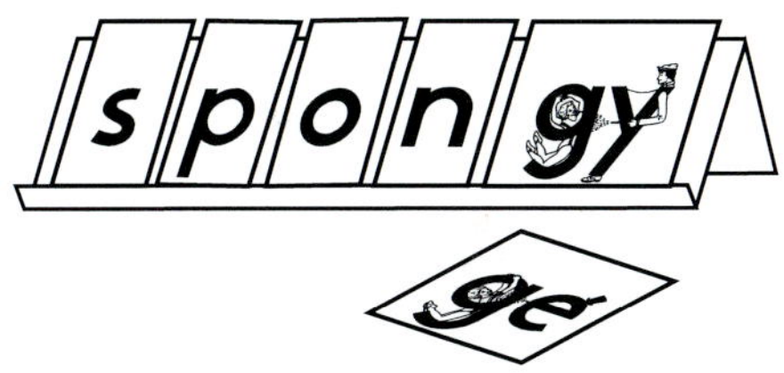

- Live spell or dictate: **page** ➜ **hedge** ➜ **magic** ➜ **gentle** ➜ **ginger** ➜ **edge** ➜ **edgy** ➜ **sponge** ➜ **spongy**.
- Use *Programme Two Copymasters* 76-78 for further practice.
- Introduce *Word Bank Copymasters* 39-40. Ask the children to look for words containing **ge**, **dge**, **gi** and **gy** in their books.

- Ask the children to look through newspapers and magazines for words containing these spelling patterns and cut them out. They then stick them on to some paper to make a **ge**, **dge**, **gi**, **gy** word montage.

Words containing gy

allergy	edgy	gymnastics	stodgy
biology	energy	ideology	strategy
clergy	gymkhana	spongy	zoology

I bought my spongy gym shoes in Egypt.

kn (as in knee)

Objectives

- To know that when the letters **k** and **n** are together, the **k** becomes a silent letter.
- To recognise and spell words containing **kn**.

What you need

- *Programme Two Picture Code Cards:* **kn** (31)
- *Programme One Picture Code Cards*
- *Programme Two Copymaster:* 79
- *Programme Two Word Bank Copymaster:* 41
- *Programme Two Songs Cassette*

Only 36 high frequency words begin with **k**. Nearly half of these words begin with silent **kn**, which is very confusing since they sound as though they begin with **n**. The most important **kn** words to read and spell correctly are **know**, **knows**, and **knew** (easily confused with **no**, **nose**, and **new**). In Letterland the confusion is attributed to Naughty Nick!

Kicking King never kicks Nick

*Kicking King loves kicking but he never kicks when he is next to Nick in a word. This is because Naughty Nick has a **kn**ack of getting in his way so that he can't **k**ick. Instead he frowns angrily and points silently at Nick for being such a **n**uisance.*

- Listen to and sing the Kicking King and Naughty Nick song on the *Programme Two Songs Cassette.*
- Write these sentences on the board and ask the children to help with picture coding **kn**.

  I know he has a knack of being a nuisance.

  I knelt on my knees looking for my necklace.

  They knew all about King Arthur and his knights.

  Do you know how to knit?

- Live spell or dictate: **no** ➜ **know** ➜ **nose** ➜ **knows** ➜ **new** ➜ **knew** ➜ **knee** ➜ **kneel**. When you say each word, put it into a sentence to give it a context and make the meaning clear.

I know he has a knack of being a nuisance.

☆ Ask a group of children to work together to make up between five and ten sentences based on **kn** words. The more **kn** words in each sentence the better. Then play an oral game where each child has a turn reading out the same sentence, but pronouncing each **k** as though it was not a silent letter, e.g.

I know a girl who knows your mother and knew your grandmother.

Did you know his address was unknown?

☆ Use *Programme Two Copymaster* 79 for further practice.

☆ Introduce *Word Bank Copymaster* 41. Write a selection of **kn** words on the board and ask the children to select those which they consider most useful to add to their Word Banks.

Words containing kn

knack	knives
knapsack	knob
knee	knock
kneel	knock-kneed
knelt	knot
knew*	know*
knickers	knowledge
knick-knack	known*
knight	knows*
knife*	knuckle
knit	unknown

* High frequency words

wr (as in write)

Objectives

- To know that the letters **w** and **r** combine to make the 'r' sound because the **w** becomes silent (as in **write**).
- To recognise and spell words containing **wr**.

What you need

- *Programme Two Picture Code Cards*: **wr** (85)
- *Programme Two Copymaster*: 79
- *Programme Two Word Bank Copymaster*: 41

Preparation

- **Wr wriggly worm words** Draw and cut out some worm-shaped pieces of paper with marked out sections for the children to add **wr** words.

Although Robber Red is a **r**obber, the **r**ingleader of a **r**obber gang (see page 92), Robber Red himself gives little trouble to young readers in words. They can **r**ely on him to make his **r**egular 'rrr...' sound at the start of words and in consonant blends (**br**, **cr**, **dr**). However, in **wr**, he comes face to face with the Water Witch. When these two troublemakers meet, one silences the other.

Write **write** and **wrist** on the board. Give help in reading them if necessary and when the children have discovered that they cannot even hear a whisper out of the Water Witch, tell them the following story.

The Witch's letter is captured by Robber Red

*Robber Red knows that the Wicked Water Witch is always **wr**iting wicked spelling spells. She is even working on a new one to get rid of every **r**obber in Letterland. Of course, Robber Red can't have that! So every time he sees her in a word he comes running up from behind and grabs her pen and her spell book so she can't **wr**ite. Then he runs off with her letter in his sack.*

Show both sides of the *Picture Code Card.*

That is why her robber spell is still ... **unwritten**

Write **unwritten** on the board very large and ask a child to picture code **wr** using a contrasting colour. Then give help, if needed, in working out the word.

*... Yes, that is why her robber spell is still un**wr**itten, and why we have nothing but silence from the **W**itch. She is still sitting right out of the picture, too startled to speak! So whenever you see the Witch's letter next to Robber Red, remember he has her letter in his sack and she is nowhere to be seen or heard!*

- Listen to and sing the Witch and Robber Red song on the *Programme Two Songs Cassette.*
- Choose several children to retell the story in their own words.

The Witch wrote the wrong word.

- Write the following sentences on the board and ask the children to help with picture coding **w**, **r** and **wr**.

  The Witch wrote the wrong word.

  The worms wriggled when they saw the wren.

  The robber wrapped the present in wrinkled paper.

  His wristwatch was lost in the shipwreck.

- Live spell these words: **wrist** → **wren** → **unwrap** → **wriggle** → **shipwreck**.

- Write some of the words in the **wr** word box on the board. Discuss the meanings of these words and ask the children to read them out loud. Whose sound can they hear and which letter is silent?

- Ask the children to write their own tongue-twister using **wr** words.

- Introduce *Word Bank Copymaster* 41. Write a selection of **wr** words on the board. Ask the children to choose the ones they consider most useful to them, and to add them to their Word Banks.

- Make some **wr**iggly, **wr**inkly worms out of paper (see Preparation). Write some **wr** words and some **r** words on the board and ask the children to select the **wr** words and write them in the sections on the worm.

- Use *Programme Two Copymaster* 79 for further practice.

- Role-play the **wr** story. One child could retell the story while two others mime the actions of **r** running in and stealing the **w** child's letter. The **w** child is so shocked, she is left silent.

write

writer

wrote

written

Words containing wr

shipwreck	wreck	wring	written*
unwrap	wreckage	wrinkle	wrong*
wrap	wren	wristwatch	wrote*
wrapped	wrestle	write*	
wrapping paper	wretched	writer	
wreath	wriggle	writing	

* High frequency words

The worms wriggled when they saw the wren.

gh (as in bought) (as in laugh)

Objectives

- To know that when the letters **g** and **h** are together, they both usually become silent (as in **bought**).
- To know these exceptions: **laugh**, **cough**, **rough**, **tough** and **enough**.
- To recognise and spell words containing **gh**.

What you need

- *Programme Two Picture Code Cards:* **gh** (26), **ou** (75)
- *Programme One Picture Code Cards*
- *Programme Two Copymaster:* 80
- *Programme Two Word Bank Copymaster:* 42

The following silent **gh** story is also included in brief in Unit 3.3, as part of the study of the 'igh' sound.

Revising silent gh

Golden Girl and the Hairy Hat Man are almost always silent when they are together

Golden Girl knows that Hairy Hat Man hates noise, so whenever he stands next to her in a word she keeps completely quiet. So does he. They just enjoy being silent together.

- Write these sentences on the board, showing silent **gh** by writing dotted letters. Ask the children to help with picture coding 'gh'.

I went straight out and bought eight buns.
She caught her cold from her daughter.
Hugh thought you brought a scarf for him to wear.

- Live spell or dictate: **ought** ➜ **brought** ➜ **thought** ➜ **though** ➜ **although**. Since there are no *Picture Code Cards* to represent the very erratic changes in the sounds of 'ou' in **-ough** and **-ought**, the children should hold up the plain letter side of Card 75. They can also cover their mouths to show when they are being silent letters (e.g. **u** and **gh** in **though** and **although**).

Words containing silent gh

although*	fought	though	Note: Also all **igh** and **ight** words listed on page 55.
bought*	height	thought*	
brought*	ought	through*	
caught*	straight*	weigh	
daughter	thorough	weight	
eight*	thoroughly		

* High frequency words

I went straight out and bought eight buns.

Introducing the 'fff...' sound sometimes made by gh

Sometimes Golden Girl and the Hat Man laugh softly in words

*In one word **laugh**, it seems that both Golden Girl and the Hat Man cannot resist laughing softly like this, 'fff, fff, fff'. Then **gh** sounds just like **f** or **ph**. This also happens in the words **cough**, **rough**, **tough** and **enough**.*

☆ Write these sentences on the board. Add little fff's in a speech bubble over the **gh** in **laughed**, **cough**, **rough**, **tough** and **enough**.

She laughed so much that it made her cough.

This rough leather jacket is tough enough to wear around the farm.

☆ Use *Programme Two Copymaster* 80 for further practice.

☆ Introduce *Word Bank Copymaster* 41. Write a selection of words on the board where **gh** is silent and include somewhere: **gh** makes a 'fff...' sound. Ask the children to sort the words and add them to their Word Banks in the appropriate places.

☆ See how quickly different children can say the following sentences. They could try saying the sentences three times each and you could use a stop watch to make it more fun.

I thought you had it thoroughly thought through.

Although he has a cough, he looks rough and tough enough.

Words containing gh saying 'fff...'

cough	laugh*	rough
enough*	laughter	tough

* High frequency words

References
For the full story explanation for **igh**, see p54.

She laughed so much that it made her cough.

mb (as in thumb) and mn (as in autumn)

Objectives

- To know that, in words ending in **mb**, the **b** becomes silent, and in words ending in **mn**, the **n** becomes silent.
- To recognise and spell words ending in **mb** and **mn**.

What you need

- *Programme Two Picture Code Cards:* **mb** (68)
- *Programme One Picture Code Cards:* **m** (8), **n** (19)
- *Programme Two Copymaster: 81*
- *Programme Two Word Bank Copymaster:* 42

Preparation

- **Look, say, cover, write, check**
  Make copies of the format on page 230.

Words containing mn	
autumn	hymn
column	solemn
condemn	

Munching Mike takes Bouncy Ben's breath away

When Munching Mike murmurs "Mmmmm" right behind Bouncy Ben's back, he takes Ben's breath away! That's why no-one can hear Ben at the end of these words.

Mike takes Nick's breath away

When Munching Mike and Naughty Nick are together, the same thing happens. Being right next to Munching Mike takes Nick's breath away. Perhaps this is why we rarely see either Ben or Nick next to Munching Mike in a word!

- Write these sentences on the board. Ask the children to help with picture coding **mb** and **mn**. To code **b** and **n** as silent, wipe them out and rewrite them with dotted letters.

  The plumber had to climb up the ladder.

  The autumn leaves swept round the columns.

- Live spell or dictate: **comb ➜ climb ➜ autumn ➜ hymn**.

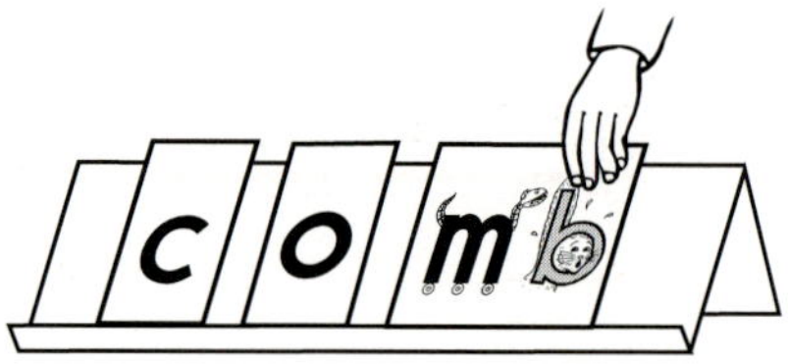

- Use *Programme Two Copymaster* 81 for further practice.
- Introduce *Word Bank Copymaster* 42. Write some of the **mb** words and all the **mn** words on the board and ask the children to enter them into their Word Banks. Explain that there are so few other words where Naughty Nick dares to be next to Munching Mike that they may never find another word to fill the **mn** lines!
- Give the children **mb** and **mn** words from the word boxes and ask them to complete the *look, say, cover, write, check* format.

Words containing mb				
bomb	comb	lamb	numb	plumbing
climb*	crumb	limb	plumber	thumb

* High frequency words

ie (as in līe) (as in fiēld)

Objectives

- To know that the letters **i** and **e** can combine to represent long ē (**ie** as in **field**).
- To recognise and spell words containing **ie** saying ē.

What you need

- *Programme Two Picture Code Cards:* **ie** (29), **ie** (30)
- *Programme One Picture Code Cards*
- *Programme Two Copymaster:* 82
- *Programme Two Word Bank Copymaster:* 43

Preparation

- **Look, say, cover, write, check**
  Make copies of the format on page 230.

This Unit revises the first sound of **ie** (as in **lie**) covered in Unit 3.1 (page 50) and introduces its second sound (as in **field**).

Mr I and Mr E do not appear on the *Vowel Men Out Walking Poster* because, unlike the other vowels, one *or the other* talks while the partner remains silent. *Picture Code Card* 30 shows the second Vowel Man talking. By analysing the vowel sound in any given word, the children decide whether *Picture Code Card* 29 or 30 applies, and are guided by these cards when picture coding a word themselves. They can also draw a circle around the digraph they are coding, using yellow when Mr I's arm is up (to emphasise long **ī**) and red when Mr E's arm is up (to emphasise long **ē**).

The alternative sounds of ie

When Mr I and Mr E go out walking they take turns with the talking

When Mr I and Mr E go out walking, sometimes Mr I does the talking and sometimes Mr E talks instead. Because they both like talking, they have agreed to take turns. They also take turns at being the look-out man. Let's see who is talking in these words.

Write the following sentence on the board:

Mr I fried a fish and made a pie.

*Yes, we can clearly hear Mr I saying his name "I!" in the words **fried** and **pie**.*

Words containing ie saying ī

allies	fried	simplified
amplified	justified	supplies
applies	lies	terrified
cried	magnified	tied
die*	pie	
flies	satisfies	

* High frequency words

Mr I fried a fish and made a pie.

Let's see who's doing the talking in the next words.

The pixie took a piece of my brownie.

Yes, Mr E clearly says his name "E!" in these words. Now let's see if we can spot Mr I and Mr E taking turns with the talking all in one sentence.

- Write these sentences on the board and ask the children to help with picture coding the two sounds of **ie**.

Mr E gave his niece a piece of Mr I's pie.

Never believe a lie.

I tied my golden retriever to a tree in the field.

- Live spell or dictate: **ties** ➜ **field** ➜ **piece** ➜ **cries** ➜ **niece**. Two pairs of children holding the different **ie** cards can take turns miming being out walking in these words.
- Use *Programme Two Copymaster* 82 for further practice.
- Introduce *Word Bank Copymaster* 43. Write on the board a selection of words containing **ie** saying **e** and ask the children to choose the ones they consider most useful to add to their Word Banks.
- Give the children a range of words from both word boxes and ask them to complete the *look, say, cover, write, check* format.

Words containing ie saying ē

		Children's names
achieve	pixie	Annie
believe*	prairie	Jamie
brief	retrieved	Sophie
brownie	retriever	Stephanie
chief*	shield	
field*	thief	
niece	thieves	
piece*		

* High frequency words

References
For the first reference to Vowels Out Walking, see p36.

Mr E gave his niece a piece of Mr I's pie.

ei (as in recēive) (as in heīght)

Objectives

- To know that the letters **e** and **i** can combine to represent long ē (**ei** as in **receive**) or long ī (as in **height**).
- To recognise and spell words containing **ei**.

What you need

- *Programme Two Picture Code Cards:* **Mr E** (2), **Mr I** (3)
- *Programme One Picture Code Cards*
- *Programme Two Copymaster:* 83
- *Programme Two Word Bank Copymaster:* 43

As with the **ie** spelling pattern, the **ei** pattern can represent either long ī or long ē. In Letterland the rule is as follows:

Mr E and Mr I both like walking and talking, so when they go out walking they take turns with the talking.

(There are no *Picture Code Cards* for these two phonemes as there are relatively few words needing the **ei** spelling pattern.)

- Write these sentences on the board and ask the children to help with picture coding the two alternative sounds of **ei**.

  Look at the height of this ceiling.

  Did he receive the eiderdown we sent him.

  Just when I had the kaleidoscope he seized it!
- Live spell or dictate: **receive** ➜ **either** ➜ **ceiling** ➜ **height**.
- Use *Programme Two Copymaster* 83 for further practice.
- Introduce *Word Bank Copymaster* 43. Write on the board a mixed selection of words from the word boxes and ask the children to choose words to enter into their Word Banks in the correct places.

Words containing ei saying ē

ceiling	deceive	receive
conceited	protein	seize

Words containing ei saying ī

eiderdown	Fahrenheit	kaleidoscope
either*	height	neither

* High frequency word

References
For **ie** taking turns with the talking, see p50 and p215.

Look at the height of this ceiling.

ous (as in famous)

Objectives

- To know that the letters **o**, **u** and **s** combine to make the 'us' sound (**ous** as in **famous**).
- To know that the suffix **-ous** means 'full of'.
- To recognise and spell words containing **ous**.

What you need

- *Programme Two Picture Code Cards:* **ous** (76)
- *Programme One Picture Code Cards*
- *Programme Two Copymaster:* 84
- *Programme Two Word Bank Copymaster:* 44

Preparation

- **Look, say, cover, write, check**
  Make copies of the format on page 230.

The omission of the silent **o** when spelling words ending in **ous** is a common enough mistake. So how does the inexperienced speller choose between **us** and **ous**?

In fact, you can greatly reduce the number of errors by telling children that the majority end in **ous**! Once they have learned the few high frequency words which do end in **us**, e.g. **circus** (see page 219), it will be even easier. Apart from those words, if in doubt don't leave Mr O out, use **ous**. Help children to notice, too, that the **ous** words are all adjectives (describing words) whereas the few **us** words are all nouns (naming words).

Mr O is too breathless to speak in describing words which end in ous

*Many describing words end in **ous**. (An **ous** ending usually means 'full of'.) Mr O loves being in all these describing words. But why is he silent in them every time? Because they fill him 'full of' excitement and that takes his breath away!*

- Write these sentences on the board and ask the children to help with picture coding **ous**. They should wipe out the **o** and write it in again as a dotted letter before adding stick man Mr O with his handkerchief, mopping his brow.

Mr O feels famous in these fabulous words.
That enormous elephant doesn't look dangerous.
Watching the poisonous snake makes me nervous.

The **ous** suffix is frequently preceded by an **i**, sounding more like an **e**. This is really the Yo-yo Man working for Mr E but wearing his neat straight **i**-clothes. The letter **e** before **ous** is only found in four words (see the word box on page 219).

-ious I am anxious that he will become curious.
-ous The courageous knight fought the hideous monster.

- Select words from the **ous** box and discuss how they are built on words like **adventure**, **danger**, **fame**, **humour**, **monster**. Point out that over 235 useful describing words end in **ous**.

Mr O feels famous in these fabulous words.

☆ Use *Programme Two Copymaster* 84 for further practice.

☆ Introduce *Word Bank Copymaster* 44. Write a selection of **ous** and **ious** words on the board and ask the children to choose some to write in their Word Banks.

☆ Give the children some **ous** words from the word boxes and ask them to complete the *look, say, cover, write, check* format.

Words (adjectives) ending in ous

adventurous	hazardous	ravenous
boisterous	humorous	ridiculous
dangerous	marvellous	strenuous
disastrous	miraculous	stupendous
enormous	mischievous	thunderous
fabulous	monstrous	treacherous
famous	nervous	tremendous
generous	perilous	vigorous
glamorous	poisonous	virtuous
gorgeous	prosperous	

–ious		–eous
envious	luxurious	courageous
furious	mysterious	gorgeous
glorious	studious	hideous
hilarious	various	outrageous
industrious	victorious	

☆ Ask the children to focus on the **us** words in the box below. Let them work in pairs to think up sentences using as many **us** words as possible. They can then exchange sentences.

Words (nouns) ending in us

apparatus	chorus	focus	minus
asparagus	circus	fungus	octopus
bonus	citrus	genius	virus
cactus	crocus	hippopotamus	walrus

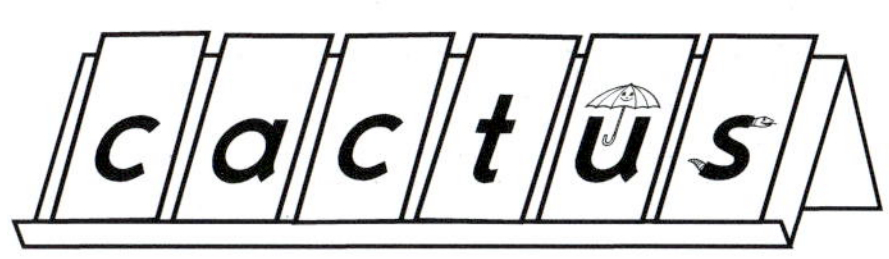

tion (as in attention)

Objectives

- To know that the letters **t**, **i**, **o** and **n** combine to make the 'shun' sound (**tion** as in **attention**).
- To recognise and spell words ending in **tion**.

What you need

- *Programme Two Picture Code Cards:* **tion** (81)
- *Programme One Picture Code Cards*
- *Programme Two Copymaster:* 86
- *Programme Two Word Bank Copymaster:* 45
- *Programme Two Songs Cassette*

Preparation

- **Word hunt**
  Bring in some old newspapers so the children can use them to hunt for **tion** words.
- **Card game**
  Have ready some fairly stiff paper cut into long strips suitable for writing **tion** words on. Write 16 **tion** words and 16 **ation** words on the board or on a sheet for photocopying.

It may be tempting to feel that there is no need to look at the **tion** ending with your children until a later stage. However, many **tion** words are informa**tion** words. (The 'Tion Song on the *Programme Two Songs Cassette* illustrates this point well.) They are also great confidence boosters. Children feel good when they can read a word as long as telecommunica**tion** – and spell it too! Any child who memorises this story's title should be able to read and spell the **tion** ending correctly in over 1500 words. Children prone to writing '-shon', '-shun' or '-toin' will be interested to know that none of these spellings *ever* occur in the English language (though a few do end in **sion**).

The aim of the 'Tion story is two-fold:

1. To preclude typical errors when a child mistakenly expects **sh** to be an acceptable way to start this suffix.
2. To teach inexperienced readers to approach multi-syllabic words with confidence.

The story below deliberately uses **tion** 15 times to increase phonemic awareness for this unit of sound. It helps to exaggerate **'Tion** and **tion** as you read it aloud.

Mr 'Tion says, "Here's the Tea I Owe Nick"

Have you ever met a teacher called Mr 'Tion? He teaches reading and spelling at Naughty Nick's school. Everybody likes Mr 'Tion because he often gives tea parties.

One day Mr 'Tion gave a tea party for all of Nick's class. Before serving tea he asked everybody to spell some easy words and then some harder words. Everyone did quite well, so he was pleased. Then he said, "I think I know a word which you can't spell; my name, 'Tion!". By then Nick was getting thirsty. He was sure he knew how to spell Mr 'Tion's name. So he said, "Let's say that whoever spells Mr 'Tion's name right first will be served tea first."

*"All right," Mr 'Tion agreed. Many children tried to spell 'tion' but they all started with **sh**, which is wrong. Then Nick said he would try. "What's more," he said to Mr 'Tion, "I'll bet that after I whisper the right spelling for 'tion' into your ear, the first thing you say after that will tell everyone else how to spell 'tion'." "How can that be?" everyone asked. Mr 'Tion called out "sh..." so that he could hear Nick whispering.*

*Then Mr 'Tion smiled. He poured Nick's tea and said, "Here's the Tea I Owe Nick". So now all of the children remember how to spell **tion** by saying to themselves what Mr 'Tion said to Nick at the party: "the **T**ea **I** **O**we **N**ick".*

Shortened version for revision

*At Mr 'Tion's tea party no-one could spell his name until Nick did. Nick then gave everyone a tip on how to spell **tion** by predicting what Mr 'Tion would say next when Nick won a bet with him: Here's 'the **T**ea **I** **O**we **N**ick.'*

- Listen to and sing Mr 'Tion's song on the *Programme Two Songs Cassette*. Listen again, counting the **tion**'s. Read the verses aloud slowly, if necessary, so the children can succeed in catching **tion** all 26 times!

- Write these sentences on the board and ask the children to help with picture coding **tion**.

Pay attention to words that mention Mr 'Tion.

His instructions were to make three corrections.

The question was about addition and subtraction.

The station master has information about my destination.

- Live spell or dictate: **action** → **section** → **infection** → **invention** → **fiction** → **information** → **telecommunication**.

Words ending in tion

action	correction	instruction	perfection
adoption	destruction	intention	portion
affection	exception	introduction	prevention
attention	fiction	invention	section
caution	fraction	mention	subscription
construction	infection	objection	subtraction

Roughly 1000 of the 1500 **tion** words end in **ation**! To picture code the fact that Mr A is a frequent visitor to Mr 'Tion's tea parties, children can draw a stick man, Mr A, announcing himself at Mr 'Tion's door and draw a house around **tion**. This will cure the most common reading error: sounding the **at** in **tion** words as 'ăt', e.g. 'operat...' and then giving up.

Pay attention to words which mention Mr 'Tion.

Whenever there is a vowel before **tion**, the chances are high that it will be a long vowel, i.e. one of the other Vowel Men coming to Mr 'Tion's tea party.

explanation   station   information

Words ending in ation

aviation	explanation	information	relation
combination	exploration	investigation	sensation
complication	foundation	limitation	station
conversation	hesitation	operation	translation
destination	imagination	population	transportation

completion   motion   solution

etion	otion		ution	
completion	devotion	notion	contribution	solution
deletion	emotion	motion	evolution	revolution
secretion	lotion	promotion	institution	substitution

There is one excep**tion**, Mr I, who always politely leaves a gift of a bottle of ink instead of turning up himself because he does not like tea.

- Use *Programme Two Copymaster* 86 for further practice.
- Introduce *Word Bank Copymaster* 45. Ask the children to look for words ending in **tion** and **ation** in newspapers (see Preparation) and to add them to their Word Banks.
- Display or hand out your lists of **tion** and **ation** words (see Preparation) for children to work with in pairs. One child makes a selec**tion** of eight **tion** words to write on the paper strips. The other child does the same with **ation** words. They take turns holding their words up for each other to read. The first pair to claim that both partners can read all their 16 words wins. They may then read them out to the rest of the class. The same word strips can be used for an easy memory game, finding two **tion** or two **ation** words when all are face down.

Exceptions: words ending in ition

addition
ambition
competition
condition
definition
edition
exhibition
expedition
preposition
recognition
repetition

Mr I is in a difficult position.

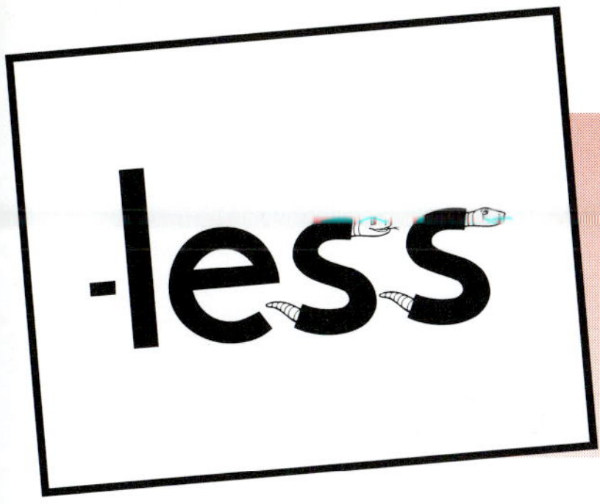

The -less and -ness suffixes

Objectives

- To know that the suffixes **-less** and **-ness** take double **s**.
- To know the meaning of these endings.
- To recognise and spell words ending in **-less** and **-ness**.

What you need

- *Programme Two Picture Code Cards*
- *Programme One Picture Code Cards:* **n** (19), **e** (33), **l** (39), **ss** (56)
- *Programme Two Copymaster:* 88
- *Programme Two Word Bank Copymaster:* 46

Preparation

- **Look, say, cover, write, check**
  Make copies of the format on page 230.

Begin by reminding the children of the meaning of the word 'suffix': an ending which you can add to a word to make a new word. Write the words **useful** and **useless** on the board. From their work on Unit 17.1, remembering the meaning of the **-ful** suffix, they should now be able to deduce the meaning of the **-less** suffix – in this case 'without any use'.

The meaning of the **-ness** suffix is more difficult to explain and understand: a 'state of being'. Explain that it is a suffix which can be added to an adjective if you want to talk about that quality, e.g. **illness**, **goodness**, **kindness**.

From a spelling point of view, the only difficulty may be in remembering to use not one **s**, but two. The following jingle will help.

-less and -ness take double s

Once you know that this is so,
if you forget the second ***s***
in ***-less*** *or* ***-ness,*** *it's simply …*

carelessness.

- Write these sentences on the board and ask the children to help with picture coding **less** and **ness**.

  It was useless and meaningless.

  This button adjusts the darkness and lightness of the TV screen.

- Write the following words on the board and ask the children to decide which fits better as a suffix for each word, **-less** or **-ness**.

great	good	help	hope	law
meaning	open	price	thought	rest
selfish	skilful	sick	tooth	value

Then decide which words could be given both endings to make new words (**restlessness, helplessness, hopelessness, lawlessness**).

It was useless and meaningless.

- Use *Programme Two Copymaster* 88 for further practice.
- Introduce *Word Bank Copymaster* 46. Write a selection of **-less** and **-ness** words on the board and ask the children to choose the ones they consider most useful to add to their Word Banks.
- Give the children some **-less** and **-ness** words from the word boxes and ask them to complete the *look, say, cover, write, check* format.

Words ending in -less

blameless
harmless
lifeless
meaningless
pointless
priceless
senseless
shapeless
speechless
stainless
tasteless
timeless
toothless
unless
valueless
worthless

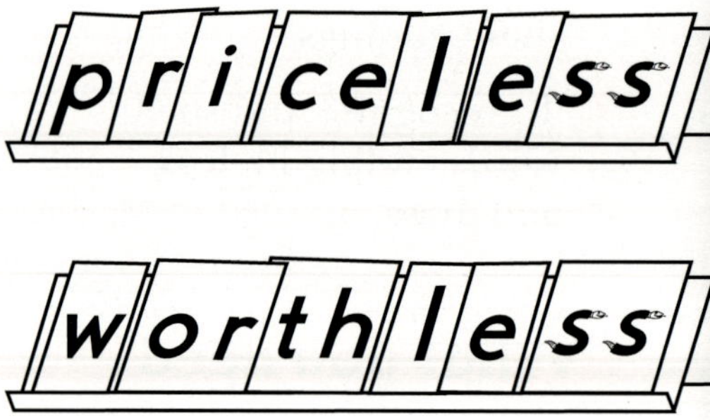

Words ending in -ness

brightness
dampness
darkness
deafness
fairness
fondness
goodness
illness
kindness
likeness
loudness
politeness
sadness
selfishness
shyness
sickness
stiffness
willingness

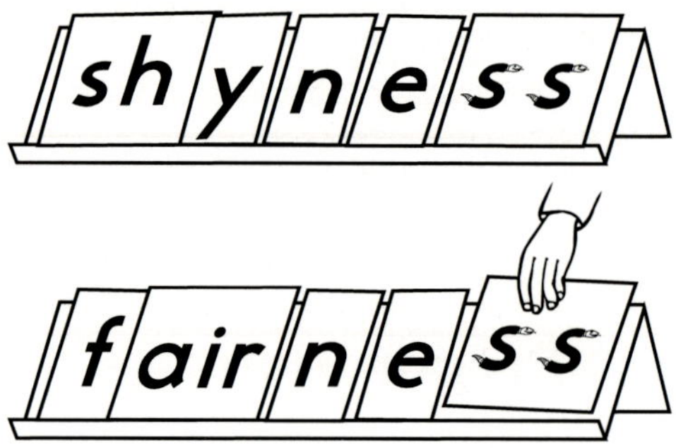

-ture and -que

Objectives

- To know that the letters **t**, **u**, **r** and **e** combine to make the 'cher' sound (-**ture** as in **picture**).
- To recognise and spell words ending in -**ture**.
- To know that the letters **q**, **u** and **e** can combine to make the hard 'c' sound (-**que** as in **cheque**).
- To recognise and spell words ending in -**que**.

What you need

- *Programme One Picture Code Cards*
- *Programme Two Copymaster:* 89
- *Programme Two Word Bank Copymaster:* 47

Preparation

- **Signatures**
  Collect some examples of signa**tures** from famous people to show the children.
- **Sculpture**
  Collect postcards of sculp**tures** and sort out a variety of modelling materials.

The -**ture** ending is easily mis-read and mis-spelt (as **c-h-e-r**). In fact, the only high frequency word actually spelled **cher** is **teacher**, whereas over 40 useful words end in -**ture.** A useful quick rule is therefore: unless the word is **teacher**, use -**ture**. The -**ture** pictogram is shown below and on *Word Bank Copymaster* 89 but there is no *Picture Code Card* for it. The Letterland explanation for **ture** is as follows.

Ticking Tess sneezes as Urgent Ur breaks Magic e's wand

*As Urgent Ur runs past Ticking Tess, he hears a sound just like Clever Cat sneezing, '**ch**!'.*

*But Clever Cat is nowhere to be seen. "So who sneezed?" wonders Urgent Ur as he rushes past Tess, crying '**ur**!' Could it be Tess? Yes, it is!*

*Notice how Urgent Ur always overpowers the Magic **e** at the end to make sure it can't turn his stolen umbrella into a Vowel Man!*

- Write these sentences on the board and ask the children to help with picture coding -**ture**.

  Who will venture to capture Urgent Ur?

  He watched the wild creatures in the nature reserve.

  Do you like the texture of this furniture?

  Let's draw a picture of that sculpture.

- Live spell or dictate: **future** ➜ **capture** ➜ **teacher** ➜ **picture** ➜ **mixture** ➜ **nature**.
- Tell the children to pretend to be someone famous who needs to sign lots of autographs. Show them some famous signa**tures** and ask them to have a go at practising their own new signa**tures**. They could go around the school collecting signa**tures** from various members of staff.
- Show the children the postcards of famous sculp**tures** and ask the children to copy one of them in minia**ture**, choosing their own modelling materials.

Who will venture to capture Urgent Ur?

- Use *Programme Two Copymaster* 89 for further practice in the **-ture** suffix.

- Introduce *Word Bank Copymaster* 47. Write some **-ture** words on the board and ask the children to choose the ones they consider most useful to add to their Word Banks.

Words ending in -ture

architecture	fixture	mixture	premature
capture	furniture	moisture	puncture
creature	future	nature	sculpture
culture	literature	overture	signature
departure	mature	picture*	temperature
feature	miniature	posture	texture

furniture

moisture

* High frequency word

Introducing the -que sound

The Queen makes Clever Cat's sound in the -que ending

*Normally you would expect Quarrelsome Queen to say '**qu**' in this ending. Instead, just to be difficult, she makes Clever Cat's little 'c…' sound. She's even silenced Mr U and E out walking. What an impossible queen!*

unique

technique

The **-que** pictogram is shown here and on *Word Bank Copymaster* 89 but there is no *Picture Code Card* for it. A quick way to remember the sound of **-que** is to cover the queen's hair and **ue** with a finger, leaving **c** (the 'k' sound).

- Write these sentences on the board and ask the children to help with picture coding **-que**. To code **-que**, the children wipe off all but the **c** shape within a **q** and write the rest of the **q** and the **ue** as dotted letters.

  She won't queue up to buy this antique.

  The unique view was very picturesque.

- Use *Programme Two Copymaster* 89 for further practice in the **-que** suffix.

- Introduce *Word Bank Copymaster* 47. Write on the board a selection of words from the **-que** word box and ask the children to choose the ones they consider most useful to add to their Word Banks.

Words ending in -que

antique	physique
cheque	picturesque
grotesque	plaque
mosque	technique
oblique	unique
opaque	

References
For more ways to spell this final 'k' sound, see p178.

She won't queue up to buy this antique.

The -able and -ible suffixes

Objectives

- To know when to choose the **-able** or the **-ible** spelling as a suffix.

What you need

- *Programme Two Picture Code Cards:* **able** (62) **ible** (63)
- *Programme One Picture Code Cards*
- *Programme Two Copymaster:* 90
- *Programme Two Word Bank Copymaster:* 48

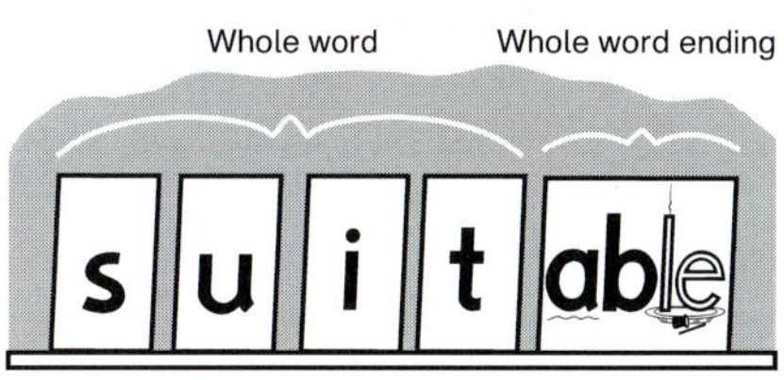

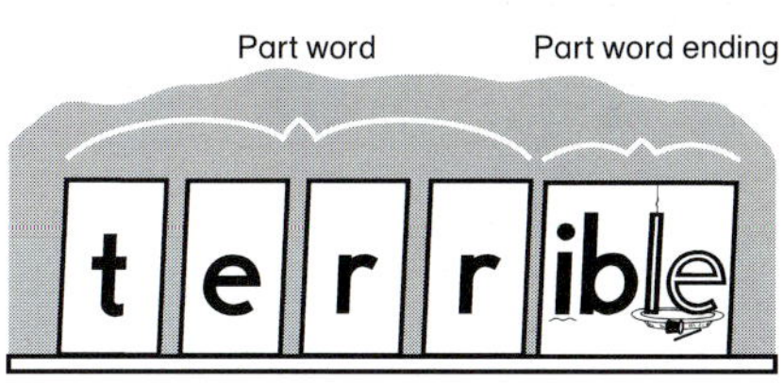

When the word **able** becomes a suffix, the **ā** becomes an 'uh' sound. The **i** in **ible** also changes to 'uh', so the pronunciation of both suffixes becomes virtually identical. In terms of picture coding, the irregular vowels are marked by wiggly lines and the Candle Magic is shown as out of action. The following guidelines are for children who are ready to learn some rules set out in more conventional terms.

When to use -able

1. Use **-able** where the root word is a whole word in its own right. The suffix **-able** is also, of course, a word in its own right. Its meaning when added to the root word (frequently a verb) is literally 'able to be…'.
2. If the root word ends in an **e** in its whole form, drop the **e** before adding **-able** (apart from a few exceptions in the list of root words ending in a soft **c** or **g**, see page 228).
3. Root words ending in a hard **c** or **g** take **-able**.

When to use -ible

1. If the root word is not a whole word when pronounced alone, it will usually take **-ible**.
2. Most root words ending in soft **ge** or **ce** drop the **e**, using the **-ible** ending to keep the **g** or **c** soft (**gi** or **ci**) instead.

- Write these sentences on the board and ask the children to help with picture coding **able** and **ible**.

  Her clothes are really fashionable.

  It was understandable that he was feeling upset.

  That looks absolutely horrible!

- Dictate: **drinkable** → **suitable** → **understandable** → **valuable** → **terrible** → **horrible** → **edible**.

- Use *Programme Two Copymaster* 90 for further practice.

Her clothes are really fashionable.

☆ Introduce *Word Bank Copymaster* 48. Write a selection of words ending **-ible** or **-able** on the board and ask the children to enter them into their Word Banks in the appropriate places. You can make the activity harder by giving just the root word for some of them, so that the children have to work out for themselves which is the correct ending.

The three -able rules

Whole words take -able

acceptable
available
avoidable
bearable
breakable
considerable
drinkable
fashionable
mendable
payable
questionable
reasonable
suitable
understandable
washable

Challenge words

perishable
predictable

Root words minus the e take -able

advisable
arguable
believable
conceivable
consumable
curable
debatable
deplorable
desirable
disposable
disputable
excitable
excusable
forgivable
lovable
movable
reputable
valuable

Exceptions

changeable
chargeable
damageable
enforceable
knowledgeable
manageable
noticeable
replaceable
serviceable
traceable

Root words ending in hard c or g take -able

amicable
communicable
delegable
despicable
inexplicable
irrevocable
navigable
practicable

The two -ible rules

Part words take -ible

compatible
divisible
edible
horrible
invisible
terrible
visible

Root words ending in ce or ige drop e and take -ible

crucible
eligible
forcible
illegible
incorrigible
intelligible
invincible
negligible
reducible
tangible

SECTION 4

We have been thinking about ph words.
ph
elephant
graph
photo
Can you think of any more ?

Name .... Date ....

Look/say	Cover/write	Check ✔	Write again

 Published by Collins Educational

Name..........................

Date..........................

Letter to Parents

Dear Parent/Guardian

As part of our teaching during the Literacy Hour, our school will be using *Letterland.*

Letterland is a programme that has been used successfully for many years to teach children the sounds and spelling patterns they need to become confident readers and writers. The programme meets the statutory requirements of the National Literacy Strategy and the National Curriculum for English and encourages the children to take a special interest in the written word.

In Letterland, your child will meet the picture-coded characters that represent the sounds and spelling patterns (phonemes) which make up the English language. The Letterland characters also interact with each other to explain why the sounds in words often change, creating new phonemes for your child to learn (for example, **p** as in **p**uppy, **h** as in **h**at, but when these same letters are side by side in a word, they make a '**fff**' sound instead, as in **ph**otogra**ph**).

Through memorable stories, rhymes and activities, your child will not only learn to recognise and spell all the new phonemes, but will gain the skills and confidence to work out more unfamiliar words for themselves. *Letterland* also aims to develop and extend children's vocabulary by providing carefully chosen examples and challenge words, relating to the relevant phoneme, for teachers to use as part of their literacy teaching. As you will soon discover, once your child can understand how the phonemes interact in words, they are on the road to becoming good writers and spellers.

We are looking forward to introducing your child to the world of Letterland and we hope you will join in the fun and learning with your child at home.

TEACHER CHECKLIST (SECTION 2)

Unit	Phoneme	Programme Two Picture Code Cards	Programme Two Copymaster	Programme Two Word Bank Copymaster	Programme Two Songs Cassette	Live Spell/Dictate
	YEAR 1, TERM 3*					
1.1	**ee** (as in feet)	**ee** (24)	1	1	*Vowels Out Walking song*	free, flee, heel, steel, green, agree, degree.
1.2	**ea** (as in seat)	**ea** (22)	2	1	*Vowels Out Walking song*	each, beach, reach, reason, season, stream.
2.1	**ai** (as in train)	**ai** (18)	4	2	*Vowels Out Walking song*	tail, snail, stain, brain, paint, faint.
2.2	**a–e** (as in name)	Mr A: **a** (1), Magic **e** (9)	5	2	*Magic* **e** *song*	tap/tape/tap, plan/plane, scrap/scrape.
2.3	**ay** (as in play)	**ay** (45)	6	2	*Vowels Out Walking song*	rain, ray, fray, stay, spray, stray.
3.1	**ie** (as in lie)	**ie** (29)	8	3	*Vowels Out Walking song*	pie, lie, lies, flies, tries, tried, cried, relied.
3.2	**i–e** (as in bite)	Mr I: **i** (3), Magic **e** (9)	9	3	*Magic* **e** *song*	pin/pine/pin, bit/bite, spin/spine, rip/ripe, trip, strip/stripe.
3.3	**igh** (as in high)	**gh** (26), **igh** (64)	10	4		high, sigh, sight, night, bright, light.
3.4	**y** (as in fly)	**y** (13)	11	4		my, fly, fry, try, shy, why.
4.1	**oa** (as in boat)	**oa** (69)	13	5	*Vowels Out Walking song*	boat, coat, coast, toast, throat.
4.2	**o–e** (as in pole)	Mr O: **o** (4), Magic **e** (9)	14	5	*Magic* **e** *song*	hop/hope, not/note, glob/globe, mop/mope.
4.3	**ow** (as in show)	**ow** (78)	15	5		lot/low, rod/row, shop, show, shadow, own.
5.1	**oo** (as in boot)	**oo** (70)	17	6	*Boot and Foot Twins song*	boot, too, tool, cool, stool, spoon, moon.
5.2	**u–e** (as in tune)	Mr U: **u** (5), Magic **e** (9)	18	6	*Magic* **e** *song*	us/use, cub/cube, tub/tube, cut/cute.
5.3	**ew** (as in flew)	**ew** (59)	19	7	*Eddy Elephant and the Witch song*	few, flew, blew, grew, chew.
5.4	**ue** (as in blue)	**ue** (36)	20	7	*Vowels Out Walking song*	true, glue, blue, clue, rescue.
6.1	**-ed**	**-ed** (50), **-ed** (51), **-ed** (52)	24-25	8		cod/code/coded, side/sided, divide/divided, skate/skated, fad/fade/faded. lifted, limped, filmed, mixed, mashed, handed.
6.2	**-ing**	**-ing** (65)	26	9	*Magic* **e** *song*	name/naming, make/making, ride/riding, hope/hoping, use/using.

* *Letterland teachers often find that their children make swifter progress than shown above and therefore adapt their teaching plans according to their children's needs.*

Unit	Phoneme	Programme Two Picture Code Cards	Programme Two Copymaster	Programme Two Word Bank Copymaster	Programme Two Songs Cassette	Live Spell/Dictate
	YEAR 2, TERM 1*					
7.1	**u** (as in pull)	**u** (12), **u** (5)	27	10		but/bull, pull, pulling, putting, cutting, push, bush, bushes, fun/full.
7.2	**oo** (as in foot)	**oo** (70), **oo** (71)	27	10	*Boot and Foot Twins song*	foot, good, wood, wool, book, brook, crooked.
8.1	**ar** (as in car)	**ar** (40)	28	11	*Apple Stealer's song*	cat/cart, had/hard, pat/part, party, partly, hardly, shark.
9.1	**oy** (as in toy)	**oy** (34)	29	12	*Roy and the Yo-yo Man song*	boy, toy, joy, enjoy, employ, annoy.
9.2	**oi** (as in boil)	**oi** (35), **oy** (34)	30	12	*Roy and the Yo-yo Man song*	boil, coil, coin, point, moist, noise, noisy boy.
10.1	**ow** (as in cow)	**ow** (77)	32	13		owl, howl, growl, brown, clown, flower, shower, power.
10.2	**ou** (as in ouch!)	**ou** (75)	33	13		loud, cloud, ground, pound, pouch, ouch.
	YEAR 2, TERM 2*					
11.1	**air** (as in fair)	**air** (34)	35	14		aim/air, fail/fair, hail/hair, hairy.
11.2	**are** (as in scare)	**are** (41), **are** (42)	36	14		care, stare, square, aware, beware, prepare.
11.3	**ere** (as in there)	**ere** (56)	36	15		there, where, elsewhere, nowhere, somewhere.
11.4	**ear** (as in bear)	**ear** (49)	35	15		beans/bear, pear, wear, wearing, team/tear, tearing.
12.1	**or** (as in sport)	**or** (73)	38	16	*Orange Stealer's song*	pot/port, spot/sport, sort, born, storm, story, corn, corner.
12.2	**oor** (as in floor)	**oor** (72)	39	16		poor, door, floor, indoors, outdoors.
12.3	**ore** (as in sore)	**ore** (74)	39	16		more, sore, snore, before, ignore, explore.

* *Letterland teachers often find that their children make swifter progress than shown above and therefore adapt their teaching plans according to their children's needs.*

12.4	**aw** (as in awful)	**aw** (43)	40	17		sat/saw, pat/paw, clap/claw, crawl, draw, awful, shawl.
12.5	**au** (as in caught)	**au** (44)	41	17		pause, because, sauce, saucer, laundry, haunted.
13.1	**er** (as in her)	**er** (54), **ir** (66), **ur** (82)	43	18	*Er/Ur/Ir Brothers song* *Ernest Er in Person song*	hen, her, ever, never, other, mother, brother, father.
13.2	**ir** (as in bird)	**ir** (66)	44	18	*Irving Ir in Person song,* *Why Irving Ir Needs Ink song*	bid/bird, girl, fir, fist/first, skirt, shirt.
13.3	**ur** (as in fur)	**ur** (82)	45	18	*Urgent Ur in Person song*	fun, fur, curl, hut, hurt, turn, bun, burn, burst, disturb.
14.1	**wh** (as in when and who)	**wh** (83), **wh** (84)	47	19	*Wicked Water Witch and the Hat Man song*	when, why, wheel, white, who, whole.
14.2	**ph** (as in photograph)	**ph** (79)	48	20	*Poor Peter and the Hat Man song*	nephew, phone, trophy, graph, sphere.
14.3	**ch** (as in school)	**ch** (46)	48	20		ache, echo, school, chorus, anchor.
	YEAR 2, TERM 3*					
15.1	**ear** (as in hear)	**ear** (48)	49	21		ear, hear, hears, near, tear, tears, fear, appear, appeared.
16.1	**ea** (as in head)	**ea** (23), **ea** (22)	50	21		head, ahead, heavy, heaven, bread, ready, read.
17.1	**-ful** (as in restful)	**full** (60), **ful** (61)	51	22		full/restful, helpful, handful, thankful.
17.2	**-ly** (as in lovely)	**ly** (33)	52	22		lovely, badly, flatly, quickly, exactly, softly.

** Letterland teachers often find that their children make swifter progress than shown above and therefore adapt their teaching plans according to their children's needs.*

TEACHER CHECKLIST (SECTION 3)

Page	Phoneme	Programme Two Picture Code Cards	Programme Two Copymaster	Programme Two Word Bank Copymaster	Programme Two Songs Cassette	Live spell/ dictate
163	**all** (as in c**all**), **al** (as in **al**most)	**all** (39), **al** (38)	53	23	*Giant All song*	b**all**, h**all**, c**all**, f**all**, f**all**en.
165	**o** (as in l**o**ve, **o**ne and wh**o**)	Oscar's Little Brother (26)	54- 55	24		
168	**a** (as in umbrell**a**, **A**meric**a**)	Parachuted Apple (6)	56	25		
169	**a** (as in f**a**ther)	Yawning Apple (7)	56	25		
170	**e–e** (as in th**e**s**e**)	Magic **e** (9), Mr E: **e** (2)	22		*Magic **e** song*	
171	Silent **e** (Magic **e** exceptions)	Burnt-out Magic **e** (10)	57	26		on**e**, gon**e**, shon**e**, lov**e**, notic**e**.
172	**y** (as in ver**y**)	**y** with **e** in sack (15)	58	27		histor**y**, stor**y**, bod**y**, cop**y**, (repl**y**, magnif**y**).
174	**y** (as in bic**y**cle)	**y** with ink bottle in sack (14)				enem**y**, env**y**, empt**y**.
175	**ey** (as in donk**ey**)	Mr E: **e** (2) and **ay** (45)	59	27		hon**ey**, mon**ey**, monk**ey**, donk**ey**, hock**ey**, hol**ey**, troll**ey**.
176	**ey** (as in th**ey**)	Mr Mean E: **e** (11), **ay** (45)	60	28		
177	**ei** (as in **ei**ght)	Mr Mean E: **e** (11), **ai** (18)	60	28		
178	Spelling the 'k' sound	**ck** (47), **ke** (67), **oo** (70), **oo** (71)	61	29		cra**ck**, che**ck**, chi**ck**, clo**ck**, clu**ck**. ba**ck**, ba**ke**, li**ck**, li**ke**, du**ck**, du**ke**, smo**ke**, stro**ke**. wee**k**, wea**k**, oa**k**, croa**k**, soa**k**, shoo**k**.
182	**y** changing to **i** (as in cr**ies**, pon**ies**)	Changing hut **i** (17), ink bottle **y** (13), and **y** with tiny **e** (15)	62-64	30-31		tr**y**, tr**ies**, dr**y**, dr**ied**, dr**ier**, dr**iest**, bab**y**, bab**ies**, lad**y**, lad**ies**.
185	Double consonants before Magic Endings: **ed**, **ing**					
187	Blocking Magic **ed** and Magic **ing**	**ed** (50-52), **ing** (65)	67-68	35-36	*Best Friends to the Rescue song*	rub/ru**bb**ed, drum/dru**mm**ing, wag/wa**gg**ed, fit/fi**tt**ing, shred/shre**dd**ed, pop/po**pp**ed.
190	Magic **en** and Magic **est**	**en** (53), **est** (57), Magic **e** (9)	65	33		eve/ev**en**, wide/wid**en**, froz**en**, late/lat**est**, white/whit**est**.
193	Sometimes Magic: **er**	Magic **er** (55)	66	34		pap**er**, dive, div**er**, driv**er**, ov**er**, clove, clov**er**, comput**er**.

195	Sometimes Magic: **y**	**y** (16)	66	34		baby, rub/ruby, lad/lady, bony, pony, stony, shin/shiny.
197	**le** (as in table)	**le** (32)	72	37	*Candle Magic song*	map/maple, bug/bugle, is/isle, stab/stable.
199	**al** (as in medical)		73	37		
200	**ce**, **ci**, **cy**	**ce** (19), **ci** (20), **cy** (21)	74, 75	38		ace, face, dance, cancel, price. decide, pencil, city, electricity. fancy, lacy, icy, bicycle.
204	**ge**, **gi**, **gy**, **dge**	**ge** (25), **gi** (27), **gy** (28), silent **d** (8)	76, 77, 78	39-40	*Gentle Ginger song* (ge, gi, gy)	page, hedge, magic, gentle, ginger, edge, edgy, sponge, spongy.
208	**kn** (as in **kn**ee)	**kn** (31)	79	41	*Kicking King and Naughty Nick song*	no/know, nose/knows, new/knew, knee, kneel.
210	**wr** (as in **wr**ite)	**wr** (85)	79	41	*Witch and Robber Red song*	wrist, wren, unwrap, wriggle, shipwreck.
212	**gh** (as in bou**gh**t and as in lau**gh**)	**gh** (26), **ou** (75)	80	42		ought, brought, thought, though, although.
214	**mb** (as in thu**mb**) and **mn** (as in autu**mn**)	**mb** (68), **m** (8), **n** (19) *(Programme One Code Cards)*	81	42		comb, climb, autumn, hymn.
215	**ie** (as in l**ie** and as in f**ie**ld)	**ie** (29), **ie** (30)	82	43		ties, field, piece, cries, niece.
217	**ei** (as in rec**ei**ve and as in **ei**ther)	Mr E: **e** (2), Mr I: **i** (3)	83	43		receive, either, ceiling, height.
218	**ous** (as in fam**ous**)	**ous** (76)	84	44		
220	**tion** (as in atten**tion**)	**tion** (81)	86	45	*Mr 'Tion's song*	action, section, infection, invention, fiction, information, telecommunication.
223	The **-less** and **-ness** suffixes	**n** (19), **e** (33), **l** (39), **ss** (56) *(Programme One Code Cards)*	88	46		
225	**-ture** and **-que**		89	47		future, capture, teacher/picture, mixture, nature.
227	The **-able** and **-ible** suffixes	**able** (62), **ible** (63)	90	48		drinkable, suitable, understandable, valuable, terrible, horrible, edible.

PUPIL RECORD SHEET (SECTION TWO)

Name ....

Unit	Phoneme	Can read some (s)/ most (m) words with this phoneme	Can spell words containing this phoneme	*Programme Two Copymaster*	*Programme Two Word Bank Copymaster*
1.1	**ee** (as in f**ee**t)		**ee**	1	1
1.2	**ea** (as in s**ea**t)		**ēa**	2	1
2.1	**ai** (as in tr**ai**n)		**ai**	4	2
2.2	**a–e** (as in n**a**m**e**)		**a–e**	5	2
2.3	**ay** (as in pl**ay**)		**ay**	6	2
3.1	**ie** (as in l**ie**)		**ie**	8	3
3.2	**i–e** (as in b**i**t**e**)		**i–e**	9	3
3.3	**igh** (as in h**igh**)		**igh**	10	4
3.4	**y** (as in fl**y**)		**y**	11	4
4.1	**oa** (as in b**oa**t)		**oa**	13	5
4.2	**o–e** (as in p**o**l**e**)		**o–e**	14	5
4.3	**ow** (as in sh**ow**)		**ow**	15	5
5.1	**oo** (as in b**oo**t)		**oo**	17	6
5.2	**u–e** (as in t**u**n**e**)		**u–e**	18	6
5.3	**ew** (as in fl**ew**)		**ew**	19	7
5.4	**ue** (as in bl**ue**)		**ue**	20	7
6.1	**-ed**		**-ed, -ed, -ed**	24-25	8
6.2	**-ing**		**-ing**	26	9
7.1	**u** (as in p**u**ll)		**u**	27	10
7.2	**oo** (as in f**oo**t)		**oo**	27	10
8.1	**ar** (as in c**ar**)		**ar**	28	11
9.1	**oy** (as in t**oy**)		**oy**	29	12
9.2	**oi** (as in b**oi**l)		**oi**	30	12
10.1	**ow** (as in c**ow**)		**ow**	32	13
10.2	**ou** (as in **ou**ch!)		**ou**	33	13
11.1	**air** (as in f**air**)		**air**	35	14
11.2	**are** (as in sc**are**)		**-are**	36	14
11.3	**ere** (as in th**ere**)		**ere**	36	15
11.4	**ear** (as in b**ear**)		**-ear**	35	15
12.1	**or** (as in sp**or**t)		**or**	38	16
12.2	**oor** (as in fl**oor**)		**oor**	39	16
12.3	**ore** (as in s**ore**)		**ore**	39	16
12.4	**aw** (as in cl**aw**)		**aw**	40	17
12.5	**au** (as in c**au**ght)		**au**	41	17
13.1	**er** (as in h**er**)		**er**	43	18
13.2	**ir** (as in b**ir**d)		**ir**	44	18
13.3	**ur** (as in f**ur**)		**ur**	45	18
14.1	**wh** (as in **wh**en and **wh**o)		**wh, wh**	47	19
14.2	**ph** (as in **ph**otogra**ph**)		**ph**	48	20
14.3	**ch** (as in s**ch**ool)		**ch**	48	20
15.1	**ear** (as in h**ear**)		**ear**	49	21
16.1	**ea** (as in h**ea**d)		**ĕa**	50	21
17.1	**-ful** (as in rest**ful**)		**full, ful**	51	22
17.2	**-ly** (as in love**ly**)		**ly**	52	22

PUPIL RECORD SHEET (SECTION 3)

Name ....

Page	Phoneme	Can read some (s)/ most (m) words with this phoneme	Can spell words containing this phoneme	*Programme Two Copymaster*	*Programme Two Word Bank Copymaster*
163	**all** (as in c**all**)		**all**	53	23
164	**al** (as in **al**most)		**al**	53	23
165	**o** (as in l**o**ve)		**o**	54	24
166	**o** (as in **o**ne)		**o**	55	24
167	**o** (as in wh**o**)		**o**	55	24
168	**a** (as in umbrell**a**)		**a**	56	25
169	**a** (as in f**a**ther)		**a**	56	25
170	**e–e** (as in th**e**s**e**)		**e–e**	22	
171	Silent **e** (as in gone)		Silent **e**	57	26
172	**y** (as in ver**y**)		**y**	58	27
174	**y** (as in bic**y**cle)		**y**		
175	**ey** (as in donk**ey**)		**ey**	59	27
176	**e** (as in th**e**y)		**e**	60	28
177	**ei** (as in **ei**ght)		**ei**	60	28
178	**ck** (as in cra**ck**)		**ck**	61	29
179	**ke** (as in ba**ke**)		**ke**	61	29
179	**k** (as in wee**k**)		**k**	61	29
180	**c** (as in pi**c**ni**c**)		**c**	61	29
182	**y** to **i** (as in cr**y**, cr**i**es)		**y** to **i**	62-64	30-31
187	Blocking Magic **ed** and **ing**		Magic **ed, ing**	67-68	35-36
190	Magic **en** and **est**		Magic **en, est**	65	33
193	Magic **er**		Magic **er**	66	34
195	Magic **y**		Magic **y**	66	34
197	**le** (as in tab**le**)		**le**	72	37
199	**al** (as in medic**al**)		**al**	73	37
200	**ce** (as in twi**ce**)		**ce**	74-75	38
202	**ci** (as in **ci**rcus)		**ci**	74-75	38
203	**cy** (as in spi**cy**)		**cy**	74-75	38
204	**ge** (as in oran**ge**)		**ge**	76-78	39-40
205	**dge** (as in ba**dge**)		**dge**	76-78	39-40
206	**gi** (as in ma**gi**c)		**gi**	76-78	39-40
207	**gy** (as in ener**gy**)		**gy**	76-78	39-40
208	**kn** (as in **kn**ee)		**kn**	79	41
210	**wr** (as in **wr**ite)		**wr**	79	41
212	**gh** (as in bou**gh**t)		**gh**	80	42
213	**gh** (as in lau**gh**)		**gh** (f)	80	42
214	**mb** (as in thu**mb**)		**mb**	81	42
214	**mn** (as in autu**mn**)		**mn**	81	42
215	**ie** (as in l**ie**, f**ie**ld)		**ie**	82	43
217	**ei** (as in rec**ei**ve and h**ei**ght)		**ei**	83	43
218	**ous** (as in fam**ous**)		**ous**	84	44
220	**tion** (as in atten**tion**)		**tion**	86	45
223	**-less, -ness** suffixes		**less, ness**	88	46
225	**-ture**		**ture**	89	47
226	**-que**		**que**	89	47
227	**-able, -ible** suffixes		**able, ible**	90	48

Index